Dedicated to the memory of my father
and the thousands of merchant seamen
like him who defied the gauntlet of
German U-boats to keep Britain alive.

1. T. H. Grossmith (1905-1979), merchant seaman,
   photographed in 1922, the year the *Laconia* was built.

2. Doris M. Hawkins (1911-1991), O.B.E.

THE SINKING OF THE LACONIA

A TRAGEDY IN THE BATTLE OF THE ATLANTIC

FREDERICK GROSSMITH

PAUL WATKINS

STAMFORD

•

Published by
PAUL WATKINS
18 Adelaide Street
Stamford, Lincolnshire
PE9 2EN

ISBN

Ordinary edition: 1 871615 68 2
Special edition: 1 871615 72 0
The special edition is numbered and signed
by the author and is limited to
200 copies only, bound in cloth

By the same author:
The Bottomless Pit
Dunkirk A Miracle of Deliverance
The Cross and the Swastika
How To Have A Faith That Works

Printed by the Alden Press, Oxford

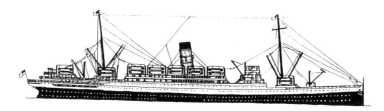

CONTENTS

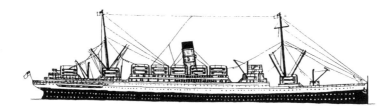

ACKNOWLEDGEMENTS

In sending out this book to the public I would like to make certain acknowledgements. Firstly, a sincere expression of thanks and appreciation to the survivors of the *Laconia*, relatives of survivors and interested persons for interviews granted and time taken out to engage in correspondence: D. Ashworth, Llandudno, North Wales (photographs); E. Bankier, Wirral; K. Bates, Liverpool and for his unpublished diary describing a serviceman's life on board; D. Blackburn, Northampton; Mrs J. Brown; Mrs A. Buchanan, Runcorn; J. Campbell, Strathpeffer, Scotland; F. Chadwick, Liverpool; J. Chappel, Coventry; J. E. Charnock, Altrincham; A. Downs, Liverpool; Mrs D. M. Edwards, West Kirby; Mrs D. Godden, Liverpool; C. Gregory, Liverpool; W. Hardacre, Liverpool; A. Henderson, Bebington, Wirral; R. Hicks, Wallasey; W. Hoyer, Liverpool; E. Johnson, Wallasey; L. Jones, Cheshire; A. Kirk, Liverpool; J. Le Brocq, Liverpool; K. Lewis, Bromborough, Wirral (ship's plans); Mrs E. Meehan, Liverpool; the Piper family, Liverpool; E. Power, Liverpool; Mrs M. Rawlinson, Wallasey; J. Robinson, Birkenhead; J. Scaife, Shipley, West Yorkshire; D. Sharkey, Liverpool; J. Sharkey, Liverpool; G. Tankard, Liverpool (photograph); M. R. Tinkler, Eastham, Wirral; D. Walker, Liverpool; P. Wallace, Liverpool; and J. White, Liverpool; A. Zamrej, Kildary, Scotland.

Grateful thanks to the Public Record Office, Kew, Surrey for all their help in locating unpublished reports and other information found in Adm. 199-1279; and to the University of Liverpool archives (Cunard Section) for information concerning ships' records and the unpublished report of Lt C. S. Mercer and the two versions of the report of Third Officer Buckingham. The first, more formal account, was written soon after his return to England in 1945; the second, more personal and more detailed, was written in 1959. The Maritime Museum at Liverpool and the Tyne and Wear Archives Services at Newcastle-upon-Tyne were also helpful in locating records and illustrations.

The Scolar Press, Aldershot, gave permission for the lengthy quotation from their *Edward Bawden, War Artist* and the Imperial War Museum, London supplied the prints of Bawden's drawings, together with a short account of *Laconia* survivor David Chawe.

ACKNOWLEDGEMENTS

The provision by General Robert C. Richardson III of *The Origins of the Laconia Order*, put together at his request by United States Air Force historians Dr Maurer Maurer and Lawrence J. Paszeck, has proved extremely helpful in determining why Ascension Island was so important to the Allied cause, why the secrecy of its operations was vital and why they took the decision to attack *Laconia's* rescuers. General Richardson also wrote several personal letters to the author. An important extract from one of them is published in these pages.

Laconia's crew list is published courtesy of The Registrar General of Shipping & Seamen, Cardiff.

Several picture agencies proved extremely helpful in locating illustrations. These are listed in the picture credits, but a special thanks to John Clarkson for waiving reproduction fees for the use of his photograph from his 'Ships in Focus' archive.

Rear Admiral Mario Maguolo, Defence and Naval Attaché at the Italian Naval Historical office, Rome, was most helpful in locating the war diary of Lt Commander Marco Revedin, of the submarine *Cappellini*. The unpublished extracts relating to the *Laconia* incident were translated by Paul Watkins.

The diary of Stoker James Rowson was supplied by his widow, Mrs H. Rowson, Essex. She also supplied the article from *The War Illustrated*, containing the contemporary account of Claude Jones.

Thanks are also due to the London Express News and Feature Services; *The Liverpool Echo*, *The Ross-shire Journal* and *The Wirral Globe* for publicity and use of their 'letter' columns; Cunard Steam Ship Company; Department of the Air Force, Washington, USA; Albert F. Simpson Research Centre, Maxwell Air Force Base, Alabama, USA; and to Shaun Tyas for his editorial surgery, encouragement and belief that the *Laconia* story should have a wide readership. He also compiled the index. Thanks also on behalf of the publisher to Ian Breakell, Brian Cocks, Marion Cutforth, Barry Ketcham, Paul Ridgway, Philip Riley, Brenda Ripley and Mike Roffe; and Martin Smith for drawing the map and the diagrams used as chapter headings.

Thanks to the Marine Safety Executive (Department of Transport, Southampton) for information on the modern specifications of lifeboats.

The photographs in *U-Boats to the Rescue* were published without an acknowledgement in both English editions. For the few we have reproduced we have tried to locate any one with a claim on the copyright, but not always with success.

THE SINKING OF THE LACONIA

We are particularly grateful to Mrs Norah K. King, sister of the late Doris Hawkins O.B.E., for permission to quote the substantial extracts from *Atlantic Torpedo*, first published by Victor Gollancz in 1943; and for supplying the photograph of her sister which we have used as a frontispiece.

A late addition was the discovery of the list of the Polish cadet officers on board the *Laconia*. This was supplied by survivor Andrew Zamrej. Unfortunately we were not able to locate a full list of the British service personnel, the civilian passengers or of the Italian prisoners. This information would be a welcome addition to any future edition.

Finally, our grateful thanks to Philip Rentell for lending us his rare colour postcards of the *Laconia*. Two of these were first used in his book *Historic Cunard Liners*, now about to be republished by Waterfront Publications of Blandford Forum. Thanks also to Harry Greaves for sending them on Philip Rentell's behalf.

If unwittingly I have made any other omission, I trust that the oversight will be forgiven. I am always interested in receiving corrections or new information via the publisher.

Frederick Grossmith

THE NEW CUNARDER "LACONIA"—20,000 TONS

3. Cunard postcard of the *Laconia* soon after launching.

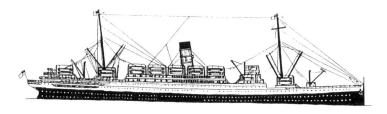

INTRODUCTION

The story of the last voyage of the *Laconia* that follows is entirely factual. In that regard I am grateful to so many people who co-operated in my research. Without such help this book could not have been written.

At 8 p.m. on Sunday, September 12th, 1942 nearly 3,000 human beings, each with hopes for tomorrow, were abruptly brought to a point in time hitherto unexperienced: challenging their untested emotions with demands for great courage and endurance. War is a monstrosity! Yet the personal experiences of human beings reacting to life-threatening situations are beyond dispute.

Of course, vital to the accurate reconstruction of the last moments of the *Laconia* are the accounts of survivors and others who took part in the drama. In respect of their willingness to give quality time designed to satisfy my quest for information, accordingly, their names together with all sources of data are listed in the 'Acknowledgements' section.

I am particularly grateful to the French writer Léonce Peillard for his excellent earlier book on the *Laconia* incident: *U-Boats to the Rescue* (Jonathan Cape, 1963) and to Doris Hawkins, a *Laconia* survivor, for her contemporary account published by Gollancz under the title of *Atlantic Torpedo* in 1943. However, Peillard's descriptive book closes with a mystery: who did bomb the German submarine U-156 whilst her gallant commander Werner Hartenstein was carrying out what must be regarded as the most remarkable and humane rescue operation of World War Two? Since 1963 new information has surfaced, sufficient to clear up the mystery left in Peillard's book. Recognition for this is due to United States Air Force General Robert C. Richardson III who in 1942 was Captain Richardson, commander of the first Composite Squadron based upon Ascension Island and the man who gave the order to sink U-boat 156. Léonce Peillard did not know of the role of Ascension Island, where secrecy shrouded every military operation. It was only after the publication of Peillard's book that Richardson told his side of the story and I appreciate his collaboration in piecing together the events for this book. It would have been interesting to have had the view of the young American pilot and his crew, for after all his action gave birth to an historical document known as 'The Laconia Order'. Regrettably, the United States Air Force were unable to help or advise if pilot and crew survived the war. It would appear that their records were possibly destroyed in a fire on July 2, 1973.

What amazes me is that the 'Laconia Order', which signalled a significant shift in the rules of warfare at sea, due to rapid technological advances in submarine detection which left the submarine disadvantaged, is grossly ignored by military historians. In fact, outside of Merseyside few realise that the *Laconia* actually existed and many major historians of the War simply omit to mention the ship and the incident. There may, however, be a glimmer of hope: on January 2, 1994 the *Laconia* found its way into the script of BBC Television's *House of Eliott* series.

In any book which sets out to mix facts together with eye-witness accounts, allowing human emotions to spill out on to the page, there is always the temptation to take advantage of imaginative licence, making the work more appropriate to a novel. This I have avoided. Any human emotions expressed are there because of the endorsement of the contributor in question.

Over thirty years have elapsed since Peillard's book. When he conducted his research Admiral Dönitz was alive, readily co-operating with a lengthy interview; so too were a few members of the submarines engaged in the *Laconia* affair. All these submarines were sunk with their commanders and crews not many months after the sinking of the *Laconia*, but some among the crews were saved by varying circumstances such as illness, leave or through transference to other vessels. In contrast to Peillard, I have relied heavily upon primary source material produced through interviews with British survivors, unpublished reports and statements. Herr Albert Speer, former Reichminister for Armaments and war production, discussed with me the Dönitz trial. Speer himself was classified as a war criminal and sentenced to twenty years imprisonment at Nuremberg. I have also included as a perpetual memory to the much beloved *Laconia* and those who sailed in her a crew list for her final voyage, indicating whether they were lost or saved, alongside the names of those who for various reasons 'signed off' before that fatal voyage and lived to fight another day.

On my office wall hangs an oil painting by Liverpool marine artist Dave Sharkey of the Cunard liner *Laconia*. The ship is anchored mid-river between the Liverpool landing stage and Birkenhead. It serves as a reminder of that cold, grey Sunday in January, 1942, when from the top deck of a Mersey ferryboat I peered up at her huge superstructure. At that time I was seven years old, but remember it well! Accompanied by my mother and brother we rode the boat backwards and forwards on its short trip from Liverpool to Birkenhead, each time waving handkerchiefs, hoping my father, somewhere on her bridge, would see us.

The *Laconia* completed her 1942 round voyage to Suez without incident. Then she prepared for what would be her final journey. My father, who had been a career navy man since the age of fifteen, later joining the Merchant Navy, transferred for service as a Navigating Officer on another ship. He was thus spared the trauma of her last voyage. But many of her crew whom he knew personally sailed down the River Mersey and into an action with an enemy submarine which would result in the loss of nearly two thousand lives ... and have far reaching consequences!

4. Cunard postcard of the *Laconia* passing through the Panama Canal.
5. *Over:* Rear view of the *Laconia* in dock (pages xii-xiii).
6-8. Ships plans, based on those of the *Laconia*'s virtually identical sister ship *Scythia.* No plans specifically of the *Laconia* appear to survive (pages xiv-xix).
9. Rear view of the *Laconia* in dock (page xx).

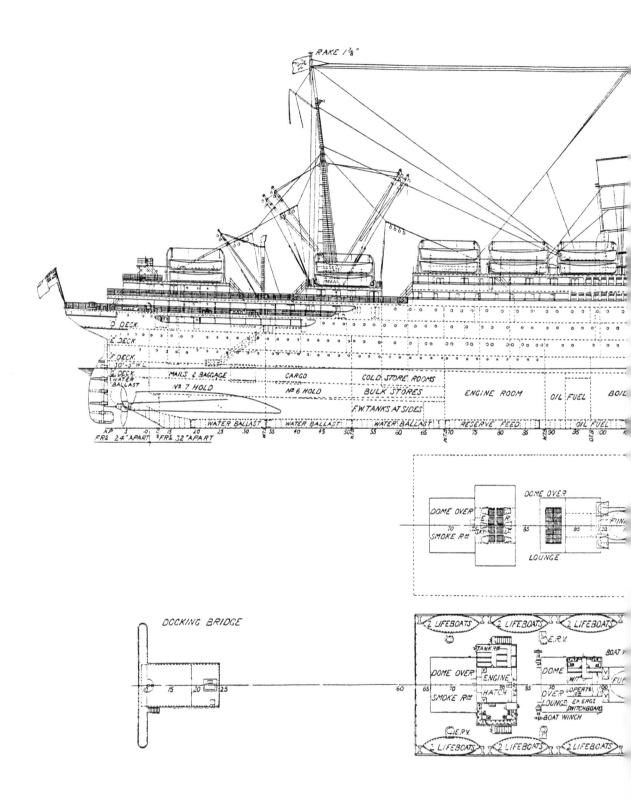

RAKE 1⅜"

D DECK.

E DECK.

F DECK.
30'-5"W.L.

G DECK.
WATER
BALLAST

MAILS & BAGGAGE		CARGO	COLD STORE ROOMS			
Nº 7 HOLD		Nº 6 HOLD	BULK STORES	ENGINE ROOM	OIL FUEL	BOIL
			F.W.TANKS AT SIDES			
WATER BALLAST	WATER BALLAST		WATER BALLAST	RESERVE FEED	OIL FUEL	

A.P. 5   10   15   20   25   30   35   40   45   50   55   60   65   70   75   80   85   90   95   100
FRS. 24" APART   FRS. 32" APART

DOME OVER
SMOKE Rᴹ

SKY

DOME OVER

LOUNGE

FUN

70   85   95

DOCKING BRIDGE

10   15   20   25   60

2 LIFEBOATS   2 LIFEBOATS   2 LIFEBOATS

E.R.V.

TANK Rᴹ

DOME OVER
SMOKE Rᴹ

ENGINE
HATCH

DOME
OVER
LOUNGE
BOAT WINCH

OPERTS
EMERGᵧ
SWITCHBOARD

80AT

W.T.

FUᴇ

E.R.V.

2 LIFEBOATS   2 LIFEBOATS   2 LIFEBOATS

65   70   85

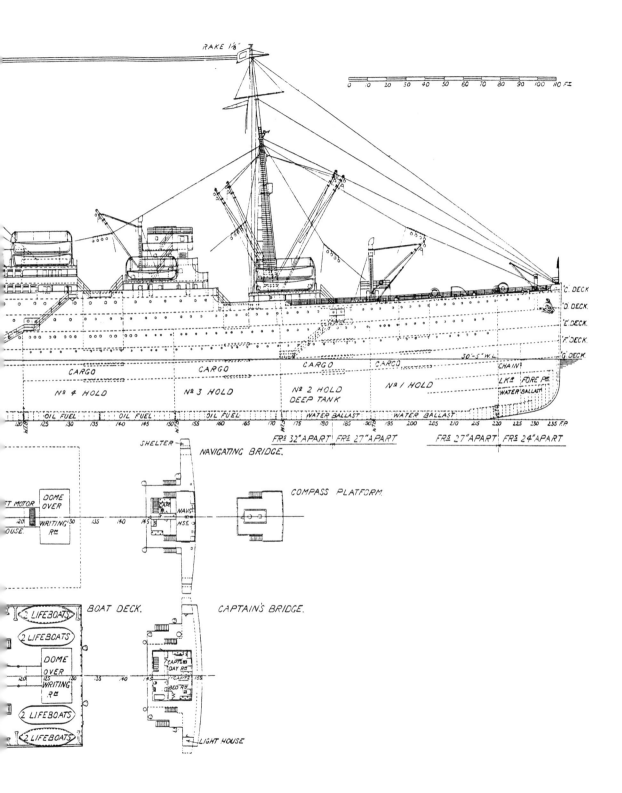

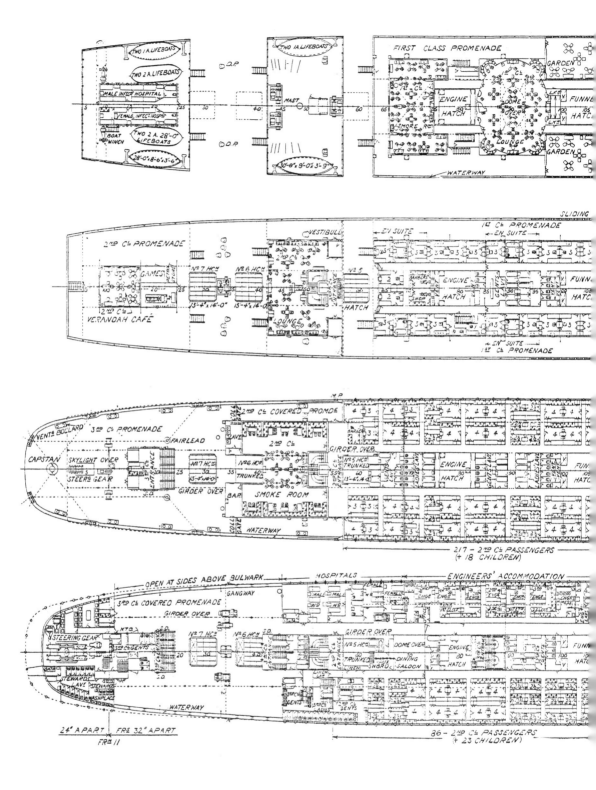

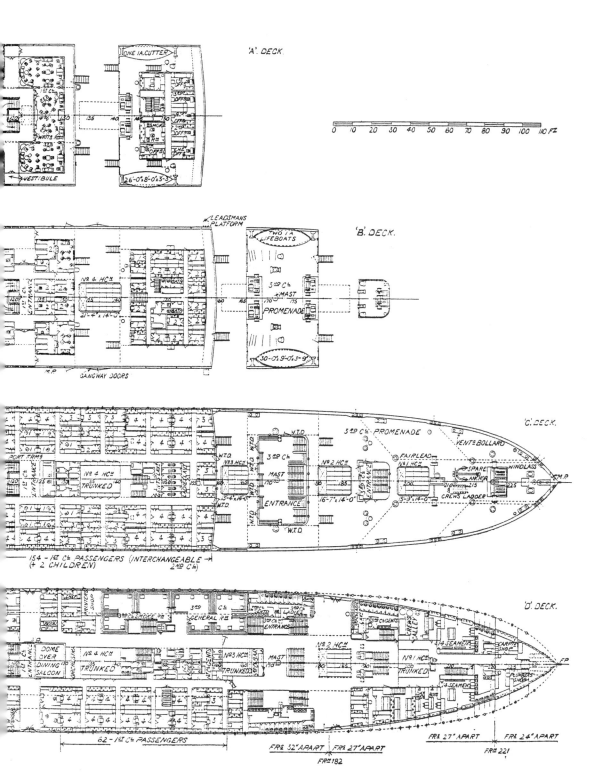

'A'. DECK.

ONE 1A.CUTTER

VESTIBULE

'B'. DECK.

LEADSMANS PLATFORM

TWO 1A. LIFEBOATS

3RD CL MAST PROMENADE

GANGWAY DOORS

'C'. DECK.

3RD CL. PROMENADE

VENTS. BOLLARD

FAIRLEAD

SPARE ANCHOR

WINDLASS

CREWS LADDER

154 - 1ST CL PASSENGERS (INTERCHANGEABLE 2ND CL) (+ 2 CHILDREN)

'D'. DECK.

DOME OVER DINING SALOON

No. 4 HCH TRUNKED

No. 3 HCH TRUNKED

MAST

No. 2 HCH

No. 1 HCH TRUNKED

CREWS GALLEY

SEAMEN

CARPRS. SHOP

PUMPRS. SHOP

62 - 1ST CL PASSENGERS

FRS 32" APART   FRS 27" APART   FRS 27" APART   FRS 24" APART

FR 182   FR 221

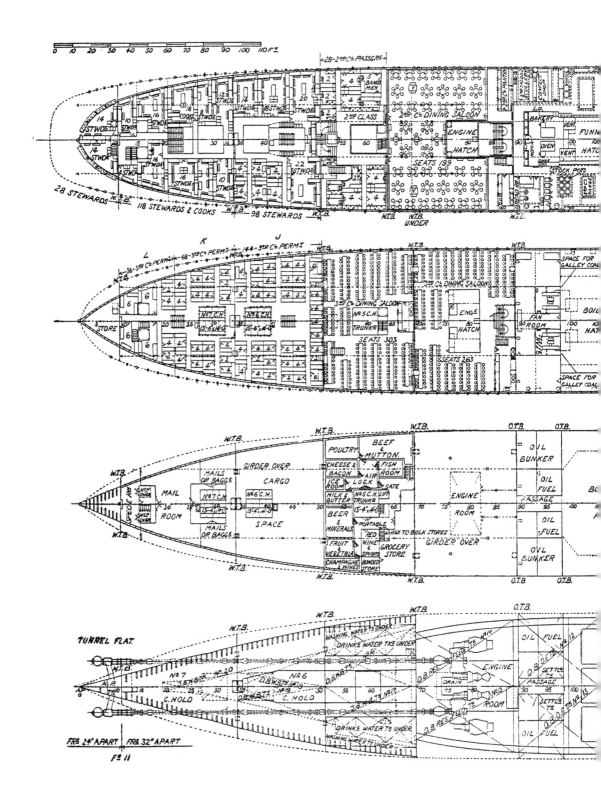

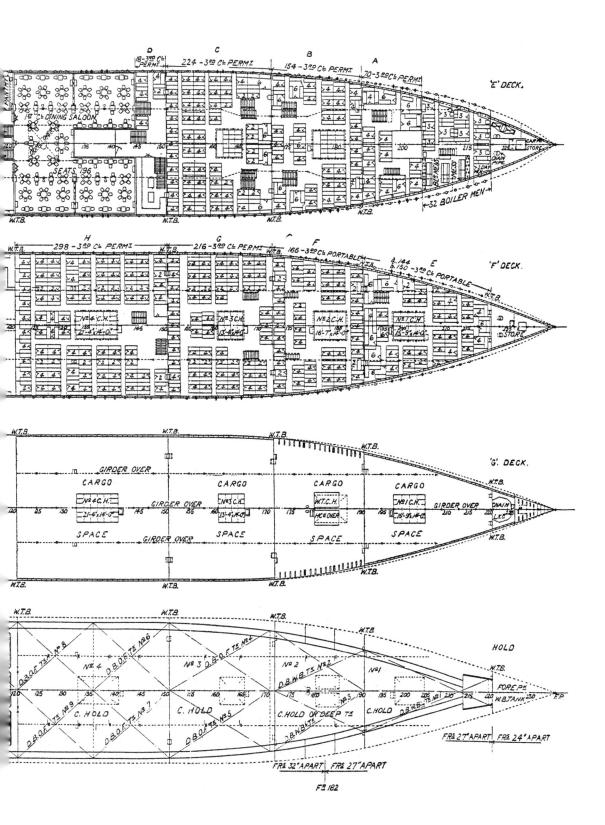

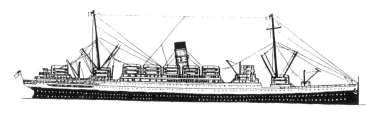

I

PREPARING FOR WAR

When the question of drama at sea is raised, inevitably minds turn to such ships as the *Titanic*, the luxury cruise liner which hit an iceberg in the Atlantic on her maiden voyage, or the *Lusitania*, sunk in 1915 by a German submarine off the coat of Ireland. But not the *Laconia*! In fact, few people outside Merseyside have ever heard of her. It is almost unbelievable in the light of her sinking and what followed that a sea drama of such importance should have attracted so little attention, as if it never took place. Yet the sinking of the *Laconia* resulted in a remarkable rescue mission, perhaps the most humane and exciting rescue mission of World War Two, and accounts of *Laconia*'s survivors are as graphic as those of the more famous disasters.

During the Nuremberg Trials of 1945/6 the prosecution tried hard to sentence to death the German Admiral Karl Dönitz for issuing 'The Laconia Order', which forbade his submarine crews attempting further rescue missions after an American Liberator bomber had attacked the rescuing U-boats. But for almost five decades since the Trials it has virtually remained ignored, even though, almost by stealth, it has become standard practice of modern submarine attacks. The *Laconia* incident is therefore extremely important as a turning point in the general history of sea warfare and in the Battle of the Atlantic in particular.

At the outbreak of war, the *Laconia* was at sea on passage from New York and Boston for Liverpool. By wireless she received notice that under Requisitions Order T98A she was now the property of the British Admiralty.

Early on the morning of 4th September, 1939, *Laconia* plied towards the familiar Wirral peninsular coastline and the Liverpool Bar Lightship. Looming up before her on the starboard side the sight of the New Brighton Pier, stretching for hundreds of yards out into the River Mersey, signalled she had reached safe waters: beyond the reach of enemy submarines. At 8 a.m. *Laconia*'s passengers disembarked at Liverpool Landing Stage.

On 7th September she put to sea for what was to be her final voyage painted in the attractive colours of the Cunard White Star Line. Upon

1

arrival at Portsmouth's H.M. Dockyard, painters quickly set to work changing her pillar box red funnel, white superstructure and blue hull into battleship grey.

Designated an Armed Cruiser, she had necessary artillery hoisted aboard and into their placements went two antiquated 4.7" naval guns which were manufactured in 1917; six 1½" anti-aircraft guns; four Bofor guns and two 2" rockets. Housed and ready for combat.

Built in 1922 by Swan Hunter and Wigham Richardson, Wallsend-on-Tyne, she was the second Cunard boat to bear the name *Laconia* (an ancient territory of SW Greece; her sister ships *Carinthia*, *Franconia*, *Scythia* and *Samaria*, all built between 1920 and 1925, bore similar names). Her predecessor was torpedoed and sunk in the North Atlantic on 25th February 1917. Due to labour troubles, the new *Laconia* was completed at Rotterdam, Holland, starting her maiden voyage on 25th May 1922 from Southampton to New York, via Queenstown (Cove, Republic of Ireland). Upon transference to the Liverpool – New York route, Liverpool became her home port. During the summer of 1923 she made a number of voyages out of Hamburg to New York. On January 24th 1938, the *Laconia* made a 52-day cruise from Liverpool, covering 14,108 miles and did much cruise work throughout the 'thirties.

Six hundred and twenty-four feet in length, with a gross tonnage of 19,695 tons, the *Laconia* was twin-screwed and, full out, steamed at 17 knots. A new device, an invention of the American Sperry, furnished her a place in history as the first passenger liner to circumnavigate the globe by gyro-compass during her world cruise in the winter of 1922/23. At that time she also boasted the world's largest floating laundry, and she was the first British liner to be fitted with anti-rolling tanks ('Frahms').

Passengers were impressed with her luxury and comfort. The eye-catching romantic garden lounges together with the surprise of seeing an oak room replica of an old English inn, complete with ingle nook fireplace, lingered in the memory. She also boasted a ballroom, a library and her own printing office for production of the on-board gossip magazine, *Cruising Topics*, a few copies of which survive at the National Maritime Museum. During the 1920s and '30s *Laconia* rose rapidly as a cruise choice. "She was really beautiful!" Liverpool marine artist Dave Sharkey told this author.

The 1928 refit increased the passenger accommodation to comprise 347 first, 350 second and 1,500 third class.

Long before the torpedoes from German submarine U-156 would tear huge holes in her side, *Laconia* was already a victim. The economic

10-11.Two early views of the *Laconia*. The first was taken soon after she was built in 1922, while she was on trials; the second soon after.

12. *Laconia*'s library and writing room. This and the following interior pictures are from Cunard publicity material held at the National Maritime Museum, London.

13. *Laconia*'s main *salon*.

14. *Laconia*'s first class dining room. Several survivors report being here when the first torpedo hit.

15. *Laconia*'s garden lounge.

16. A double bedroom on the *Laconia*

17. Cruising on the *Laconia* in happier days: Clarice Maine, Ivor Novello and party pose next to one of the lifeboats.

18. *Laconia* with *HMS Hood* in Madeira. The *Hood* was sunk by the *Bismarck* in 1941.

19. Fancy dress ball during *Laconia's* cruise to the West Indies in 1934.

FIRST CLASS SMOKING ROOM
LACONIA

20. The famous first class smoking room with its inglenook fireplace. *Laconia*'s sister ships also enjoyed this feature.

8

recession during the early 1930s necessitated drastic surgery in national expenditure. As the economic plague cut a swathe through the British way of life, living standards sank to a deplorable level. Resultant cut-backs starved funds available for research, creating a technological 'vacuum'. In 1933 the *Laconia* carried a record cargo of fruit from New York and Boston to Liverpool, numbering 41,000 cases of grapefuit, apples and plums.

By the mid 1930s, a gentle wave of new prosperity lifted the spirit of the nation. It appeared the 'bad old days' were now a mere historic memory and it is not surprising that exclusive attention to materialism gave birth to a crapulent attitude. In consequence, the British people found it easy to ignore the turbulent events in central Europe. But Germany's Fuhrer, the unduly schismatic Adolf Hitler, saw himself as a man of destiny. Consistently, he punctured the idyllic optimism of fanciful dreamers hopeful of a better world with his contest for attention. Demonstrating audacity of intellect and imagination, authoritative speech, figure, symbol and trope, he arrested attention.

In January 1933, Hitler became Chancellor of Germany and from that time British politicians viewed him from various stances and with various opinions. Repeatedly, the voice of Winston Churchill communicated a strong warning of the German menace. He ridiculed the Government's ineffectual approach to the nation's defence programme. Hitler was a threat!

Labelled a warmonger, Churchill was out in the cold, spending much time working upon a biography of his ancestor, the Duke of Marlborough. Following the Abdication Crisis of King Edward VIII, Prime Minister Baldwin retired to the House of Lords with an Earldom. He was succeeded by Neville Chamberlain, the youngest son of the famous Victorian statesman. The new Prime Minister overlooked Churchill for a Cabinet post and ignored the warnings of a growing band of Conservatives, led by Churchill, who declared that Germany was re-arming for another assault on the freedoms of Europe. Yet, Churchill was the one Englishman whom Hitler feared, frequently referring to him in speeches.

German rearmament had now advanced to the extent that Hitler was able to use the threat of war for territorial gains. He accused the Austrian Government of not treating properly those who wanted Austria to be joined to the Third Reich. So, in March 1938, he marched his army in and annexed the country. The reaction of the British Government that no great danger faced the nation was applied like a healing balm to soothe away the fears of a British public aroused to the reality of renewed conflict with the German nation.

21-22. The Cunard publicity paintings always exagerated the proportions of the ship (see also front cover and pages viii, xi, 151 and 223), but (plate 23) she was beautiful enough without exaggeration. Several photographs illustrate the prominent smoke which made her an easy target for U-boat 156.

10

Laconia. "Nautical."

On the last day of September 1938, Chamberlain added his signature to the Munich Agreement. Cheering crowds greeted his arrival at Heston Airport where he waved the paper signed by Hitler and himself. When he read the part of the text signifying the desire of 'our two peoples never to go to war with one another again', cheers resounded from the crowd. Later outside No 10 Downing Street he announced to a large gathering: 'This is the second time in our history that there has come back from Germany to Downing Street peace with honour. I believe it is peace for our time.'

The dark night of uncertainty was dispelled. Britons celebrated! In their merrymaking, fear, doubt and unbelief were banished to other realms as the nation experienced a new impetus in working and looking forward to a better tomorrow. Nestling in hope, a new faith was nurtured – a faith in her leaders. 'Appeasement', promulgated as a doctrine by the politicians, found seed-bed acceptance in the minds of the people. Winston Churchill thought otherwise: 'peace in our time' appeared to him an aphorism of absurdity.

Thus, *Laconia* entered a war for which she was unprepared. To face a revived Germany ready to continue where she left off following the First World War, by waging unrestricted submarine warfare on Britain's trade routes.

Sadly, the admonitory aspect of lessons learned, in particular from 1917 onwards, remained neglected. Undisturbed, Britain continued to put her trust in the battle fleet, with the emphasis on fire power. Accordingly, the meagre Defence Budget was channelled in that direction. In 1937, the British Admiralty informed the 'Shipping Advisory Committee': 'We have means of counteracting a submarine which are very effective, and which will normally reduce our losses from that weapon. It will never be a fatal menace again as it was in the last war. We have taken effective steps to prevent that.'

The 'effective steps' referred to their 1917 invention – ASDIC. Interest in a means of detecting underwater objects was highlighted by the problem of icebergs, underlined in 1912 by the sinking of the *Titanic*. By 1916, an inert system of submarine detection made use of a hydrophone; an underwater microphone, plus an amplifier to pick up the sound given out by a submarine's engine. In the following year, scientists developed an active system consisting of a transmitter/receiver which sent out impulses under the sea: its rebounding echo could be used to detect a submarine even with its engines shut down.

It was a tremendous breakthrough for science and a giant step forward in dealing with the submarine menace. Two sound beams could be sent out

12

in a similar manner to a searchlight or radar beam in the air. The vertical beam bouncing off the sea bed supplied depth determination, whilst the horizontal beam, aimed much higher, proved capable of detecting underwater objects nearer the surface.

Such was the growing confidence in ASDIC (Allied Submarine Detection and Investigation Committee) to deal with any attack from U-boats upon Britain's vital sea lanes that it was generally believed that Germany could not seriously employ this strategy. When war came, 180 naval vessels were fitted with ASDIC, which at that time was the only known method of discovering the presence of a submarine. It was thought appropriate to call it ASDIC as this was the original name of the underwater sound-ranging apparatus for determining the range and bearing of a submerged submarine, derived from the initial letters of the committee which was set up as an Anglo-French project in 1918. The invention was mainly French in conception and is also known as sonar.

However, Germany had planned differently. The sinking of the Donaldson liner *Athenia* on the first day of hostilities by U-30 with the loss of 128 lives telegraphed realisation to the British Admiralty of Germany's intention to wage an unrestricted underwater onslaught upon her vessels. Kinder Admiral Karl Dönitz, Commander-in-Chief of U-boats, set the objective to attack Britain's trade routes. He was determined to wreak havoc by depriving Britain of life-sustaining supplies, especially food, motivated by the expectation of her suing early in the war for peace terms.

From the outset, Dönitz calculated that the 'tonnage' war was the all important key to success. Provided shipping losses exceeded replacements, then the U-boats would win the battle. At the same time, his planned building programme would by far exceed his own losses. He believed he held the advantage as ASDIC could not detect a surfaced submarine and at night U-boats adopted the tactic of attacking on the surface. Nor had a weapon been invented to kill a submarine from the air or sea. To score, an attacker needed to drop depth charges to explode within seven yards of the vessel. Whilst ASDIC with much accuracy could measure the range of a submarine through its fixed beam, it could not ascertain the depth at which a submarine lay. This meant that when going into an attack the vessel passed over the submarine before it could activate the stern method of dropping depth charges. In consequence, very early during the run-in, contact was lost with the enemy.

These problems regarding the efficiency of ASDIC detection and depth charge attack called for urgent attention. British scientists worked around the clock in an endeavour to make up for twenty wasted years.

13

Historically, too, *Laconia* was a victim. One hundred years before armaments manufacturer Frederick Krupp presented the first U-boat to the German Navy, Britain was carrying out experiments. In 1804, the American Fulton interested Prime Minister Pitt in his invention and design for a Nautilus submersible boat and electric torpedo. A mast and sail were added for the purpose of surface versatility. Pitt was enthusiastic, much to the disgust of the First Sea Lord, Sir John Jarvis, who bluntly advised: 'don't touch it'. Pitt ignored the advice, allowing Fulton to proceed with a demonstration. On 15th October 1805, the hulk of the Danish brig *Dorothea* was towed into Deal harbour off the Kent coast and, to the satisfaction of Britain's Prime Minister, Fulton's new weapon blew the brig into two halves. Sir John Jarvis saw Pitt 'encouraging a mode of war which they who commanded the seas did not want'. He further advised Pitt: 'If we take it up, others will and that will be the strongest blow against our supremacy on the sea.'

Six days later, Lord Nelson excited the nation with a great victory over the French at Trafalgar. Britain forgot about submersible craft, but the Americans continued and in 1893 the United States Congress invited designs for an underwater boat. By 1900 a design found acceptance with a new feature – a 50 h.p. petrol driven engine for propulsion when operating on the surface and an electric motor for use when submerged.

The French took an active interest and by 1901 boasted 29 boats. Britain followed with an order for 5 boats, then every maritime nation of note began to order or bought rights to build their own under licence.

Whilst fellow Europeans engaged in this revolutionary pursuit, Germany just observed, taking no action herself. But it couldn't last and Frederick Krupp spearheaded pressure on the German Admiralty for action. In September 1904, Krupp was instructed to build the first U-boat. When he handed U-1 to the German Navy a vision was born. Although late starters, they contracted to build a fleet. In 1912 they carried out a major alteration by replacing the petrol driven engines with diesels.

The advent of World War One forced Germany to assess the might of Britain's sea power. There was no doubt as to her supremacy but they had faith in the ability of U-boats to level a severe challenge. Britain didn't have to wait long. On 5th September 1914, a month after the declaration of war, H.M.S. *Pathfinder*, a flotilla leader of the Fourth Destroyer Patrol, was torpedoed and sunk off St Abb's Head. She sank in four minutes with the loss of nearly all hands.

Over a century had elapsed since Britain had engaged in a naval struggle. At that time the British rested in the triad of Nelson's achievements: Copenhagen ... the Nile ... Trafalgar. News of the sinking of H.M.S. *Pathfinder* caused the British sailor to feel he had been hit below the belt and there was something underhand about this 'sneaking' mode of warfare. A stand up fight seemed the fair way of doing things – the way it had always been done.

Since time immemorial, the sea has stood as silent witness to man's warring against each other. As Napoleon developed the 'Lozenge' system for tactical land warfare, so too the maritime nations through sea battles learned the strategy of ideal deployment. By a wrong deployment, the commander of a superior fleet may situate himself in a position of tactical inferiority obviating the advantage he may possess in number of ships and weaponry. The ideal deployment ensured that when the enemy was sighted and came within gun range, every gun in the fleet would bear upon them, whilst only a small proportion of the enemy's gun power could be employed.

Principles of action at sea, even to the tactical use of visibility and wind, had been developed into a science by mariners. However, the dawn of the twentieth century introduced a new destructive power at sea – the submarine. From depths below, this new menace was poised to attack at any time, from any direction, without warning.

More was to follow: early on the morning of 22nd September 1914, Lt Otto Weddigen, commander of U-9, torpedoed and sank three British cruisers whilst they were patrolling at 10 knots off the Dutch coast. H.M.S. *Aboukir* was hit first; twenty-five minutes later she was floating bottom-upwards and subsequently sank. Assuming she was hit by a mine, H.M.S. *Hogue,* assisted by H.M.S. *Cressey,* steamed to the wreck area. Both ships lowered boats to pick up survivors. Minutes later torpedoes from U-9 also struck *Hogue* and *Cressey.* In the space of one hour, three ships had disappeared beneath the waves with the loss of 1,300 officers and men.

The moral effect of these successes proved a stimulant to Germany, showing conclusively the changed conditions of war – the fact that warfare at sea had taken a new turning, and one to Germany's advantage.

When hostilities ended, the Allied Powers met to discuss the chastisement of Germany. Apart from losing all her colonies, the terms of the Treaty of Versailles limited Germany to an army of 100,000 men and she was forced to deprive herself of heavy guns, military aeroplanes and to submit to the occupation of the Rhineland by an Allied Force which remained there until 1929. Furthermore, the Treaty prevented Germany building submarines. However, the 1935 Anglo-German Navy Agreement mitigated the Versailles ruling, granting U-boat construction on a restricted basis.

At the outbreak of World War Two, Germany had 57 U-boats. Of these, 24 were 'Einbaume' – coastal boats – of 250 tons, not suitable for the Atlantic. In the mind of Admiral Dönitz lay the uncompromising quest to build up a large submarine fleet capable of penetrating the Atlantic Ocean and able to remain at sea for long periods of time. Cutting across the miscalculations of others, he declared that 300 operational boats would pronounce German mastery of the seas. Had he received full co-operation, the Battle of the Atlantic might have been recorded far differently. But it was not to be. Internal battles fronted by Hermann Goering, Chief of the Lutfwaffe, subjected Dönitz to frustration. Coveting the meagre raw materials available, Goering, a World War One hero, believed the Luftwaffe should receive priority attention. His campaigning overtures to Hitler scored precedence over naval demands, neutralising any hope for U-boat ambitions. For Dönitz, the war came six years too early.

Following the *Athenia* incident, Dönitz concentrated on military targets for a short time. On 19th September 1939, the aircraft carrier H.M.S. *Courageous* was torpedoed and sunk. The following month, U-Boat Command plotted a daring raid by sending U-47 into the heart of the Royal Navy at Scapa Flow. Immaculate navigation by her captain, Günter Prien, gained access through guarded waters, resulting in the sinking of the battleship H.M.S. *Royal Oak*. Winston Churchill, soon to become Britain's Prime Minister, told a packed House of Commons: 'such is the U-boat war – hard, widespread, and bitter – a war of groping and drowning, a war of ambuscade and stratagem, a war of science and seamanship'. During 1940 merchant shipping losses amounted to 2,186,150 tons. Losses for 1941 attributed to U-boats totalled 2,171,754 tons (432 ships). Added to this the ships lost in action with raiders, aircraft or through striking mines brought the disturbing total to 4,328,558 tons (1,299 ships).

From 1939 to 1945 U-boats sank 2,800 Allied merchant ships as well as 148 Allied warships (not taking into account those of the USSR). Amongst their victims were the battleships *Royal Oak* and *Barham*; aircraft carriers *Courageous*, *Ark Royal* and *Eagle*. Of the 1,131 U-boats commissioned, 754 were sunk or damaged beyond repair in port. Of the 39,000 officers and men who served on U-boats, 27,491 are recorded as killed in action or missing presumed lost at sea. Historians are agreed that the Battle of the Atlantic was decided about the middle of 1943, but crucial work in 1941 by the Royal Navy helped to seal the fate of the U-boats. In that year the Royal Navy boarded U-110. Before she sank, British naval officers captured charts, codebooks and a major prize: the submarine's Enigma coding machine. They also received the surrender of U-570 and sailed her to a British port. Later, the Royal Navy took U-570 for extensive sea trials, producing information of great value to the anti-U-boat forces.

After the first conversion to war work the *Laconia* did troop carrying and convoy duty in the north Atlantic. Canadian Fred. B. Grahame served on her in convoy in April 1941, just before the *Hood* was sunk by the *Bismark*. The captain at the time was G. G. P. Hewett and the convoy travelled from Halifax in Nova Scotia to Reykjavik in Iceland. Fred Grahame took photographs on the voyage of the guns which had recently been fitted.

On 25th September 1941, the *Laconia* was handed back to her owners by the Admiralty for duties as a merchant troop carrier (Y21). In command was Captain Rudolph Sharp, O.B.E., R.D., R.N.R. Aged 62, he had nearly thirty years experience as a captain of famous Atlantic liners. This venerable seaman, who had passed out as master in his home port of Liverpool back in 1908, held a commission in the Royal Naval Reserve. At the outbreak of World War One he was in command of the *Lusitania*, torpedoed and sunk in 1915 off the coast of Ireland with a loss of 1,198 lives, but Sharp had transferred to another command before that tragic voyage. He also commanded the four funnelled *Mauretania* and the *Olympic*, sister ship of the *Titanic*. For a while he served as Staff Captain of the giant *Queen Mary*, but by far his widest experience was in command of Cunard's smaller ships such as the *Lancastria*. On 17th June 1940, crammed with 5,000 British military personnel and 300 crew members, *Lancastria* was preparing to leave the French port of St Nazaire when a strong formation of German Junkers dive bombers attacked. A salvo of bombs passed through the dining room saloon exploding in the engine room. Almost immediately, the ship took on a list and thirty minutes later she sank. That day 2,833 persons perished in the action. But for the bravery of the ASDIC trawler *Cambridgeshire*, losses would have been greater. Assigned to the Navy Patrol with a Grimsby crew, she defied further bombing attacks and machine gun fire to rescue over 1,000 passengers and crew from the stricken liner. Captain Sharp was amongst the last batch to be rescued. Two weeks later, Sharp took command of the *Antonia* and in October of that year was awarded the O.B.E. for war service.

Many of *Laconia's* crew served under Sharp on the *Lancastria*, amongst them First Officer Walker. Mrs Ethel Meehan of Liverpool, whose husband was later to join the *Laconia*, recalls waiting at Liverpool's Lime Street Station for the arrival of her husband. When the last passenger passed through the barrier she stood alone, tearful, fearing there had been a mistake in listing his name as a survivor. Later she learned he had passed through the barrier only yards from where she stood; exhausted and barely recognisable because he was black through having spent nine hours in oily water.

On 7th January 1942, after refitting at Charles Howsons, the Liverpool ship repairers, Captain Sharp sailed *Laconia* to the Middle East via the Cape of Good Hope and the Red Sea. She completed the four month return voyage without incident. Most of the crew were Merseysiders, including Chief Officer George Steel and First Officer John Walker whom Sharp had especially requested to join him on the voyage.

Laconia went back to Charles Howsons in Huskisson Dock, who set about 'blanking' the bottom deck port-lights with steel plates about 17" in diameter. In total 90 were welded on the starboard side; whilst they were preparing to treat the port side, orders were received to sail.

Between *Laconia's* January sailing and her return to Liverpool, Admiral Dönitz strengthened the U-boat arm from 91 operational boats to 150. By the end of 1942 he would build the unit to 190. Speaking later, Prime Minister Winston Churchill described the 1942 U-boat onslaught as 'our worst evil', but many of the ships which escaped the Atlantic U-boat wolf packs headed for Liverpool with cargoes of food and raw materials only to find the seaport was targeted for major bombing raids.

On 12th March 1941, the largest air armada to attack Liverpool, comprising 339 Heinkel and Junkers bombers, dropped 70,000 1-Kg incendiaries and 270 tons of high explosives on the city. Barrage balloons prevented the Luftwaffe flying below 5,000 feet but German Intelligence didn't know about the Hurricane Squadron and Defiant Night Fighter Unit, or of the reinforced heavy anti-aircraft guns. Such was the ferocity of opposition that over half the bombs fell outside the target area, causing severe damage to private property with death and injury to the civilian population. More was to follow. Since the first raid on 29th July 1940, Liverpool had been continuously attacked. The May 1941 'blitz' surpassed all other raids. For eight consecutive nights between 500 and 600 bombers rained destruction upon Merseyside. Large sections of the 6½ miles of dockland and those on the Birkenhead side were laid waste. In Huskisson Dock, the freighter *Malakand*, loaded with 1,000 tons of explosives, blew up. In that week 70 ships were sunk at their moorings or in the River Mersey. Vast areas of the docks and city, in particular the shopping centre, burned furiously. The acrid smell of burning permeated the atmosphere; the city was alight with fires. At the end of 68 aerial attacks, 3,966 were dead with as many again injured. 6,500 homes lay totally destroyed, 125,000 badly damaged. But Hitler failed! Debris was cleared and life went on undeterred. Vital shipping continued to reach and leave the battered port.

The *Laconia* left Huskisson Dock on Friday 28th May 1942, dropping anchor mid-river between the Cunard Offices and Birkenhead Landing Stage. As she cast her shorelines for what would be her final sailing, the Battle of the Atlantic was swinging in Germany's favour, notwithstanding British propaganda which stated otherwise.

At 11.30 a.m., two tug boats accompanied her down the River Mersey. Packed with military personnel, she sailed to join a large convoy consisting of such well known names as *Britannic*, *Aquitania*, *Mauretania*, *Orcades*, *Oranto*, *Viceroy of India*, *Santa Elena*, *Staffordshire* and *Empress of Canada*. The battleship H.M.S. *Nelson* was escort together with H.M.S. *Renown* and the Dutch cruiser *Heemskirk*, making up a convoy of seventeen ships.

As she cleared the Mersey, heading for the Irish Sea, the traditional one o'clock gun fired from Birkenhead, sending hundreds of pigeons flying into the air from both banks of the Mersey. It was as if a final salute had been made to a familiar friend ... *Laconia* was not to keep her next appointment at Howsons.

24. *Laconia* after her 1928 refit: the most obvious difference is the extra white line at the top of the hull.

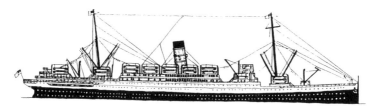

II

LAST DAYS

On Sunday morning, 26th July 1942, *Laconia* weighed anchor at Port Tewfik ready to disembark 3,000 military personnel, their equipment and supplies. Orders were to complete the operation as quickly as possible due to the regularity of bombing raids by the Luftwaffe upon the Suez Canal zone.

For her return voyage from Suez, she took on board returning servicemen, including some badly wounded cases, about twenty civilians and British officials with their families fleeing the theatre of war.

On 12th August *Laconia* weighed anchor and sailed out of Suez Bay southwards towards Aden. Standing beside Captain Sharp, Third Officer Buckingham gazed at the bare undulating sand dunes of the coastline, prodigiously picturesque, exhibited in a grandeur of silhouette as far as the eye could scan. The night passed quietly and by daylight on the 13th specialised look-outs were stood down. Sharp was satisfied he was now out of range of enemy bombers.

Before leaving Port Tewfik, two surprises were in store for the crew. First, some 200 women were taken on board. They were prisoners, of various nationalities and captured in several different cities, accused of prostitution and fifth column work. The ship was to take them to Mombassa. Then, shortly before sailing, fifty heavily guarded lorries parked alongside the quay. From them emerged 1,793 Italian prisoners of war. Boatswain's Mate Le Brocq watched them hurried up *Laconia's* gangplank by their Polish guards, most of whom he considered not much more than 18 years old. Captured in Libya, the Italians appeared unkempt with few belongings. Some only carried a mandolin or guitar. Sighs of relief, even pleasure, showed on their faces as they boarded the ship.

During the next five weeks *Laconia* made calls at Aden, Mombassa, Durban and Cape Town. Crew and passengers were allowed ashore whilst the ship took aboard fresh supplies of oil, fuel, water, food and new passengers. Military police boarded the ship and took charge of the 200 women prisoners. The sight of British warships at Mombassa, base of the

25. A view of Aden taken from the *Laconia* in 1942.

Royal Navy Indian Ocean fleet, furnished psychological comfort to passengers, though a warning of Japanese activity in the Mozambique Channel was given before they set sail.

The passage to Durban, however, was completed without sighting a single vessel. On 28th August, *Laconia* berthed some distance from the main quays of the town. The next port of call was Cape Town where all available cabin space was filled with new arrivals. The Italian prisoners were allowed a relaxation period within the confines of the jetty. Upon leaving Cape Town on 1st September, Captain Sharp faced a 7,000 mile, unescorted voyage to England, plus the responsibility for the safety and well-being of 463 officers and crew, 286 military personnel, 80 civilians, mainly women and children, 1,793 Italian prisoners of war and 103 Polish guards. In total, 2,725 people. A course was set due south to the 100 fathom contour before rounding the Cape of Good Hope, a necessary precaution in order to avoid mines reported laid in the coastal waters by German craft. Once clear of the Mozambique Channel although out of range of enemy aircraft, they were fully exposed to the unseen menace – U-boats. Steaming north to the west of Africa, extra protective measures were adopted. The number of gun positions was doubled and stocks of ammunition increased with additional racks assembled at the gun placements. Keeping well away from the coast, Sharp plotted a zig-zag course by day, proceeding full steam on a normal course under the cover of darkness.

21

THE SINKING OF THE LACONIA

By 9th September, the *Laconia* had covered 2,800 miles and there was an obviously relaxed attitude amongst the passengers, most of whom had been on board for over a month without incident.

Since embarking, life for the servicemen had been unpleasant. Billeted on 'E' Deck, almost level with the water-line, requiring port holes to remain closed, they suffered a lack of fresh air in a hot sticky humidity. Some of the men underwent bouts of claustrophobia. Head room was virtually nil, except in the place where the hatch came through the centre of the deck. Boards covered the hold and the surrounding wooden rails gave it every appearance of a boxing ring. When first shown their quarters, some men thought this was the messing area with a sleeping accommodation located elsewhere. That is, until a steward pointed to racks above their heads where hammocks were stored.

Mess tables, fixed to bulkheads on both sides of the deck, seated 16 men. Plates were stored in a cupboard at the head of each table. Water was rationed; available daily from fresh water taps. In the best of tradition, the servicemen adjusted to their new environment but it was somewhat ironic to be surrounded by so much water, yet to be on a water ration. During the short daily period when the fresh water taps available to them were switched on, everyone ensured his water bottle was full.

Each mess table detailed three men as orderlies who collected the food at meal times, then cleared up afterwards. Calculating men, with strong stomachs, volunteered as orderlies, becoming friendly with kitchen staff in the hope of receiving special favour. During bad weather they capitalised upon their comrades' misfortunes, eating as much as they could consume. Mess orderlies assumed a mediatorial role, as well, carrying solicitations to the kitchen concerning the standard of meals and their suitableness. An insuperable task! The only respite was welcomed by kitchen staff when the obstreperous sea rolled and pitched the ship, causing men to be sick. On such occasions the mess deck was a shambles, the floor covered in servicemen sighing for relief surrounded by broken crockery which had cascaded out of cupboards at the head of the mess tables, smashing in piles on the floor.

In bad weather, service at the two shops, small modified cabins with hatches opening onto a passageway on 'D' deck, was excellent. In calmer weather, long queues formed to buy sweets, cigarettes, crisps and tinned beer.

The psychologists' jargon about extroverts, introverts and ambiverts tells us that we are all different. Subjected to the conditions on 'E' deck, men discovered themselves. Some underwent bouts of claustrophobia, hardened combat soldiers conditioned to survival endeavoured to remain circumspect. Bad feelings festered. 'Barrack-room' style lawyers, capitalising on the situation, questioned the legality of the order placing all first class accommodation, cabins, public rooms and restaurants out of bounds, except to officers, senior N.C.O.s and civilian passengers, arguing that in combat all gratefully share the same shell-hole irrespective of rank or inconvenience. The question of morale constantly challenged those in command but the absence of attention from officers and senior N.C.O.s suited the men; except the innate moaners who discovered another ground for complaint, alleging that they kept away deliberately lest they realise the true facts of conditions below decks.

On a voluntary basis, physical training classes were held daily from 0930 to 1100 hrs on the port side of 'A' deck. Men found the facilitated privilege of the Promenade Deck more congenial surroundings than their own quarters, spending as much time as permissible there to write letters home, read and relax. There was an appreciable build up of overnight sleepers, overlooked by their superiors.

The improvisation of canvas tents, erected around the ship to draw in fresh air for circulation to the mess decks, galleys and engine room, provided a little consolation. But it could not erase the general grievance that the inconvenience of overcrowded conditions should be borne entirely by other ranks. The men re-named the ship *Altmark*, after the German supply vessel renowned for collecting from German warships survivors from British merchantmen they had taken on board. *Altmark's* Captain Dau, taken prisoner in the First World War, did not like the English and threatened that rather than surrender, he would scuttle his ship with all the prisoners in the hold. Considering subsequent events, the nickname was not inappropriate.

Even slight swells added to the exhaustion of the servicemen. Daily the sick list grew, characterised by conditions such as vertigo, nausea, retching and prostration, with the added indecency of only six W.C.s and six urinals available to them. Sick Parade convened at 0800 hrs on 'B' Deck attended by the ship's Orderly Officer and Orderly Sergeant. The officer inspected the men dressed in accordance with Part I Orders: Battle Dress or Shirt Sleeve Order; F.S. Cap, boots, haversack, small kit and life-jacket.

The Medical Inspection Room dealt with R.A.F. sick at 0830 hrs and Army at 0930 hrs. Before attending Sick Parade the remainder of the servicemen's kit was handed in to the stores. Urgent cases admitted to the hospital were taken in at any time of day or night; provided an officer signed the requisite form, anyone could see a doctor in the interim between Sick Parades. Apart from seasickness, the main stream of complaints comprised tropical colds, headaches and sunburn, with a few cases of sunstroke. Nevertheless, regardless of conditions, accentuated by strong opinion that merciful alleviation of their state was overlooked, the mischief of the moment could not dam up the servicemen's thankfulness for being British ... and not Italian.

Sympathy went out to the Italian prisoners. Each morning they climbed vertical ladders from the holds which incarcerated them at the bottom of the ship. Battened down, they slept in rows of hammocks, subjected to fears at being imprisoned below the water-line. They looked bedraggled, exhausted through the buffetings of the elements, stinking from their own vomit. They were issued with soap then herded to improvised showers which were nothing more than punctured buckets hung above a man's head, filled with sea-water.

Assistant Butcher Edward Johnson got along well with the prisoners. A favoured few helped out in the butcher's shop level with the engine room. They were so anxious to please, exhibiting cordiality to the extreme, that he found it hard to think of them as his enemy. Daytime temperatures of seldom less than 100 degrees in the shade did not seem to bother them too much; irrespective of language barriers, he could see these young men were just glad of a few hours away from the wretched hold.

Each day Boat Deckman Hicks chose twelve Italians to keep the boat deck clean; he found them good workers, amiable, anxious to impress. With Chief Deck Steward Wallace rested the responsibility of feeding the prisoners; it was a task of great difficulty to balance food supplies against keeping a man alive in dreadful conditions. English food, consisting of two slices of bread and jam, cup of soup and tea, became their daily diet. Wallace, aged 46, had sailed the Cunard Liners since his teens. Apart from two trips, *Laconia* had been his home from the day of her maiden voyage. In 1935, on a five week cruise of the Mediterranean he had waited upon the Prince and Princess Arthur of Connaught. After 30 years at sea, he was used to people coming or going; he keenly anticipated bidding farewell to the Italians, likeable as they were.

Third Officer Thomas Buckingham in addition to bridge watch, was assigned the nightly task of inspecting the ship, ensuring blackening out regulations were in force, no tell-tale light telegraphing the ship's position. Exceeding his duties, he visited the prison hold and ordered guards to open the prisoner deck gates. His authority went unquestioned as guards allowed him to move amongst the Italians, choosing the obvious

24

exhaustion cases for transfer to the sick-bays where they could spend the remainder of the night in comparative comfort

'It was always a touching business to have the gates closed again upon so much pathetic human pleadings', he recalls, 'but the spare cots in the hospital were limited in number and my doubtful authority was limited to only a token gesture.'

With the advent of the dawn of Saturday 12th September, stocks in the shop of 'D' deck were depleted, offering only plain biscuits, tea, razor blades, soap and toothpaste. The special soap sold at the shop was vital if the men were to enjoy one of the few luxuries left – a sea-water shower.

Most of the books had been read and the men searched for some new interest to relieve boredom. They had taken down the stage on 'E' deck following a successful concert put together with the help of a borrowed piano. Something else had been accomplished: the concert proved a means of bringing together the three services. Up until then, the general attitude had been to keep themselves to themselves, except for the occasions when a representative visited the other's mess to check on conditions. The concert organisers, drawn from the three services, came up with the idea of a boxing tournament between the Army, R.A.F. and Royal Navy, using a hatch cover for a ring. Suddenly, servicemen developed a renewed pride in their uniform and its colour. Determination to show which was the senior service pervaded the respective messes, each resolute in a quest to be the victor as they sought to put together a worthy team. It was just the right therapy needed to punctuate the awful boredom, discomfort and seemingly long drawn out days. New friendships were formed; now, with a sense of greater unity between the three services, they searched for some new interest they could pursue.

As night approached, Third Officer Buckingham satisfied Captain Sharp that, consequent upon his inspection of the ship, security was in accordance with regulations. At 7 p.m. they watched the setting sun. Even after many years at sea, they never ceased to marvel at its wonder and beauty, which since the beginning of time has been generous to the artist's mind and a continuous source of inspiration to the poet. Yet, art and beauty formed no part of their thoughts that fatal September night, as their eyes scanned the trackless expanse of sea. Submarines plagued their minds!

Sharp calculated the *Laconia's* position was 900 miles south of Freetown and 250 miles north east of Ascension Island. Until the previous day, *Laconia's* captain and officers were of the opinion they were bound for Liverpool, although this was never confirmed. However, a coded message from the Admiralty in London was received at midnight on 10th September whilst Junior First Officer Hall-Lucas and Third Officer Buckingham were on bridge duty. Buckingham handed it to Purser Hurst for decoding. At 1.15 a.m. Captain Sharp read the deciphered message instructing a major alteration of course two hours after sunset on the 11th. The new course took *Laconia* into the middle of the South Atlantic, further away from the African coast, to cross the Equator midpoint between the coasts of Africa and Brazil. No reason was given for the change of course, opening the subject to conjecture as regulations prohibited them breaking radio silence to ask questions. Sharp and his officers reasoned it might be only a temporary diversion based upon intelligence reports of U-boat activity in the area. Should the new course be maintained, it was obvious Liverpool was not their destination, but possibly Canada or the West Indies. The fact that they were transporting prisoners of war made this assumption quite credible. In compliance, *Laconia's* course was altered at 10 p.m. on the 11th.

For several days the weather had remained fine, which added comfort to all on board. Saturday, the 12th, was no exception and a kind of 'week-end' atmosphere was sensed amongst the passengers on the upper decks, now more relaxed. Civilians and military officers dressed for dinner. In normal circumstances the Captain would have his own table with selected guests to talk the evening away, an experience to remember long after the voyage was ended. On this voyage there was no captain's table; *Laconia's* master ate alone and slept fully clothed in the Chart Room, ready to be summoned at a moment's notice. Such was the burden and loneliness of command.

At 7.30 p.m. bearings were taken and the captain ordered a cessation of zig-zagging procedures, putting the ship on a normal course. Hall-Lucas and Buckingham were given permission to leave the bridge to have dinner in the officers' mess. Elsewhere nightly formalities received attention. Children, tired from the heat and playing games on deck for most of the day, were tucked into cabin bunks, sleeping in warm pyjamas and life-jackets which offered as much protection from the cold as their clothes would do if they had to take to the lifeboats. Shoes and overcoats were arranged in readiness at the bottom of their bunks. Some cabin doors were slightly ajar and here and there a mother's voice was heard reading from a favourite story book, or a child's voice saying prayers.

Shortly after 8 p.m. with dinner over, dancing was underway in the First Class lounge. Officers of the three services sat comfortably in plush chairs. Larger groups occupied the lounge corners from where voices, often loud, engaged in discussion upon a host of topics. The inter-mixture of human expression seasoned with outbursts of laughter competed with the music.

Laconia's plumber, Charles Gregory, a native of Liverpool, decided to have an early night. In his cabin on 'C' Deck he stretched out on his bunk with a migraine headache, not wishing to be disturbed. At 25 years old he was unrelenting in his determination to survive the war. By his bunk within hand reach lay a carefully prepared survival bag containing a yellow overall suit complete with hood, food, cigarettes, matches and a torch. But sleep that night ignored the cry from his weary body. His tortured head, whilst seeking relief, was filled with anxious thoughts about the safety of his family, which like other households throughout the British Isles was attending to similar nightly chores, drawing heavy curtains over windows, many of which were fitted with home-made shutters. The official blackout time commenced at 7.30 p.m., lasting until 6.04 a.m. In order to comply with the 'total' blackout regulations, violation of which could produce hefty fines, it was a common sight to find blankets and rugs hung up as an extra precaution over the windows. Policemen and Wardens patrolled the pitch black streets devoid of any lighting. The 'Week in Westminster' broadcast on the B.B.C. Home Services and Forces programme was in its final minutes, bringing news of Prime Minister Winston Churchill's return from Russia and the Middle East in time to hear Lord Leathers announce that during the three years of war, 2,551 bravery awards had been issued to Merchant Navy personnel. Also, an announcement in Moscow stated that 12 British officers and men were to receive the 'Order of the Red Flag', the 'Order of the Red Star' and the 'Order of the Patriotic War', the first time such awards named foreign recipients. Over Germany, the R.A.F. were heavily bombing Bremen, their seventh attack upon the enemy that month. A few days previously they had spent ninety minutes over Karlsruhe near Stuttgart.

Satisfied their homes were safe, the people drew up their chairs to the fireside in readiness for the ever popular hour long 'Music Hall' programme.

The blackout resulted in few people walking the dark streets, in a sense cultivating an unofficial curfew. Effective as any drug, the blackout turned the nation into compulsive 'Nine O'clock News' listeners; at the chimes of Big Ben an almost holy hush permeated homes in Britain. So much so, that Major Wellesley Tudor-Pole and Colonel W. H. Carver, M.P., hit upon an idea for uniting the nation. As a point of contact they chose the chimes of Big Ben, urging the people at 8.59 p.m., as they prepared to listen to the nine o'clock news, to observe a one minute silence. It was to be a rallying point for the renewal of courage, determination and faith. This 'Dedicated Moment' was shared by millions on land, sea and even in occupied territories. The King, Prime Minister and Church leaders lent their wholehearted support to Sir Waldron Smithers, chairman of the 'Big Ben Silent Minute Observance Council'. News of R.A.F. attacks upon Germany brought glimmers of hope to the people.

At 8 p.m. engine room fitter Billy Hardacre came off duty, relieved to get away from the bottom of the ship. Sanguine in nature and not easily frightened, he felt uneasy aboard *Laconia*. Now in his sixteenth week as a crew member, the nauseous disturbance in his spirit suffocated life's simple joys and laughs with his friends. At times he felt trapped in a confusion of his own making, unable to relate emotional and real life principles. When *Laconia* docked at Cape Town, her last port of call, he went ashore, meeting up with his cousin Charlie Jackson. After leaving a shop where he purchased a gift for his mother, he handed the item to his cousin asking him to take it home as he had a feeling he would not be seeing her again. Time is an abstraction. It is not perceptible to the senses of sight, touch, hearing, smell and taste. Yet it exists. Billy Hardacre could not shrug off the deep seated conviction that time was running out for the *Laconia*.

Each night after dinner, he spent an hour of his time with younger crew members, who, to relieve boredom as well as wanting to keep themselves in trim, joined his boxing training class. In a space near the ship's 'Shell door', a space reserved for bringing the oil aboard, he set up a practice punch bag. Upon arrival two boys were already attacking the punch bag with much energy and hostility. At 25 Hardacre was not much older than them, yet they looked upon him as their elder brother, wanting to benefit from his vast boxing experience. As a professional fighter, he had progressed well in the 'middle-weight' division until his career was abruptly marred by the accidental death of an opponent in the ring, followed by a serious injury to another. These unfortunate incidents proved a blockage in obtaining further contests. Hardacre exchanged a few words with the two boys, promising to join them after supper.

Royal Naval Gunner Robert Tinkler swept the trackless expanse of sea with high powered binoculars. The afternoon gunnery practice, always an attraction to passengers, earned him and the gun crew words of commendation from Lt. Tillie. The exercise was good for morale, too, as onlookers went away feeling more secure.

His duty colleague, Gunner John Hennessey, preferred standing watch on a warship to being aft on an ageing liner and expected to perform marvels with ancient weaponry. As a boy he listened intently to the stories his father told about naval actions, shipwrecks and how he survived the sinking of the *Lusitania.* Our memories retain the counterfoil of life's experiences and long ago John Hennessey distanced himself from the twilight worlds of boyhood imaginations, far different to the realities of war at sea. He knew the odds were still strongly in favour of the U-boat as they entered the fourth year of belligerency. Due to shortage of shipping, *Laconia* was overcrowded, sailing without escort, without any means of detecting a submarine other than by the naked eye. Since January 1942 the British had possessed a radar set known as Type 291, containing a revolving aerial to give all round search capability, and able to detect a surfaced U-boat at 5,000 yards or submerged at 3,000 yards. Regrettably, manufacture of the new equipment was too slow for *Laconia* to benefit.

Ship's Butcher Edward Johnson exercised on the Boat Deck before going to his cabin to change out of his working clothes. Then he remembered a promise made to his colleagues at the meal table. An intelligence report received from a steward attached to the military revealed that somehow the soldiers had come into possession of an excellent gramophone. All agreed some music would be cheering, suggesting Johnson with his winning personality as the very man to send on a mission to 'E' Deck and ask the soldiers if they would be willing to lend out their gramophone and records. Finding the soldier who was the custodian of the sought after treasure, Johnson felt stifled in the clammy atmosphere on 'E' Deck, made worse as blackout regulations required all portholes to remain closed. He rolled a cigarette whilst the amiable soldier rummaged around to find the gramophone handle.

Barely a mile away, in the veiling darkness, a German U-boat surfaced. And waited!

26. Lieutenant Commander Werner Hartenstein, commander of U-156

30

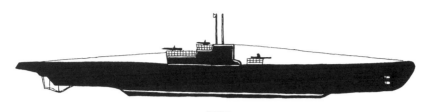

III

UNSEEN OBSERVER

Since 9.30 a.m. that morning, Commander Werner Hartenstein had stalked the *Laconia*, working out her zig-zag course, waiting for nightfall before he attacked.

A regular officer, he was 32 years old with a university education, joining the navy in 1928 and coming through the ranks to officer. Born in the Saxon town of Plauen which had adopted his submarine U-156, he was unmarried and distinguished by a duelling scar down his left cheek.

U-156 was built at Bremen in the Deshimag Wesser dockyards, classified as a Type 1XC submarine. She had a displacement of 1132 tons, capable of carrying 208 tons of fuel with a range of 13,450 nautical miles. She was launched in September 1941 and was commissioned at Kiel; Hartenstein commanded the new boat on her maiden voyage, returning to Lorient on 8th January 1942 without firing even one of his 22 torpedoes. However, U-156's 4 bow and 2 stern torpedo tubes received their baptism on February 16th 1942, when Hartenstein torpedoed two oil tankers at Aruba, in the Caribbean, carrying oil for the Allied cause. Then they attacked the oil refineries with their deck guns, causing considerable damage. In June, Hartenstein surface-attacked the Lamport and Holt vessel *Willimantic* (4,858 tons). Torpedoes were unnecessary as U-156's guns were sufficient to halt the *Willimantic's* trip to Baltimore. In August, the *Clan MacWhirter* (5,941 tons) was destroyed by one torpedo, sinking with the loss of ten lives, including her captain – Capt Masters. One torpedo was also enough to send the *Norman Prince* to the bottom of the ocean with the loss of seventeen crew and her master, Capt Harries. Between February and September U-156 sank twenty two ships totalling 105,232 tons.

Since the *Athenia* affair, which occurred only eight hours after Britain and Germany had entered into a state of war with each other, U-boats had engaged in unrestricted warfare in contravention of international law. At the time Germany denied being responsible for the sinking because Fritz Lempke, commander of U-30, did not mention the matter in his wireless report. The German propaganda machine got to work, at first stating the

31

Athenia must have struck a mine. Later they changed the story in an attempt to discredit Churchill, then First Sea Lord, whom they alleged instructed a British submarine to sink the *Athenia* so as to inflame American opinion against Germany. It was not until the end of September that U-30 docked and Dönitz learnt the truth. Hitler, still hoping to avoid serious hostilities with Britain, ordered U-boats not to sink passenger ships. According to the London naval Treaty of 1930, to which Germany was signatory, merchant ships must first be stopped and searched. Except in cases when a vessel refused to stop or offered resistance, a U-boat should not take action to destroy a merchantman without first having ensured the safety of crew and passengers.

Pressure from Dönitz and his superior Raeder forced Hitler to rethink the issue through, claiming that ships stopped for search could easily radio a U-boat's position, thus increasing the possibility of attack from the air. This actually happened to a Royal Navy submarine, H.M.S. *Salmon,* which sighted the German liner *Bremen* in the Skagerrak. H.M.S. *Salmon* surfaced and signalled the liner to stop. Wireless messages from the *Bremen* brought Luftwaffe patrols to the spot and H.M.S. *Salmon* was forced to submerge.

By stages, Dönitz was allowed more freedom in ignoring International Law, extending each time his area of activity, until by the end of 1939 he had complete freedom in all oceans.

British ships were ever aware that their 'unseen observer' could strike at any time, in any ocean, without warning. The biggest shock Hartenstein received was on 18th May 1942 through his encounter with the *San Eliseo* en route to Barbados. Disregarding the advice of his commander-in-chief not to attack during daylight hours, Hartenstein fired two torpedoes at the British tanker. Watching through the periscope Hartenstein saw the first torpedo hit the target exactly as planned, but the second torpedo was off course. Captain Johnson on the bridge of the *San Eliseo* spotted a line of disturbance in the water forming an obvious curve and calculated it was spinning out of control. Immediately, he reduced speed, allowing the projectile to pass him by. Although his ship was damaged, Johnson maintained a zig-zag course, ordering his gun crew to open fire at U-156's periscope. The shells exploded so close that the submarine was severely shaken. Hartenstein dived, steering his boat to a safer distance. Unwilling to break off the action, he took up the challenge, firing a third torpedo, which tore into the *San Eliseo.* Captain Johnson kept to his course even though further damaged and handicapped to 8 knots. A fourth torpedo caused devastation to *San Eliseo's* engine room, reducing the apparently doomed oil tanker to 5 knots. Hartenstein fired a fifth torpedo which like the second spun off course, missing the target by a matter of a few feet. Convinced his adversary could not stay afloat for long, U-156's commander surfaced determined to terminate the contest with gunfire. Seeing what was about to happen, Captain Johnson headed *San Eliseo's* bows in the direction of U-156, set on a collision course. The tactic took Hartenstein by surprise, who then cleared decks and took his submarine deep into the ocean and away from the scene. Two days later the *San Eliseo* reached Barbados.

Repeatedly, Dönitz preached to his U-boat commanders the sense of night surface attacks when the small outline of the submarine was extremely difficult to spot by look-outs. It was a strategy that should not have taken the Allies by surprise. All that was required was to spend a few marks at a German bookshop for Dönitz's book *Die U-bootwaffe* (The U-Boat Force). Published in January 1939, its pages clearly document his intentions. Any reader would have interpreted the message in the same manner as a ship having a warning shot fired across her bows. Much of the book was devoted to an in-depth look at the considerable advantages gained by submarines attacking on the surface at night. In 1937, before Dönitz translated his thoughts to print, he demonstrated the shape of things to come when the German Navy carried out full scale manoeuvres observed by Britain and other leading maritime nations. At the manoeuvres Dönitz's U-boats rehearsed his scheme for attacking convoys of ships using the 'wolf-pack' approach. The plan of attack was simple. Upon discovering a convoy the vigilant U-boat would report the position to base command, continuing to shadow the convoy throughout daylight hours. In the meantime, wireless messages were passed to U-boats in the area and as night fell the 'pack' converged on the convoy. In a surface attack the U-boat was at her best. She benefited from maximum speed, could utilise all armaments and fire torpedoes with greater accuracy. Shrouded by darkness she was virtually invisible.

U-156 had two main diesel engines capable of delivering a surface speed of 18 knots. Although primarily designed as a surface vessel, it was also a diving vessel fitted with battery operated electric motors to propel the boat when submerged. Underwater, she had a top speed of 7 knots. Hartenstein kept the number of men on the bridge and deck to a minimum, aware as none other that his boat could only submerge when she was underway. The space between the periscope and bridge coaming was small. In an emergency the bridge watch scrambled down the narrow conning tower, one man at a time. Saving precious seconds was crucial, especially if under attack, and could mean the difference between life and death. Superinduced jumping with two crewmen at the foot of the ladder waiting to catch each man, dragging him aside before the next man landed substantially increased speed, the ladder only coming into use for climbing and more leisurely occasions. Last off the bridge, Hartenstein would hear the bellow of the diesel engines, the boat starting its downward plunge as he slammed closed the hatch cover. As soon as the boat submerged the only source of oxygen was the supply left in the boat, which the diesel engines would consume in an instant, suffocating the crew. At the right moment the chief engineer cut off the powerful diesels, at the same time turning on two battery operated electric motors, which drove the boat under with the help of selected crew members who ran forward to give extra weight to the bow. The main ballast tanks outside the boat opened to release air, then flooded with sea water, reducing the vessel's buoyancy. While submerged, a further complication arose. The life of the electric batteries, whose function was to drive the diesel engines, was limited to a few hours. This meant the U-boat had to surface to charge its batteries, an impossible situation if being hunted for several hours by destroyers.

For this, his fourth combat mission, Hartenstein was fitted out with an experimental 'schnörkel', a Dutch pre-war invention largely forgotten about. Dönitz saw its value! At least as a temporary measure until such time as his 'back room' designers adapted something better. The 'schnörkel', a floating valve attached to an air line, allowed U-boats to run their diesel engines while submerged. Although it was invulnerable from airborne radar incapable of picking up an object as small as a 'schnörkel' head, Allied intelligence passed on to the anti-U-boat forces a useful tip – the 'schnörkel' left a trail of effervescence. For a while aircraft used up valuable fuel, time and explosives in attacking any resemblance to this description, but real sightings were few, most of their effort being spent in dropping depth charges on water spouts thrown up naturally by the sea.

As 'guinea pigs' Hartenstein and his crew soon discovered the major problem with 'schnörkel' experimentation. Often, the sea closed over the 'schnörkel's' top, which activated a mechanism shutting down the float valve, preventing water pouring into the boat. Such occurrences introduced unpleasant discomforts to the crew. The diesel engines rapidly burnt up oxygen from the boat's interior, leaving the men gasping for breath. They also inhaled exhaust gases blown back into the boat.

Submarine crews, whether Allied or German, lived in a close-knit community. Each individual accepted the importance of his personal level of morale, realising the security of his vessel depended upon his efficiency. Ever conscious of the possibility of sudden attack from the air, Hartenstein made it his business to know his boat and crew intimately. Regular exercises

34

were carried out in cutting the diving time by urgent life saving seconds, to the extent of counting the revolutions on each electric motor to ensure maximum silence while gliding slowly underwater. Oftentimes, sucking undersea currents and swells presented him with difficulty in keeping the boat level in the water, requiring expertise in harmonising the forward and aft ballast tanks. Mature, trained hands moved positively over the extensive array of levers and switches, regularly adjusting the diving planes. Quite unofficially, Chief Engineers improvised ingenious means to give the boat an extra couple of knots speed in an emergency.

Dönitz was of the opinion that, just as important as combat strategy, a contributing factor to morale amongst crews at sea for several months was good food, as the health of each member depended upon a well ordered diet. So he ensured that careful arrangements existed for provisioning boats. Before setting off on a patrol every available space was packed with fresh food, placed where it was within easy reach, usually in the crew's living compartments. Food had to be eaten in reverse order to storing and once stocks of fresh food were exhausted, cooks turned to tinned and dried foods.

In order to maintain the physical fitness of the crew, exercise and fresh air for each man augmented the fighting efficiency of the boat. Because the only way into a U-boat's interior was through a hatch large enough to admit one man at a time, sessions for relaxation were strictly limited to a man's turn on deck, in case of emergency.

As Hartenstein battled at sea, in Germany, scientists fought the battle for technological excellence. As new developments were put to use, Hartenstein's role demanded new skills. Since sailing from Lorient on 17th August, in addition to the 'schnörkel' he was carrying another new piece of equipment. Dubbed 'the Biscay Cross', this simple instrument, a radar search receiver, effectively located radar impulses up to a range of fifteen miles. Rough in design and temporary until a more sophisticated radar location set could be manufactured, it consisted of a wooden base with wires strung around it to connect with the receiving set below deck. Its main disadvantages in use were that it had to be dismantled and taken below before the boat could dive, and that Hartenstein had to station a rating permanently in the conning tower.

In June 1942, Dönitz convened a meeting with Kinder Admiral Stummel, Director of Naval Communications. He was troubled because Allied technology had surpassed German progress: notwithstanding the principles of radar having been recognised in Europe as early as 1930, Germany knew very little about it. Since the beginning of 1942 a number of

U-boats, particularly in the Bay of Biscay, had been sighting enemy aircraft long after the aircraft were sighting them. Unexpected losses were sustained. The Germans concluded that the British aircraft were equipped with a new, highly sensitive location device, especially as some aircraft appeared out of low cloud ready to attack. Dönitz was further disturbed by reports received from trusted and experienced U-boat commanders, baffled as to how, on a dark night, an aircraft could take them by surprise and with great accuracy switch on a high powered searchlight, lining them up in its beam, making the submarine as accessible as in daylight. Dönitz was quite correct in his assumption. British advances in the field of radar enabled scientists to produce a 1½ metre radar set sufficiently compact to be carried in an aircraft. The 'Biscay Cross' saved many U-boats from being caught unawares and Hartenstein became one of the first commanders to test it.

Dönitz was not happy about U-156 operating in waters 6,000 miles from home. Strong words of disapproval for the scheme were exchanged with Supreme Naval Command over the commission given to the new 'Eisbär' (Polar Bear) Group, consisting of U-156, four other U-boats and a 'milch cow' – U-459 – a supplies submarine much larger than the others, carrying fuel, torpedoes and food to replenish the boats at sea. Dönitz was in contention with the whole idea of the operation of U-boats in the Cape Town region where they had not functioned before, maintaining that it was not worth the risk so far from home base when he could acquire the same success by merely crossing the equator. Naval Command thought otherwise, overruling the exigent U-boat commander-in-chief, arguing that the Allies would be taken by surprise, opening up to U-boats a fresh period of immunity in a new area. But there were other players in the game. British Intelligence had gained knowledge of the plan, which influenced the Admiralty to re-route shipping away from Cape Town's usual sea lanes. The soft spot German Naval Command anticipated was denied Polar Bear Group, who had to search for victims, contrary to briefings which assured them of a galaxy of easy targets, unescorted troopships.

The only solace Dönitz found in the 'Polar Bear' Group was in the quality of his commanders. Hartenstein graduated from training school before the Nazi era. A regular officer, he transferred out of destroyers into the U-boat arm and was eyed by his chief as a candidate for high rank. An agglomeration of losses amongst experienced commanders and crews brought new worries to Dönitz, and he was forced to send younger and less skilled crews into battle. Constantly, he studied reports on U-boat losses, his analytical mind reviewing causes for loss and deducing that older and more experienced commanders like Hartenstein, who underwent extensive educational programmes, were top of the league in sinking enemy ships. Even in bad weather they had the expertise to get close enough to release their torpedoes. The number of U-boats at sea in September 1942 exceeded 300 – six times the number in September 1939 – and more were under construction. New conditions necessitated new thinking and Dönitz shifted his training policy, deciding that new skills could not be taught in schools. Rather, they should be learnt in action. In consequence he reduced the training programme to five months for new crews, who were then sent out into combat.

Laconia's course alteration received at midnight on 10th September took her further south into water where U-boat activity was not known. Or so it was thought. When Hartenstein sighted her, U-156 was only just within the zone Dönitz had set for attacks. As the sun set in orange and ochre tones the crew were taking an early supper which meant that, once it was dark, they would be in action.

27. A late view of the *Laconia*.

28. Captain Rudolph Sharp, OBE, RD, RNVR.

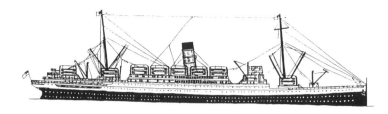

IV

ABANDON SHIP!

As the hand of Commander Hartenstein's stop watch touched 8.07 p.m. the first torpedo tore into the *Laconia's* side, sending shock waves of destruction through the liner's steel frame as the warhead exploded violently. Tons of water poured into the huge gaping hole, the smitten ship lurching to port under the force of the blast. She then rose and began listing to starboard only to be flung again from side to side, rocked by a further explosion thirty seconds later as the second torpedo entered the engine room. Hissing steam escaped from shattered steam pipes and scalded those not killed in the explosion, settling like a heavy mist to conceal the carnage of twisted steel, decapitated bodies and human flesh strewn about machinery and walls.

Everyone in the firemen's quarters perished in their cabins, which collapsed like cardboard boxes, victims of the impetuous blast; flying metal, debris and huge steel girders fell on to them from above.

In No 2 hold, where Italians were imprisoned, the first torpedo spread speedy death to the majority of them crammed in their dingy prison.

Lights suddenly failed! In the darkness stunned passengers returned to their senses upon hearing the loud shrill of the boat stations alarm echoing across the ocean like the cry of a helpless victim, contested by the eerie shuddering of a mortally wounded ship.

Dancers in the First Class lounge were thrown off balance, those sitting around tables spilled onto the floor, their drinking glasses smashed across the room.

Army Lieutenant Mercer was standing outside the First Class Dining Room, relaxing; dinner was over and he was the last to leave. Regaining his feet he heard a huge bang behind him as the mainmast came crashing down on the bridge and the dining room roof caved in.

The force of the blast flung Dorothy Davidson, a colonel's wife, and Molly her teenage daughter across the lounge floor, where couples were dancing. Recovering their balance their only thought was to make for the

Boat Deck. As they reached the stairs, the second torpedo tore into *Laconia*'s hull, causing the ship to list further to the starboard side. As the lights suddenly failed, the Davidsons returned to their senses upon hearing the loud shrill of the boat stations alarm. A determination gripped them to climb the stairs. And survive!

* * *

Missionary nursing sister Doris Hawkins was returning home after five years service in Palestine. Entrusted to her care was fourteen-months-old Sally whose young mother had said to Miss Hawkins, before leaving: 'Never forget if anything happens and Sally has to go, that you must do all you can to save yourself ... we cannot replace you and you have a lot of work to do.' Doris Hawkins described *Laconia*'s sinking and her experience of twenty-seven days in an open boat in a book entitled *Atlantic Torpedo*, written in 1943 when she eventually arrived in England. And home! She describes the moment of impact:

'Calmly, until suddenly there came a shattering explosion. The ship shivered, then stood still; and the air filled with the smell of explosive. It had happened; the first torpedo had struck.

'I fled to Sally. She was still asleep, and I wrapped her in her woollies, picked up her shipwreck bag, and turned. As I did so the second torpedo struck. The ship rocked; we were flung across the corridor. Sally remained in my arms, unhurt.

'Just ahead of me was Mary [this was the name Doris Hawkins gave her companion throughout her account. The book *U-Boats to the Rescue* identified her as Lady Grizel Wolfe-Murray], and together we made our way upstairs. We were carried on a surging wave of people, some with their emergency outfits, many without, for they had been unable to reach their cabins. As we went the lights failed.'

* * *

Third Officer Buckingham left the dining room on 'D' Deck a few minutes before 8 o'clock with Junior First Officer Hall-Lucas, who reminded him of a promise to visit a Royal Navy officer and his wife in Cabin 17 on 'A' Deck, quite close to their own. Together they walked along the starboard alleyway leading to their cabins when Hall-Lucas decided Buckingham should make the visit alone, saying he would see him at midnight for their bridge watch. As Buckingham raised his hand to knock on the cabin door, a violent explosion from below decks shook the ship. The cabin door disintegrated into hundreds of pieces, the air filled with a thick cloud of fine grey-white dust, the pungent smell of explosives pierced the atmosphere. Inside the cabin by the faint glow of a light bulb fixed on the bulkhead, Buckingham

40

could see two figures enshrouded in the fog-like conditions. Alarmed and fearful the bewildered couple instantly obeyed Buckingham's order to leave everything and get to their boat station.

* * *

When the first torpedo struck the *Laconia's* starboard side Army Captain Ben Coutts was in the sick-bay, his foot swathed in bandages. Everyone who had seen the tall Scottish artillery officer would remember him for the large dressing which covered the hole in his face where his nose should have been due to the wound sustained at the battle for Tobruk. Instinctively, he reached for the haversack, containing a survival kit which he had carefully prepared for such an emergency. Placing his injured foot on the floor, he was resolved it would not let him down in his determination to survive, regardless of this handicap. Hurriedly, he slipped on his greatcoat before setting off to the Boat Deck, checking that his revolver was loaded, then dropping it into his greatcoat pocket. By the time he reached the Boat Deck all the boats had gone. Finding a rope ladder on the port side of the ship now listing perilously, Captain Coutts negotiated the tilted hull until the sea was only a few yards beneath him. And jumped!

* * *

Butcher Edward Johnson stood appalled for a few seconds, which seemed an eternity. Co-ordination between mind and muscle was non-existent; fear like an invisible lava threatened to overwhelm his whole being as he searched his mind. 'We're done for. Won't need it,' he told the shocked soldier facing him, with a gramophone handle in his hand. Everyone on the Mess Deck moved as one man when Johnson urged them to evacuate the place. Uppermost in the mind of Johnson, a non-swimmer, was the life-jacket in his cabin.

* * *

In the darkness pandemonium reigned. Gone were the constituting class distinctions. Civilians, army, air force and navy personnel, crew members, prisoners and those who guarded them, attempted to keep a firm foot on slippery, tilted decks littered with debris and sprayed with burst pipes.

Voices competed for attention:

'This way to the boats.'

'Have you seen ...?'

'I've no life-jacket.'

Children crying.

Some in utter confusion, bemused, huddled together waiting for instructions. People bumped into each other.

41

Heavy machinery, lashed to the deck because of shortage of space below, now loose from its anchorage, posed new dangers at every turn.

To make matters worse, crazed Italians emerged from the holds. They headed for the boats, pushing each other and anyone else in the way. By some miracle, some prisoners from the disastrous No 2 hold, bloodied, barely clothed, screaming, joined the seething throng intent upon escaping their floating tomb.

* * *

Boatswain Le Brocq was scheduled for duty at midnight. Feeling quite fresh he decided after dinner to forego his usual 'snooze' and join friends for a social evening in a cabin on 'C' Deck. Five minutes later the first torpedo hit the forward hold over which the firemen and engine room crew lived. Thrown off a comfortable cabin settee, Le Brocq and his friends, all crew members, instinctively, without a word passing between them, ran out of the cabin to take up their duty stations. Le Brocq set off in the direction of his cabin to collect a life-jacket but changed his mind, knowing he could easily obtain another somewhere on the large ship.

Before he could reach the Boat Deck, Hartenstein's second torpedo hit the *Laconia*, throwing him off his feet as the blast up the ship's side came just ahead of him. None the worse for the fall, Le Brocq arrived at the Boat Deck, now thronged with anxious passengers, as were the connecting corridors between port and starboard side decks. The *Laconia's* engines had stopped and in the changing moonlight, strong then clouded, he could see the starboard Boat Deck covered with the remains of at least six lifeboats thrown inboard by the force of the explosions.

* * *

Darkness and canted slippery decks covered in wreckage were not envisaged during the orderly if not light-hearted boat drills when passengers queued in small groups, always in daytime. The crewman's demonstration of how the lifeboat worked appeared straightforward. For over twenty-one years, *Laconia's* lifeboats had more or less been ornamental, except for the occasion on 24th September 1934 when she had collided with the United States tanker *Pan Royal* in fog off Cape Cod, severely damaging this vessel. Passengers were mustered at Boat Stations as a precaution. Now reality interposed the drill's missing ingredient – the will to survive.

* * *

When Plumber Charles Gregory reached the main staircase leading up to 'A' Deck, he stopped to gather his thoughts. Minutes earlier he had switched off his cabin light hoping he could sleep, a damp handkerchief across his sore head. Seconds later he was lying on the floor; the explosion below decks, which instantly he knew was caused by a torpedo, triggered within him a compulsion to run. As he reached the staircase, his lungs were nearly bursting, his thoughts troubled by the tremors reverberating through the dying ship, and from the feel of the planking beneath his feet he knew the *Laconia* was sinking fast. Panic seized him when he realised the survival bag he had carefully prepared was still in his cabin and in the darkness he deliberated as to whether he should go back for it. Men's voices nearby distracted such thoughts as he peered to see what was happening. Unexpectedly, darkness was turned into light as emergency lighting benefited parts of the ship. At the bottom of the staircase, struggling soldiers were piled up on each other, covered in oil. Down the staircase poured the black substance from the ruptured tanks above, bringing with it more soldiers unable to keep their feet or grip the slippery handrails. The sight was horrific! Charles Gregory felt scared and trapped. He decided to move away from the scene and try to escape along the working alleyway leading to the stairs which would take him up to the pantry and eventually to 'A' Deck. He wasn't sure what he would discover on the way but he set off as the ship turned more dangerously on its side.

* * *

Meanwhile, Third Officer Buckingham reached the damaged bridge. Captain Sharp, unhurt, was out on the wing of the bridge, leaning over the rail trying to see where the torpedoes had entered. Junior Second Officer Stokes told Buckingham that all telephone communications had broken down and that the captain had ordered 'Abandon Ship!' Upon instructions from the captain, messengers conveyed the order to all parts of the ship. Chief Officer Steel and First Officer Walker left the bridge to go to the Boat Deck in order to assist in launching all possible lifeboats into the water. Buckingham's responsibility if the *Laconia* came under attack was to jettison confidential mails, which were kept in lockers in the captain's chartroom. 'The quartermaster will help you,' Sharp said, urging Buckingham to attend to the matter with all haste. In the chartroom, Buckingham opened the lockers removing the secret documents including deciphering codes already stored in canvas bags perforated with holes and heavily weighted at the bottom to make them sink. The lights were out in this part of the ship and they flashed torches. Carrying the heavy bags along the sloping deck, through the officers' mess, to the bridge was tiring work. Ten minutes later they tipped the last consignment over the rail. Unfortunately, a few of the bags fell on survivors swimming away from the ship. In his own report, Buckingham commented 'Even in these few minutes the sea was alive with persons and prisoners who had jumped overboard. I could faintly see them; black shapes in the disturbed phosphorescence along the port side... Whilst dropping the confidential mail overboard I knew it was falling among people in the water but this could not be avoided.'

Buckingham's next order was to go to the radio room and find out if distress signals had been transmitted. The radio shack was behind the funnel and to get to it Buckingham had to go down two decks, then cross a short length of deck leading to the vertical emergency ladder he intended to climb. After refusing to be stopped by passengers who had so many questions to ask, he found his path to the emergency ladder blocked by Italian prisoners who cost him valuable minutes, but by sheer force he powered his way through them. In his personal report he added 'Several of them held religious tracts in hands outstretched over the heads of their companions, and with uplifted faces the intonations of men in prayer seemed to make my journey to the radio room more of a compelling and imperative errand...'

The two radio operators were seated in front of their switchboards in a listening attitude. They seemed calm, almost oblivious to what was happening around them. Bad news awaited Buckingham. Due to the collapse of the mainmast, the wireless transmitter had been destroyed and an effective S.O.S. could not be sent. Using the emergency set, the wireless operator flashed the captain's message hoping someone within its limited fifty mile range would intercept the signal.

Buckingham decided to return to the bridge by a different route, by way of the alleyways below decks and through the officer's quarters. He was shocked to come across groups of passengers congregated together, unwilling to go up to the boat decks. He talked to some of them, emphasising the urgency to disregard the unreal security given by the ship's lights and the brief comfort of the companionship of people they knew. His words seemed to have no influence in moving them from their dissenting position.

When Buckingham reported to Captain Sharp, he was examining a chart by torchlight on the wheelhouse bench. 'Thank you, Buckingham,' he said with sadness in his voice, 'better go to the Boat Deck yourself, now.'

* * *

Billy Hardacre left his cabin in the firemen's quarters, knife and fork in hand, ready for supper. A terrible, scorching force seized his powerful body, depositing it in a semi-conscious state halfway down the companionway. In the darkness, his battered form was all that remained alive in the firemen's quarters.

Covered in debris, befuddled, his mind screamed out for intelligence. Slowly, senses returned, dispelling the fog eclipsing struggling thoughts only to present dark forebodings about his physical condition and what was happening around him. Pushing away the lumber covering his body, he slouched to his feet, steadying his aching body against the buckled companionway wall, to discover he was completely naked. Except for a leather belt dangling slackly around his waist.

He had difficulty in opening his eyes, matted by blood flowing from a head wound. Blood was also pouring from a deep cut on his right arm. Billy Hardacre realised his position was precarious but overshadowing all his circumstances was the strong determination to live.

* * *

At 8.20 p.m. Lt Tillie ordered the *Laconia's* gun crews to 'Stand Down'. 'Look after yourselves, lads,' he said. They were to be the last words Gunners John Hennessey and Robert Tinkler would hear this gallant Royal Navy officer speak. Hennessey climbed the ladder up to the Boat Deck and the scene awaiting him shattered his optimistic hopes of getting away in a lifeboat. Frantic Italians had swamped the boat stations, several British Army officers, revolvers in their hands broke through the language barrier, menacingly aiming their weapons at them. Polish guards with 'fixed bayonets' supported. Convinced they would be considered last for boat spaces, the prisoners would not take any notice. Passengers fought with the Italians, making their own contribution to restore some resemblance of order.

Lt Col Baldwin, officer in charge of the prisoners, took stronger measures to calm the situation. After escaping their prison hatch, they tried to reach the upper decks by using the main staircase. Baldwin, assisted by Capt McCordick and Lt Dickens (RA) together with some Polish guards, took up a position designed to cut off their path to the staircase and fired a hail of bullets into their surging mass. In the darkness it would be difficult to distinguish Italians from British and surviving crew members believe that some of the *Laconia's* catering staff were shot dead, mistaken for desperate prisoners.

* * *

Amidst the clamour, Boat Deckman Robert Hicks, Boatswain Le Brocq and other crew members worked tirelessly to launch the lifeboats. In the best of conditions this can be a long and arduous task but with the occasional shot ringing out, operating on oblique decks, under the stress of not knowing how much time was left to get the job done, it was extremely difficult, especially as a number of boats showed signs of damage. John Hennessey judged he would only prove to be an extra burden and with the thought that perhaps some child might live if he withdrew, he retraced his steps, returning aft to take his chance in going over the ship's side.

Checking the knot of one of the many ropes tied to the stern railings, he took it in his hands and climbed over. Suspended between sky and sea he started to manipulate his hands and feet in a motion which although making his descent slow, ensured he was in complete control of the rope. At all costs he wanted to avoid hitting the water with rope burns on his hands. Not all who chose to venture over the ship's side on a rope found it manageable. Many released their grip after looking down at the sea. Some could negotiate the method of using hands and feet in their descent. Some, like the *Laconia's* barber, overwhelmed with fear, dangled on the rope for a considerable time until aching limbs forced them to make a further effort. Several of the lifeboats hung out too far and had to be lowered first into the water. Passengers willing to experiment swarming down a rope to claim a coveted place got into all sorts of difficulties. A Polish guard, complete with an unloaded rifle (they were not issued with ammunition), fell from a rope ladder, his fixed bayonet penetrating the bottom of the lifeboat.

In the water, Hennessey swallowed a great deal of thick oil and sea water. He found the life-jacket extremely buoyant, assisting directional progress with the minimum of effort. The ship towering above his head, hissing like a sea monster, augmented new fears, importunate, urging Hennessey to strike out and keep swimming until well away from the doomed liner. As a sailor he knew that when a ship sank, it created a circular eddy of water, sucking downwards, too powerful for anyone caught in its currents.

* * *

At 8.24 p.m. Boat No 11 on the starboard side, full with women and children, was the first to leave the *Laconia*. Naval Rating Robert Tinkler helped to get it away then assisted in getting others away for as long as he was needed.

* * *

Boat No 9 containing only women and children squashed tightly within her slender frame, crashed against the ship's side, spilling already frightened passengers headlong into the sea. Missionary Doris Hawkins, who had just taken a small baby into her arms, felt the little life wrested from her grasp as she was flung into the ocean. Doris Hawkins recalls:

'So we waited for what seemed an age; really it was only for about fifteen minutes. Then we were told that our lifeboat had been blown away. We wondered what to do. It was pitch dark. Sally never once cried, either then

46

or throughout the whole experience, despite the noise and confusion around; she remained quite still in my arms, making only gentle little talking sounds.

'There was no one to direct us. Just as Mary and I were considering feeling our way round the deck, Squadron-Leader H. R. K. Wells came upon us. Taking Sally from me, he led us from boat-station to boat-station; but all the boats seemed to have left, or to be full, or else jammed so that they could not be launched. Nearly three-quarters of an hour after the torpedoes had struck we saw below us a lifeboat, already in the water but still alongside the ship. A young Fleet Air Arm lieutenant volunteered to carry Sally. He tucked her down inside the back of his greatcoat, tied a blanket round his waist just under Sally's foot level, to prevent her from slipping, and so he carried her, papoose fashion, down a swinging rope ladder, and into the crowded lifeboat, heaving and tossing like a cork. It was well done.

'Mary and I followed as quickly as possible. We found ourselves on top of the arms and legs of a panic-stricken mass of humanity. The lifeboat, filled to capacity with men, women and children, was leaking badly and rapidly filling with water; at the same time it was crashing against the ship's side. Just as Sally was passed over to me, the boat filled completely and capsized, flinging us all into the water. I lost her. I did not hear her cry even then, and I am sure that God took her immediately to Himself without suffering. I never saw her again.'

* * *

Knowing the layout of the ship helped Plumber Charles Gregory to reach 'A' Deck. As planned, he passed through the ship's pantry, running most of the way, along narrow angled companionways which reeked of fumes from the explosion. Swinging cabin doors threatened every step. Several times he stumbled over debris and twisted linoleum covered with oil. Relieved to breathe in the night air and expel from his lungs the suffocating gases inhaled during his nightmare trip, he arrived at his allotted boat station to find that Boat No 17 had just been lowered. Without thinking, forgetting he was without a life-jacket, he grabbed a rope and slid down it. The waves of the Atlantic were now seen from a different angle as he looked down and noticed outstretched hands waiting to grab him.

A Royal Navy Gunnery Rating assumed command, from the outset earning respect for his decisiveness. Anxious to get the lifeboat away to the safe distance of three hundred yards from the foundering ship. Charles Gregory was glad to be under his authority. In the boat were over fifty men, calm, with little to say, apart from the chattering Italians. The *Laconia* was now well down at the bow but more on an even keel attributable to the bulkheads holding.

* * *

Billy Hardacre couldn't remember much about his agonising passage up to the Boat Deck. The cut on his head had stopped bleeding and his arm, although sore and stiff, was not as bad as he had feared. Still naked, for the first time he was aware of the scratches encircling his whole body, left there by the heat of the titanic explosion which stripped him of his clothes. The air cleared his misty mind and he began to think about the boys he had left around the punch bag. Discretion dictated he should stay on the Boat Deck. Resonant, death-like groanings from below, chilling bone and marrow, warned that trapped water behind watertight bulkheads would soon give way under the pressure of thousands of tons of water swirling round the lower decks. As though indifferent to this danger signal, he found a torch and headed for the working alleyway which led to where he had last seen them. Ahead, his torch spotlighted the punch bag, swinging similar to the pendulum of a grandfather clock and then on to the lifeless form of teenager Assistant Storekeeper Stanley Buchanan. Two other bodies were nearby, badly disfigured. Against the passageway wall a crew member with his head nearly severed from his body fought the air with his hands. There was nothing Hardacre could do for the man. Hurrying back to the Boat Deck, spurred on by the erupting noises around him, he found the narrow companionway blocked. His torch flashed upon another outrage of the night. Moving towards him was a crew member whom he thought he recognised but wasn't sure, for the man's face was partly blown away, his eyes dangling on his cheeks.

* * *

Below decks, *Laconia's* Third Officer overtook the ship's doctor, Geoffrey Purslow, escorting a stretcher case carried by two sick-bay attendants. They struggled along a narrow steeply sloped corridor, actually lying on the side wall yet keeping the stretcher in a horizontal position. Buckingham went ahead of them holding the torch. It took five minutes to reach the outside decks, where, fortunately for the man on the stretcher, a boat still seaworthy was being man-handled by Chief Officer George Steel and a couple of crewmen. By sheer physical strength they moved it until it rested outboard, still hanging by its tackles from the davits. It rocked dangerously, scraping and bumping the protruding rivets of the hull as the stretcher was placed along the side bench.

* * *

Dotted around the lifeboats, survivors in life-jackets, distinguishable by the red battery operated lights, swam around seeking the refuge of some boat, raft, or other piece of flotsam. Screams penetrated the night air. Cries rang out: 'Sharks!' Shoals of sharks, carnivorous with a well developed sense of smell in their search for food, infested the waters around the sinking *Laconia*. Attracted by the red lights on the life-jackets, these voracious creatures who eat any kind of animal life, including each other, introduced a new terror to those in the water.

* * *

Steward Golding, whom Charles Gregory recognised, pleaded to be hauled out of the water. As hands assisted to pull him aboard an agonising cry burst from his lips – a shark had torn his calf muscle clean out of his right leg.

Gregory helped to fish others out of the water until Boat No 17 was dangerously overcrowded. The Naval Rating in charge decided that to admit one more person could have disastrous results for them all. Somehow, the frantic Italians in the water, frightened, pleading for help, must be dissuaded from further attempts to enter the boat. Several clumsy efforts had scared everyone who thought they were about to capsize. Charles Gregory was handed an axe and told to chop off their fingers. Reluctantly, he raised the axe only to lower it again. He couldn't carry out the dastardly act. Meanwhile, the Royal Naval Rating who was slicing off as many encumbering fingers as he could see, and telling the men to row, yelled at Gregory to take action quickly against an Italian who was part way into the boat, now leaning insanely, the choppy sea threatening. Gregory hit the offending man firmly on top of the head with the blunt side of the axe and watched his body float away. For a moment he stared out into the night, disgusted.

* * *

Gunner John Hennessey paused for a rest. Swimming through waters strewn with mats of drifting oil patches, wreckage, boxes and pieces of wood, taxed his energy. Looming up before him he traced the grey form of a lifeboat. It was not full and he found himself sitting amongst young R.A.F. men dressed in greatcoats and carrying side haversacks. There was a lot of water in the boat and despite strenuous baling efforts the water level was rising. Hennessey discovered the bung was missing and it was too late to do anything about it, the boat was too low in the water and sinking. He shouted to everyone that baling was useless; that he was going to evacuate, that everyone should follow him. As he swam clear he was surprised to see the R.A.F. men still in the boat, they appeared to be mesmerised by a hidden force, bound by invisible chains, unable to act.

49

THE SINKING OF THE LACONIA

John Hennessey was to spend the next eighteen hours swimming in waters which he knew were powerful enough to uphold him and strong enough to drown him.

* * *

Hennessey's gunnery partner, Robert Tinkler, opted to jump overboard. It was the quickest way to get off the ship. Some people near him lost their hold on the deck and slid down and over the side into the sea. Tinkler found that everything seemed to happen to him intuitively. He was jumping without even thinking about other options open to him. He landed amongst wreckage tossing about in the swell and decided to keep swimming until he was well away from the tragic sea. Scud off the ragged tops of the waves stung his eyes, the mixture of oil and sea water filling his lungs. Added to this misery, new problems faced him: blood curdling screams out of the darkness sent shivers down his cold body. Sharks! Not far away large sickle shaped teeth were tearing survivors to pieces. The sudden jar of a wooden plank barring his way ahead injected a much needed psychological boost. It was comforting to hang on to something solid. A few minutes later voices becked: 'Come to the boat!' Tinkler struck out and each stroke brought the voices clearer. Nearer! The lifeboat was not full, its occupants mainly women and children. At intervals the women continued to shout their message in all directions, hoping some other soul would hear.

* * *

Boat 13a, on the port side, near the *Laconia's* bridge was the only boat left. Hardacre joined the four men trying to release it. The Boat Deck was now quiet and the men could talk to each other in normal voices. Gone was the din of trampling feet and a thousand voices, each demanding to be heard. Each wanting to live and not to die like the Italians whose bodies bearing gun shot and bayonet wounds lay around them.

The presence of Captain Sharp caused them to relax their efforts to free the boat. He calmly suggested they were wasting valuable time and should put on a life-jacket and evacuate the ship as soon as possible. He wished them good success, asking before he left them if anyone had a cigarette. Unhurried, he walked towards the bridge. Hardacre and his colleagues stuck to the challenge of leaving the *Laconia* in Boat 13a. Soon they were rewarded. Now it was a race against time, the *Laconia* was sinking fast and they wondered if the lifeboat could be lowered before she slid under the ocean. When the lowered lifeboat passed the Promenade Deck a pathetic sight awaited them. Two small children, forlorn, stood hand in hand. The boy, around six years old, asked if they had seen his mum and dad. Billy Hardacre reached out towards them and brought them into the boat. The boy kept asking about his parents, but all Hardacre could think of telling him was that they had gone for a swim.

* * *

Boatswain Le Brocq saw the last boat leave. He considered jumping over the starboard side, then changed his mind, believing that he might get dragged under the water by absorbing undercurrents along the side of the ship, caused by the two large holes in her plating where the torpedoes had entered. Swarming down a rope he joined Boat 13a as it reached the water. British Army Major Creedon saw Le Brocq take to the rope and followed him down it. Altogether six men and two children pulled away, aghast at how high out of the water stood the *Laconia's* stern.

* * *

Captain Rudolph Sharp and First Officer George Steel chose to stay with the doomed liner. Buckingham later commented that he had asked Steel what he intended to do next: 'He said: "I'll go and see the Captain." As if, steadfast in the essential and customary ways of the sea, whatever the tide of its fortunes, the final and absolute execution of his duties was a personal report.' From the wing of the bridge on the port side, Le Brocq and Hardacre saw the glow of two cigarettes. Gradually, they pulled away from the floating nightmare towering above them, picking up lone swimmers on the way, drawing their cold, oily bodies out of reach of the sharks. R.A.F. Wing Commander Blackburn, who was yet to play an unusual role in the *Laconia* epic, assisted Hardacre in baling as Le Brocq stuffed cloths into the offending hole where the bung should have been (this is the second lifeboat mentioned with a bung missing and there were probably more).

* * *

Fifty minutes after the first torpedo struck, Buckingham was alone on the Boat Deck. He examined several boats, unshipped from their cradles, which lay useless on their sides. The deck, covered with loose gear and debris brought down from above by the impact of the two explosions, moved with each shudder of the ship. As he took off his jacket and shoes, a violent sound coming from a porthole only fifteen feet away urged him to act quickly. Buckingham recalls:

'The air below decks trapped and under tremendous pressure was escaping with a steadily increasing roar, obliterating all other commotion in its alarming crescendo. I did not hesitate but steadied myself on the upper edge of the ship's side and eased my way down the inclined hull. The bilge keel protruded some few feet above the water and I was able to pause there long enough to find a foothold and plunged out, headlong, into the chasm of the ocean.'

51

30. Lt Commander Werner Hartenstein.
Previous two pages: U-156 in harbour, built in 1940/41. The functional design is in marked contrast to that of the Italian *Cappellini* submarine on pages 206-207.

V

UNEXPECTED HELP

Very slowly U-156 headed her bows in the direction of the disaster area, solid water breaking along the forward casing, passing down her flanks and spreading widely past her bulging saddle tanks. The sea was running a heavy swell, as if a token of her anger over the dark deed of that night. In the changing moonlight, the waves showed white-caps – and wreckage from the *Laconia*.

Hartenstein decided to implement Admiral Dönitz's directive issued early in 1942 to capture, if possible, her captain and chief engineer. Chugging along on her diesels the *Laconia* was getting nearer and larger. Wreckage was tossed about in the swell which he was careful to manoeuvre well away from. From the inelegant space of the bridge coaming, Hartenstein trained his binoculars on *Laconia's* stern, his gun crew ready to finish her off in the event of resistance. The guns did not appear to be manned. However, his professionalism, and a mental catalogue of stories shared by others in a similar position, warned him not to rule out the unexpected – a ship playing possum – luring the proud hunter into a trap. He would not be the first to be sent to the bottom by a dying ship firing a final savage salute.

Lifeboats came into view. They passed several by and his deck officers were sure they saw women and children in them. Rafts and lone swimmers were sighted and corpses lolling in the water, upheld by their life-jackets. This was the first time U-156 had attacked a liner, which Hartenstein realised must be carrying thousands of people, possibly civilians. He was puzzled by repeated reports from his deck crew that not all of the cries of distress from the shipwrecked were English voices. They were sure some of the voices were in the Italian tongue. He decided to investigate, giving orders to pull several of them aboard.

Hartenstein had a difficult choice to make: he had successfully torpedoed a large liner exactly as planned, his greatest achievement in three years of war, but shocked to learn she was transporting nearly two thousand prisoners who belonged to a partner nation fighting the same war against the British. If he stayed in the wreck area, he risked the safety of his submarine and crew. The S.O.S. signals from the *Laconia*, although weak, might have been intercepted by a hostile vessel and passed on to a warship or aircraft. Allowing his heart to rule his head he proceeded to initiate a rescue, without discrimination.

* * *

At 9.20 p.m. black smoke emitting from her funnel, roaring, her stern high out of the water, apparently hanging from some unseen strand in the sky, the *Laconia* paused for a moment then slipped out of sight between the waves.

Edward Johnson could see the propellers and rudders as the liner went into a dive by the head. As she slid beneath the surface, he wept.

Boatswain Le Brocq experienced a sensation of abject loneliness as if iron had entered his soul. As they watched, a great surge of water spouted high over the *Laconia's* grave, issuing in a crashing sound through the air and across the water. Depth charges stored on the ship, set to detonate at fifty feet in the hope that some unwary U-boat might get caught in the eruption, sent debris hurtling through the air, the shock waves overturning some lifeboats.

* * *

Lt Mercer, caught in the blast of the explosion, was knocked unconscious. He had jumped overboard shortly before the ship sank, undergoing some bad moments in the water due to the unwanted attention of Italians trying to cling to him for support. Exhausted by the trauma, having swallowed a good deal of water, he managed to struggle free, summoning enough energy to swim away from those who placed his life in jeopardy. Then his right leg became entangled in a partially submerged rope and the strain of setting himself free of it bit further into his waning energy.

* * *

Charles Gregory thought of fellow plumber and friend, John Heslop, who rarely went ashore. Having served in the *Laconia* for many years he preferred the comfort of his cabin. Almost a recluse, his off-duty hours were spent there. He couldn't erase from his mind the bewildered look of his cabin neighbour as he passed him when dashing from his cabin. Heslop was standing in the doorway of his quarters when Gregory stopped briefly to suggest he left everything and followed him. His friend made no reply, just stared compendiously and turning around locked himself in the cabin.

* * *

56

UNEXPECTED HELP

Andrew Zamrej was one of the Polish guards on board. He had joined the Polish army in the USSR and ended up in officer cadet school at Pietermaritzburg, Natal. With his colleagues he had joined the ship at Durban to guard the Italians:

'We Polish cadet officers kept guard on the prisoners, changing every two hours. On 12th September at exactly 8.07 p.m. the first torpedo hit the ship, then other.

'I had finished my duty below the decks, guarding prisoners, at 8.00 p.m. and had gone upstairs for a cup of coffee before the ship was hit. If I had stayed another 5 minutes or my change had been late I would have been killed there and then. Right away the water became red.

'Everybody realized that the ship was sinking and the crew started lowering boats and rafts. I started helping women and children into the boats exactly as we were trained to do. We all felt that they should be helped first. Not all the lifeboats could be launched. Some were stuck.

'I was so busy helping that I did not realise that the ship was going down rapidly. I jumped into the water and swam as far as I could because I knew that I would be drowned if I stayed near the ship. It was pitch black and cold. When I found myself a good distance from the ship, I turned around. The ship was going down and the captain and a few of the officers waved to us. It is a picture you would not forget in your life. They made no attempt to save themselves. I got hold of a passing raft and pulled myself onto it, making sure I was safe.

'Then a second person came and boarded the raft, he was Italian. He whispered the words 'Santa Maria'. During the night I must have dozed because when I opened my eyes my companion was no longer there and dawn was breaking.

'I never discovered what happened to him, whether he was drowned, was eaten by a shark or got into a boat. Shortly after dawn a boat was passing and picked me up. In the boat was another Polish soldier, seven Italians and the rest were crew from the ship, in total 82 persons. Together we spent 5 days just waiting for help.

'When the submarine came across us, I was sitting at the end of the boat and I was asked to go to submarine, where I saw rescued Italian prisoners of war. I was asked questions for which I had no answers. After that I was put back into the boat with over 80 cigarettes and matches and was told to tell my comrades not to stray too far.'

* * *

THE SINKING OF THE LACONIA

James Campbell was one of the R.A.F. personnel on board the *Laconia*. He remembers:

'Four of us, R.A.F. lads, were returning home after service in the Western Desert and had got into the habit of a nightly game of cards before turning in. It was the turn of my pal Jock Jarvie to go up to the small tea bar for our nightly cuppa when the first of the two torpedoes struck. The ship listed right away and the second torpedo followed. We grabbed our life belts and went up the staircases as quickly as we could until we reached the upper deck. Some of the passengers who had been having a walk on deck had panicked and jumped into the sea. Others had thrown in small Carley floats in response to their cries for help but in fact the floats killed a few by landing on them. In addition they had slid down the exposed ships hull and badly lacerated their buttocks on the barnacles. I think that someone later mistook the lacerations for Barracuda bites.

'Our lifeboat station was the top most aft port boat but obviously couldn't be launched because of the steep list to starboard. Our deck seemed deserted but we found two naval ratings on the starboard side trying to free the last lifeboat on that side. We helped them and, after some time, managed to free it. I said to one of the ratings, "you get in and we'll lower you down." He drew himself up and declared, "We are the Navy and *you* get in the boat." When we turned, the boat was more than full of people and we just had to take a run down the sloping deck and land on them. When the boat got into the water it took in water right away. I was wearing desert boots which I gave to two of the lads and told them to bale out whilst I went under to see the damage. I could have swam through the hole which had been caused when the lifeboat had swung back into the side of the ship. I surfaced and was thinking of what to do next.

'Jock Jarvie was still baling out with one of the boots, and an R.A.F. Corporal who was sitting nearby, up to his waist in the sea, said "Stop it Jock you're splashing me". I said to my pal we had better get out of here. We swam away from the ship and got hold of a floating oar and then got a second oar. These oars helped us a lot and we got a fair distance from the ship when she went down. Even then when the boilers went up it was like a severe kick in the stomach.

'We eventually met up with a lifeboat which had dozens of Italians clinging to the sides. We shouted and asked if they had room for two more. A huge Scots Guardsman was cracking the Italians heads open with an oar and shouted that he'd soon make room for us. To him they were still the enemy although in reality we were all fellow survivors. I shouted to him in strong language to stop this. About this time the submarine surfaced and

58

came amongst the boats and swimmers. They were taking people aboard and (how naive can you be?), we agreed to swim away from the sub thinking that a British ship would soon pick us up. This had been said on the *Laconia* tannoy when "abandon ship" had been ordered. In fact there wasn't a British ship within a thousand miles of us!

'We came across a Welsh army sergeant with a Carley float and an R.A.F. sergeant and the four of us clung to it throughout the night. When dawn came it was pretty desolate with mainly small bits of wreckage and an occasional dead body floating about. We must have drifted a lot during the night as, about mid-day, we saw the submarine surfaced at least a mile away. We agreed that this was our only chance and started to swim towards it. No easy task pushing a float and in fact only the Army N.C.O. and myself were in any way fit. We reached the sub at 1.30 p.m. and the crew pulled us out along with an army W.O. who had lost an ankle to a barracuda. A crew member came along and offered us a lump of bread but we were so exhausted we couldn't lift our hands to take it. The sub took us to where they had tied seven lifeboats together and put us into one of them. The W.O. who had lost an ankle died soon afterwards through loss of blood.'

* * *

When Third Officer Buckingham reached the surface, he remembers: 'The sea seemed... in a tremendous upheaval. Huge columns of spray were bursting upwards through its surface in a wild chorus of incredible noise. I could not see the sky, only a pale green phosphorescent shroud of frothing, turbulent water. But I could breathe freely and realised from all the swarming maelstrom of the sea around, that I was being blown... about in the water by powerful blasts of escaping air. This went on for a minute or so, then to my relief slowly eased away, and when I saw the starlit sky again, all seemed strangely quiet and peaceful. No ship, no voices... only the sounds of the sea itself as the night breezes gently ruffled its surface. On the surface of this boundless ocean, the loneliness seemed infinite and eternal, and as I lay floating on my back, the myriad of stars seemed to look down without sentiment or judgement.'

At a distance Buckingham saw the white beam of a small searchlight sweeping the ocean. He swam towards it but when he looked again, it had disappeared. He kept on swimming in the direction in which he had seen the light, hoping it might be turned on again. After about ten minutes he came across an upturned lifeboat and two men holding on to its lifelines. One of the men was the *Laconia*'s Second Officer, Stokes, who told him he had broken his leg. Buckingham tested the upturned boat cautiously with his weight before the two men dragged Stokes out of the water and astride the keel. The injured officer was in great pain but sufficiently alert to lie along the keel, grasping the rope grab-lines on each bow. Buckingham reviewed the situation, wondering if the two men might have a better chance of survival without his extra weight resting on the waterlogged boat. Promising to return if he found a lifeboat, Buckingham swam away in the direction of the light he had seen. It was the last time he saw Second Officer Stokes. Buckingham takes up the story:

'I was not wearing a life-jacket and after swimming and floating for what must have been half an hour, I thought it best to stop and conserve my strength. The breeze had freshened and with the sea incessantly breaking over me, it became most difficult to lie effortlessly afloat. I wondered why I had not come across wreckage and then made up my mind to stay where I was but to keep myself in an upright position for the remainder of the night. But about 2 a.m. (...I had judged the time by the altitude of the stars I had seen rising from the east), I started off with easy movements swimming towards the west, hoping to come upon something, indeed anything, that may have drifted that way in the current. But my strength and endurance were slowly waning, and for the first time I became alarmed about my prospects. I had no idea what complete exhaustion... [meant], except that it must eventually overcome all human effort, to leave behind a beaten and defeated body to succumb without sense or feelings. And if that was to be the way of things, there appeared no purpose in waiting for its ignoble conclusion.

'I struck out and swam for what must have been five minutes or so, then stopped and listened, and swam again, but no sound other than the fretful breaking of the sea interrupted the profound solitude around me.

'The night seemed endless and without compassion. I wondered if I had been right in swimming, or if it would have been better to have remained near the sinking. With some effort I stripped off my undershirt and my socks... I began recklessly to swim back, and soon, almost breathless and before I could avoid the encounter, I swam headlong into something solid, yet yielding. I was almost half over the top of it before it sank beneath me, then surfaced again... It was a dead body floating in its life-jacket. It floated face-down, and with arms outstretched... However gruesome it seemed, at least there was some... relief in having something to hold on to...

'The two of us bobbed up and down... with monotonous regularity at least a thousand times before I saw the pale glow of the approaching dawn in the eastern sky.'

* * *

Unknowingly, lifeboat No 17 with desperate men at her oars was in the path of a German submarine. In her stern conserving his energy for when it would be his turn to row, Charles Gregory busied himself attending to the comfort of Steward Golding, fortunate enough not to have had his whole leg torn off by the shark. Gregory hated himself for taking action against the Italian in the water, who like himself only wanted to live a bit longer. He kept telling himself that he had no choice in the matter. That they would have all ended up in the water and his friend Golding would certainly not have survived for long.

Occasionally, he had turned to look at the *Laconia*, overwhelmed by an incredible sadness. Nevertheless, he was glad to see in the changing moonlight boats pulling away, some clear, some obscure in the ship's shadow. As he strained his eyes, at times imagining he could see the ship he loved, he wondered if it was all a soporific dream, perhaps happening to someone else and he was a mere observer.

It was difficult to know who else was in Boat 17, apart from the grateful Italians who just kept talking and talking. Someone lit up cigarettes and passed them around. As each man drew on it the brief glow lit up a face that he thought he recognised.

The throb of engines close at hand caused the men to stop rowing. Seconds later they were startled, almost blinded by a searchlight which lit up their boat, then turned in a wide arc to reveal the presence of other boats not very far away.

'It's a U-boat,' a voice shouted from the bow, 'and they've manned the gun.'

Fearfully, the occupants of Boat 17 cowered low, expecting any moment to be cut down by bullets.

Through the hailer, Hartenstein asked if they had the *Laconia's* captain or an officer on board. Gregory was surprised to hear a German speaking perfect English. The man sitting next to him, cheekily, in a strong Liverpudlian accent suggested it would be improper to speak with the enemy. The Naval Rating in charge shouted back that there were no officers, just crewmen and a few Italians.

Gregory noticed the U-boat crew pulling survivors out of the sea, which was unexpected – it gave him hope for tomorrow.

* * *

After Sally had slipped from her grasp, Doris Hawkins had found herself in the water: 'among numbers of Italians screaming and struggling in the water. One, in his terror, grasped me, both arms around my neck, and dragged me down, down under the water... I struggled and I came to the surface.

'My hand touched a piece of wood, and I clung on. Another Italian began to drag at me. Finally I came up to a raft, to which I managed to hold. There were already four Italians hanging on to the sides, but they were quiet; they helped me up on to the top. I lay there, and we drifted away from the ship.

'When we were about 120 yards away I saw the ship rear half out of the water, and then she sank like a great monster, hissing and roaring – an awe-inspiring sight. I thought of the men who had built her, the money that had been spent upon her, the work she had done in peace-time and in war. I thought of the cargoes which she had taken safely back and forth, and of our men whom she had carried to and from the theatres of war. Her epitaph perhaps would be: "The Admiralty regrets to announce that a ship of 20,000 tons has been sunk in the Atlantic. The next of kin have been informed..." Not even her name might be mentioned; many would hear unmoved the voice of the announcer telling of her loss. And in sharp contrast I pictured the homes where the shadow of anxiety and of death would lie, of men and women and little children, whose loved ones would never return: "Lost at sea by enemy action, September 1942..."'

Just as the explosions came from the sunken ship, Squadron-Leader Wells and Lt Tillie joined her raft. They were each slightly injured by the force of the blast.

'I was helped on top. Nine or ten men were clinging to the sides of the raft. Later we put the Italians on to another raft, to which some more of their compatriots were clinging, then all we who remained were British.

'In the water we had swallowed a good deal of thick oil from the wreck, as well as sea, and in turn we were all violently sick. Our hair and faces were thickly covered with oil.

'We were cheerful and even optimistic. I remember Squadron-Leader Wells saying "This is a lie – it can't have happened to us!" – and so it seemed – unreal, fantastic. We felt detached from it all.

'Lieutenant Tillie appeared to be in splendid form; he cheered us with assurances of rescue on the morrow, leading us in community singing and making us confident and at times almost merry.

'Suddenly he became quiet, and I felt suspicious. He changed places with the man beside me, and leaned heavily against me. I felt his pulse and found it very weak, and I became really anxious. He spoke slowly and a little thickly in answer to my questions, though he declared that he was "all right". Only then I noticed that his right shirt-sleeve was soaked with blood.

We had nothing out there on a small raft with which to stop the hæmorrhage. He refused to remain more than the allotted minutes out of the water; Squadron-Leader Wells supported him with one arm as he gradually became exhausted. After some time he lost consciousness, and at about midnight he died, facing death with the same high courage and cheerful optimism which had always been his outstanding qualities.

'I learned afterwards that when the ship was torpedoed, he had rallied the small naval draft of whom he was in charge, and had told them to help in getting the women and children away. Only when he saw the last boat go did he clamber over the side. As the ship was about to sink he jumped, and he injured his arm on the way down. Homeward bound after several years, he had served in the Narvik campaign, where he had won his D.S.C. [Distinguished Service Cross], and in the Mediterranean he had gained the bar.

'I took his watch and promised that if I should ever reach safety I would somehow get it to his mother. It is in her keeping now; his name is engraved on the back.'

* * *

31. Lifeboat overflowing with *Laconia* survivors.

Hartenstein continued to pick up survivors from the wreckage littered sea, the hum of U-156's engines a familiar sound to those in the lifeboats. He knew that unless rescue came soon, many in the boats and certainly those in the water would not survive another night.

Accordingly, he instructed his wireless man to send the following message to Admiral Dönitz:

'British liner *Laconia* sunk by Hartenstein. Ship unfortunately carrying 1,500 Italian prisoners of war. So far 90 rescued. Request instructions.'

The *Laconia's* survivors spent the night on the sea, cold, huddled together in lifeboats, anxious about loved ones, friends from whom they were separated. Hundreds were still in the sea, fatigued, fearful of falling asleep. Bravely, they gripped planks of wood, lay on rafts or clung to them. Others just bobbed up and down in their life-jackets waiting for the morning.

The fortunate few to be taken on board the U-boat could hardly believe that the enemy responsible for their condition was now doing his utmost to ensure their comfort. Members of the crew served them coffee and hot soup, gave medical attention where needed, even to surrendering their quarters for the more exhausted cases. Others were housed in the torpedo compartments.

Messages flashed between Hartenstein and Dönitz, who requested further details. In the interim he continued to take on board further survivors. Finally, when instructions from Dönitz arrived, the pink flimsy handed to him simply ordered him to stay on the spot but be ready to submerge.

Before the message arrived, he had rescued 193 British and Italians and could hardly submerge in an emergency with the speed he was accustomed to. Like all U-boat commanders, he constantly practised emergency dives, logging the time taken, commending the crew for the slightest fraction of a second saved off their best performance. Always, their last dive had to be their best.

New problems faced Hartenstein.

32. U-156 preparing for a mission.
33. Cross section plan of U-156.
34. *Laconia* survivors on the deck of U-156.

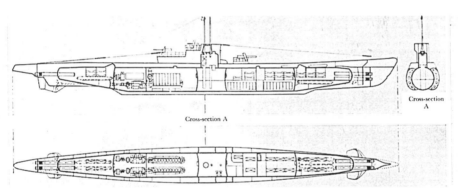

Cross-section A

Cross-section A

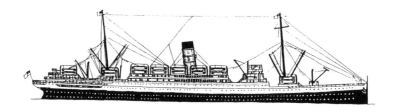

VI

THE ADMIRALS ACT

At 6.00 a.m. on Sunday 13th, Hartenstein handed to his wireless operator a message to be transmitted on the 25 metre band in English:

'If any ship will assist the shipwrecked *Laconia* crew, I will not attack her provided I am not being attacked by ship or air forces. I picked up 193 men 4 52' south 11 26' west. German submarine.'

At 6.10 a.m. the message was repeated on the 600 metre international wavelength. Dönitz was later adamant that the British must have intercepted Hartenstein's 'en clair' signal, but there is no record or admission to support this claim.

Admiral Dönitz was used to receiving calls during the early morning hours but unquestionably Hartenstein's dilemma distinguished itself in its uniqueness. When the signal arrived, he was asleep in his quarters situated in a large building on the Avenue Maréchal Maunoury, Paris, France – the headquarters of U-Boat Command. He was no stranger to Paris, for on 1st September 1940 U-Boat Command moved its headquarters from Sengwarden near Wilhelmshaven to the Boulevard Suchet in preparation for the invasion of England, part of the systematic arrangements to align all the command posts. Consequent upon the decision to postpone the invasion, Dönitz moved his headquarters to Kernevel close to Lorient, with a good view of the sea and the harbour. However, following the British commando raid on St Nazaire, direct orders from Hitler forced U-Boat Command to return to Paris.

From this cradle of German aspiration to control the seas, Dönitz, ably assisted by the impeccable organising genius, Admiral von Friedburg, directed operations, planned training programmes, dealt with matters of discipline and continuously mailed letters to next of kin of crews lost in combat. In the previous month, he had submitted to Hitler a detailed report showing 105 U-boats lost since the first day of war, accounting for 3,803 officers and men killed, captured or missing.

THE ADMIRALS ACT

Each morning Dönitz would be found in the operations room next door to his quarters, applying his keen mind to the study of reports covering the activities of the previous night. On a large chart, the position of each submarine was carefully plotted and with the artistry of a chess player, he schemed to outwit his enemy, adroitly manoeuvring the small U-boat force into strategic positions.

There was no time for delay. A decision had to be taken in response to Hartenstein's appeal for 'further instructions'. The choice was simple, although far from easy. Either instruct Hartenstein to put the survivors back into the sea or support him in the rescue. Pin-pointing U-156's position on the chart, it appeared Hartenstein was reasonably safe from air attack. The nearest British base on Ascension Island was two hundred and fifty miles from the wreck area, virtually harmless, with, it was believed, no aircraft. Nevertheless, a German submarine with a large number of its crew on deck, he deliberated, was hardly a boat in a state of alert. He agreed that the prerogative to rescue the shipwrecked, having considered the action completed, lay with the boat's commander, being in complete conformity with the law of the sea. Raeder, Commander-in-Chief of the German Navy, warned that the safety of U-boats must not be jeopardised. Times had changed, he argued; the use of radar regularised the determining point when an action could be considered over. What that point was posed an open-ended question defying interpretation by either the Germans or the British. Admirals Karl Dönitz and Erich Raeder faced a situation that was new to them. The extremely cautious Raeder, answerable directly to Hitler, made no attempt to squash the idea of a rescue mission functioning in some form. Germany's relationship with her ally Italy, was sensitive and the aid given to her countrymen in the South Atlantic would be viewed favourably.

Dönitz made up his mind to support Hartenstein and ordered the Polar Bear Group submarines engaged off Cape Town to break off operations and hasten at full speed to the disaster area with the sole intention of assisting Hartenstein. The Admiral reasoned that a full rescue of the shipwrecked could be undertaken, but it would be impossible to keep the rescued aboard submarines for any lengthy period of time. His plan was to land them at a point on the French Ivory Coast.

In Berlin, Admiral Raeder informed Hitler of the unusual drama being played out on the other side of the world, which displeased him, warning Raeder that he would hold him responsible if unnecessarily any of the submarines were placed in danger. Dönitz was glad it was Raeder who spoke to the Fuhrer and not himself. He always complained after visiting

67

the Berlin headquarters of feeling tired – exhausted! – through endeavouring to disengage himself from Hitler's strong powers of suggestion and preserve his own power of initiative.

Raeder devised his own plan: through the Franco-German Armistice Commission, sitting in permanent session at the Hotel Nassauer Hof, Wiesbaden, he approached the Vichy Government, requesting their co-operation by sending French warships out of Dakar for a rendezvous with the U-boats, who would transfer the survivors to them.

On 22nd June 1940, an Armistice had been signed between France and Germany. In his negotiations with the French, he referred to this instrument under Article 8 which stated:

'The French war fleet is to be collected in ports to be designated more particularly, and under German and (or) Italian control, there to be demobilised and laid-up – with the exception of those units released to the French Government for protection of French interests in its colonial empire. The peacetime status of ships should control the designation of ports.

'The German Government solemnly declares to the French Government that it does not intend to use the French war fleet which is in harbours under German control for its purposes in war, with the exception of units necessary for the purposes of guarding the coast and sweeping mines. It further solemnly and expressly declares that it does not intend to bring up any demands respecting the French war fleet on the conclusion of a peace. All warships outside of France are to be recalled to France, with the exception of that portion of the French fleet which shall be designated to represent French interests in the colonial empire.'

Raeder anticipated that the French might not give his request easy passage, when they discovered that not only Italians but British servicemen and civilians were to be rescued. The Vichy Government was still smarting from what they considered harsh and unnecessary treatment at the hands of the British. On 16th June 1940, six days before the Armistice was signed, the French Premier asked the British Government for a formal release from their agreement that a separate peace should not be concluded by either nation.

Churchill replied: 'Provided that the French fleet was dispatched to British ports and remained there while the negotiations were conducted, His Majesty's Government would give their consent to the French Government asking what terms of armistice would be open to them.'

The British Government discounted any 'solemn' assurances issued by Hitler, whose word could not be trusted. On 3rd July French warships berthed at Portsmouth, Plymouth and Sheerness, were seized. The French offered no resistance except on the submarine *Surcouf* when due to a misunderstanding, a scuffle broke out, resulting in two deaths and four woundings. Over two hundred vessels, a major part of the French fleet, including two battleships, two light cruisers and eight destroyers fell into British hands.

France was a major maritime nation, possessing large battleships which worried Prime Minister Winston Churchill. Under German control, they would always represent temptation to violate the terms of the Armistice by pressing them into service with German crews.

At Oran and other ports on the North African coast were berthed the 26,500 ton battleships *Dunkerque* and *Strasbourg*, cruisers, submarines and other vessels, plus the 35,000 ton battleships *Richelieu* and *Jean Bart*, almost completed but not yet commissioned.

Churchill offered the French an alternative: on 3rd July 1940, a British Task Force arrived at Oran and a message was sent to the French Admiral Gensoul asking him to meet with a British delegation for talks. Gensoul refused the invitation, whereupon the British presented a document which demanded that French warships sail out of Oran with them to continue the fight against the Nazi oppressors. However, if they were honour bound by the armistice terms not to use their ships against Germany or Italy, the document made provision for the French ships to be escorted to a French port in the West Indies where they could be demilitarised to British satisfaction. The document ended with a warning of intended British action against their ships should the terms be refused.

Admiral Gensoul and his staff took little time to consider the proposals before them, replying that rather than accept them he would turn his guns upon the British Task Force.

At 6 p.m. Vice-Admiral Sir James Somerville took the initiative and ordered British warships to open fire. Swordfish torpedo 'planes from the aircraft carrier H.M.S. *Ark Royal* scored hits upon the battleship *Dunkerque*. The battleship *Bretagne* sank and two others, severely damaged, later capsized. At the end of the action over three hundred Frenchmen were either dead or wounded. There were no British casualties.

Five days later, the British Task Force sailed into Dakar, a port in French West Africa. Similar terms to those offered at Oran were made and rejected by the French. The British response was to send a motor boat into Dakar harbour with the objective of placing demolition charges under the stern of the battleship *Richelieu* as she lay at anchor in shallow water. The explosions damaged her steering gear and propellers. Then followed an air attack upon other targets by torpedo 'planes from the aircraft carrier H.M.S.

Hermes. Later that day, in a broadcast to the French people, General de Gaulle said:

'There is not a Frenchman who has learnt without grief and anger that units of the French fleet have been sunk by our allies. That grief and that anger come from our very hearts. There is no reason to gloss over these feelings, and I must express them openly. Therefore, speaking to the British people, I ask them to spare us and spare themselves any interpretation of this tragedy as a direct naval success. It would be unfair. The French ships at Oran were in fact incapable of fighting. They were at their moorings unable to manoeuvre or scatter. They gave the British ships the advantage of the first salvoes, which as everyone knows, are decisive at sea at such short range. Their destruction is not the result of a battle. This is what a French soldier tells the British allies all the more clearly because he respects them in naval matters.'

Sharply, de Gaulle brought balance to his message by concluding:

'There could not be the slightest doubt that on principle and out of necessity the enemy would have used the ships either against Great Britain or against the French Empire, and I say without hesitation that it was better they should have been destroyed.'

Admiral Raeder wanted the U-boats back doing their main job sooner than Dönitz planned. His talks with the Vichy French Government concluded satisfactorily and they agreed to send warships manned by French crews to meet up with the U-boats. Dönitz revised his plans: sending four U-boats was no longer necessary, two would be quite sufficient. Subsequently U-506 and U-507 were instructed to proceed at full speed to assist Hartenstein. From their position on his chart, he calculated they would be in the rescue area on the 14th and 15th.

The whole mission was fraught with danger. Raeder was aware that French ships putting to sea might be misunderstood by the British who by their silence on the *Laconia* sinking either did not know of the rescue bid by Hartenstein, or were sitting back to see how it worked out. If they did not know, then the presence of French warships at sea opened up the possibility of an observer assuming they were aiding Germany, subjecting them to becoming legitimate targets to attack. Uppermost in his mind was the thought of German submarines in an unprecedented position, crammed with survivors, virtually defenceless. Only a fine line divided a success not paralleled in the history of warfare at sea and a disaster of titanic proportions. Raeder wanted the whole affair over as soon as possible.

THE ADMIRALS ACT

Admiral Collinet, Commander-in-Chief of the Vichy French Government, ordered the sloops *Dumont-d'Urville* and *Annamite* together with the large cruiser *Gloire* to set sail.

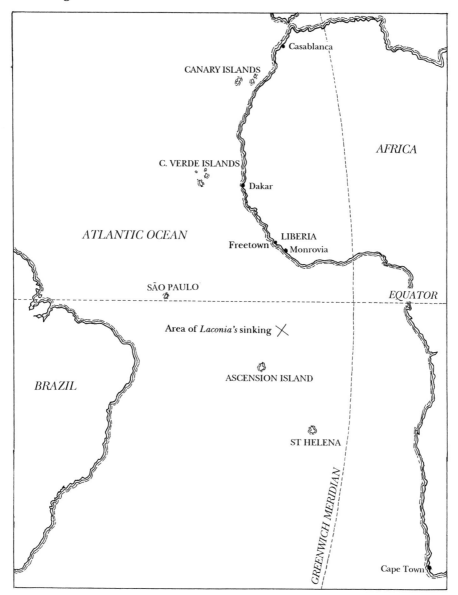

35. The location of the *Laconia* sinking and other sites mentioned in the text. The isolation of the shipwreck and the distance from Dakar is immediately apparent.

36. Lieutenant Commander Erich Würdemann, commander of U-506.

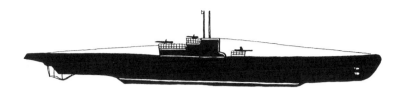

VII

FACE TO FACE WITH THE ENEMY

As the stars faded, the early morning light of Sunday 13th September dawned on a weary British Army officer. Lt Mercer, after a night of supporting himself with pieces of the *Laconia's* wreckage, was spotted and taken aboard Boat 9a. In Boat 14, Chief Deck Steward Wallace was made as comfortable as circumstances would permit. In much pain through sustaining a broken leg when lifted from the sea into the boat, he was gladdened when in the early morning light he identified Storekeeper Jack Moore who had been with him in a cabin on 'A' Deck at the time of the torpedoing. For eighteen years the *Laconia* had been his home; now dogged determination reinforced his resolve to survive.

* * *

Thirty-three-year-old Boat Deckman Robert Hicks viewed the dawn revelation of an unbroken line of sea and sky and scanned the horizon for signs of life. He thought about his friend Bill Royal (minutes before the attack he had been ironing his pyjamas ready to take them to the sick bay, where he had been confined as a result of an accident).

Confronted by a seeming emptiness, bleak and desolate, postures of weariness among the boat's occupants appeared more profound. Deprived of material comforts accepted as normal in better days, hopes of rescue raised in the night now sadly diminished. They were alone! Or so they thought: fifty yards away a submarine surfaced, her diesel engines coming to life with a thundering roar. Two figures emerged from the hatch, one easily distinguishable by his white cap against the dark grey background. The clang of the engine room telegraph responding to the captain's orders sounded across the water.

Using a hailer, Hartenstein, in perfect English, addressed the abandoned, ordering them to come alongside. A number of the Royal Naval Ratings, when they realised it was an enemy U-boat, expressed fears that to do so would make them prisoners-of-war. Other voices, disconsolate, added that U-boat crews were bad fellows, devoid of feelings, with orders to murder even the helpless. Hicks decided such ambivalence could not be left to conjecture: considering their state, he felt there was nothing they could do but obey the order.

Face to face with his enemy, Hicks eyed the tall, lean commander whom he guessed would be somewhere around his own age. To hear a German speaking perfect English, exhibiting courteous manners, was almost offensive. After enquiring if there were any of the *Laconia's* officers amongst them – the boat held solely crew and naval ratings – Hartenstein told Hicks to stay in the area as help was on its way. Out of the hatch a crewman appeared with jugs of hot coffee, indicating to Hicks that they were for him.

As the coffee was served, Hicks felt his spirits veer wildly from the deep despair of minutes before, to an excited belief that the German commander was telling the truth. If he had known that his enemy would wait upon him in the middle of the ocean, he would not have allowed the *Laconia's* dentist to have extracted all his teeth on the previous day. The hard biscuits drawn from the lifeboat's store presented a new challenge.

* * *

In Boat 13a, Billy Hardacre and Boatswain Le Brocq were near a state of exhaustion after a night of baling water to keep the boat afloat – a night penetrated by the fearful cries from Italians in the water – some of whom they had rescued. The strain of the ordeal was beginning to tell but they couldn't let up now. Several times during the dark hours, the hum of engines was heard. Once quite close, but nothing could be seen. At first light a raft was spotted; the lone resident, without invitation, swam to their crowded boat to become its seventy-third occupant.

* * *

The warming sight of sunshine brought cheer to the women and children for whom Robert Tinkler was responsible. It had been a cold night of discomfort in which the boat rolled endlessly, and spray stung their faces. Tinkler counted seven lifeboats close at hand, around them hundreds of bodies, swirling aimlessly, grotesque in the morning sun. A distressing reminder of the horror of war.

Intransigent thoughts concerning the enemy were displaced as a new quality of suspense touched their lives. Less than one hundred yards away a submarine surfaced. Water broke spuming over the bridge, spreading widely over her bulging saddle tanks until she was clear. Hartenstein signalled the eight boats to come alongside.

Tinkler, who was only wearing naval issue shorts and vest, had seen the submarine's searchlight during the night. He was one of the last to leave *Laconia*, clinging to a wooden plank for several hours hoping a lifeboat

74

would appear before his energy failed. Numb and dazed, he did not feel in a co-operative mood when Hartenstein asked for his name, rank and number. Staring hard into the German commander's face, he refused to answer. A fellow naval rating, whom he knew well, pleaded with him to answer the question, otherwise his parents would not be told of his survival.

'Robert Tinkler, A.B. Gunner, Royal Navy No D/JC/290087,' he replied.

Hartenstein smiled, 'Well – Tinkler,' he said, now grinning broadly, 'You'll Tinkle no more.'

The surprised Royal Navy man wondered what he meant.

Other boats arrived, crewmen fending them off from the U-boat's rusty saddle tanks. Each boat was assisted to ease in alongside until it was safe to lift aboard the women and children and anyone who was suffering from wounds or exposure. Tinkler and his fellows in charge of lifeboats detailed personnel in readiness to collect hot soup from the submarine's kitchen.

37. A recent photograph of Robert Tinkler.

Silent with incredulity, Tinkler's hostile attitude, openly displayed toward the German commander, underwent a change. It appeared fallacious and absurd to respect a man who had caused so much death and suffering. Yet, he believed Hartenstein meant well and would keep his promise to return to them that night. In the meantime, the lifeboats were instructed to stay close to each other and make an inventory of their supplies. Regularly checked and inspected while the *Laconia* was at sea, each boat was supposed to contain:

1 mast and sails (sails dyed crimson)
2 axes
2 boat hooks
8 pulling oars and one steering cap
1 rudder
2 bottom plugs
4 provision tanks holding biscuits, etc.
4 fresh water casks holding 40 gallons of water
2 water dippers
2 caskets
1 baler
1 canvas oil-bag for use in heavy weather
1 canvas sea-anchor
1 magnetic compass
1 oil lamp
1 box of matches
1 box of distress rockets
1 heliograph
1 first-aid kit
2 drinking measures
2 heaving lines
1 electric torch and spare batteries

* * *

About mid-morning, Boat 17 carrying Charles Gregory, the *Laconia's* plumber, and the ship's butcher, Edward Johnson, received a second visit from U-156, which now had several boats in tow. Hartenstein was engaged in gathering the boats together in groups, searching the sea for lone swimmers fortunate enough to survive the night. And the sharks! The U-boat's deck was lined with over a hundred bedraggled looking survivors. Special look-outs were positioned to scan the ocean for signs of life.

* * *

Miss Hawkins was sure that there was a second submarine, but research does not confirm this. What she probably saw was Hartenstein's U-156 on separate occasions. She recalls:

'It was Sunday, and the day wore on. I pictured my family in church. I knew they and my friends, both in Palestine and at home, would be praying that day that I might reach home safely. In that moment I felt a conviction that somehow I should be saved.

'The sun was low when a second submarine appeared, cruised around and then submerged. The sun set; we began to dread a second night. Suddenly the first submarine turned and came straight towards us. German sailors threw us a life-line, and we were all taken aboard.

'We could scarcely stand; our legs were swollen and stiff from the sun and salt water, and we were helped along the deck and down the conning-tower by the U-boat commandant and his men. I was taken to the officers' ward-room, where, to my joy, I found Mary, who had been picked up five minutes before. Altogether about 200 survivors had been picked up during the day from rafts, floating wood and suchlike, and put into our own lifeboats. When those were full the remainder of the survivors, another 200 in all, had been taken on board the submarine before nightfall. They included about 150 Italians. It was interesting to note that more consideration was shown to the British than to the Italians.

'The German officers took charge of our women (four altogether). Our clothes were taken from us and dried, and we were given hot tea and coffee, black bread and butter, rusks and jam. We found it difficult to eat, but we drank everything we were offered. Four of our officers who were in the worst condition, and we four women, remained in this cabin, which served both as sleeping quarters for the German officers and as dining-saloon for the whole crew. The officers gave up their bunks to us, and many of the crew gave up theirs to our men and to the Italians, themselves sitting up all that night and Monday night, and snatching only a rest for themselves during the day.

'The Germans treated us with kindness and respect the whole time; they were really sorry for our plight. One brought us eau-de-Cologne, another cold cream for our sunburn, which was really bad; others gave us lemons from their own lockers, articles of clothing, and tinned fruit. The commandant was particularly charming and helpful; he could scarcely have done more had he been entertaining us in peace-time. He and the captain spoke perfect English. I did not hear 'Heil Hitler' once; I saw no swastikas...'

* * *

Charles Gregory counted eight boats in their group. Again, hot soup and coffee were served, the women and children taken inside the submarine for extra care. Some of the boats were overcrowded, others had space to spare;

some contained too many Italians, or civilians or military, with few seamen. Hartenstein tackled the problem by re-distributing personnel on a basis which ensured adequate manning by skilled seamen with a capable person in charge.

Aboard the submarine all noises seemed non-resonant and gentle, in comparison to the multitudinous creaking of the lifeboats and slap of the sea. Edward Johnson, a non-swimmer and still without a life-jacket, was thankful that thus far he had kept his feet dry. One of the U-boat's officers, with a cine camera in hand, tried to be friendly. He thought Edward was a good name. Another officer told Charles Gregory they had watched the *Laconia's* Saturday afternoon gunnery practice which they considered excellent. Johnson noted the apparent priority attention the British received over the Italians, who although not overlooked or neglected in any way, nevertheless seemed to be treated more from obligation. Hartenstein's boat was woefully unequipped for coping with the situation. He knew there was barely enough room below for his crew.

* * *

Boatswain's Mate Le Brocq, who joined the *Laconia* as a deck boy of fourteen years old, was impressed by the perfect conduct of Commander Hartenstein, profusely apologetic at sinking a vessel carrying women and children. Le Brocq, used to the British cartoonists' jibes of Hitler, sampled the German opinion of Churchill. Boldly painted on the U-boat conning tower was Britain's Prime Minister with a yoke around his neck. Lt Mercer, in Boat 9a, which he now commanded by virtue of the fact that he was the only commissioned officer of the eighteen British on board, found Hartenstein quite talkative, if somewhat boastful. Freely, Hartenstein declared that he had followed the *Laconia* for the whole of Saturday and decided to attack her at 8 p.m. Furthermore, he was in full possession of shipping movements and intended to torpedo the *Stratheden, Pasteur, Ile de France, Nieu Amsterdam* and the *Duchess of Atholl* – all large ocean going liners requisitioned to transport British troops.

Hartenstein's Churchill cartoon was also remembered by twenty-one-year-old crew member William Hoyer. He had, together with his friends David Chawe and Gerald Partridge, considered themselves fortunate to abandon ship in *Laconia's* prized motor launch, only to find that the interior of their salvation craft had been completely stripped out by a work party in preparation for a fresh coat of paint. Furthermore, their vision of powering away from the shipwreck area turned to disappointment when their frantic endeavours to start up the motor failed because the fuel tank was empty. However, Third Radio Officer Cooper, anticipating the cause of

38. William Hoyer, utility man aboard the *Laconia* at the time of her sinking.

the problem, examined a seemingly empty petrol can found inside the cabin which housed a wireless transmitter. In Cooper's mind the transmitter was secondary to getting the launch away from *Laconia*'s side, still towering above their heads. Cooper discovered that the can was not entirely empty and William Hoyer was amazed when the young Radio Officer was able to start the motor on a mere cigarette tin full of petrol drained from the larger can. Soon the motor died out, but by then they were a safe distance away from the doomed *Laconia* and had even taken in tow five vulnerable lifeboats.

William Hoyer's study of the conning tower on U-156 was interrupted by the voice of Commander Hartenstein telling the sole woman taken on board the submarine from the motor launch how much he deeply regretted her circumstances. Hoyer detected a ring of sincerity in Hartenstein's manner: 'Sorry, Fraulein', he said, 'but war is war.' The forty occupants on the launch (designed to carry twenty-five persons) were hoping that Hartenstein would not discover their wireless transmitter before the promised food was served to them from the submarine. If he did, then they would have expected Hartenstein to submerge quickly. Not that the transmitter was of any further use: the batteries were completely flat after Cooper had sent out two distress messages.

William Hoyer had abandoned ship with some personal documents in his pocket. One was his crewman's identification pass, signed by Captain Sharp, which became sea-stained. Others included his last wage slip and emergency lifeboat stations card (see page 222).

THE SINKING OF THE LACONIA

Hartenstein continued his search of the sea. Miraculously, an unaccompanied baby was lifted from a raft, alive and well. He did his utmost to provide medical attention for the injured. Billy Hardacre, still naked except for the belt around his waist, accepted clothing but refused medical help, suggesting to Hartenstein, who had noticed the burns on his body, that the women and children should come first.

* * *

Eighteen hours had passed since Naval Rating John Hennessey opted to swim clear of the sinking lifeboat. A little after 2 p.m. on Sunday, a look-out on the German submarine spotted him in the water, swimming in their direction. Hartenstein took a special interest in a man who could survive for so long in the sea, allowing him space below to rest and sleep. Later, he congratulated him on the previous day's gunnery practice.

* * *

Mercer, in Boat 9a, was advised to stay in the area, as a truce was being arranged to enable British ships to contract a mercy mission. Thirty Italians and two British Naval ratings joined him in the boat. He discovered that one of the Italians, Colonel Major, spoke French; a language he could speak and understand. In order to overcome the language obstacle, he explained to the colonel that organising for survival was vital and he must communicate this to his men. In the event of rescue ships failing to find them, the African coast was 600 miles away and as a safety measure, he would institute a system of rationing based upon a thirty-one day period. Colonel Major assured Lt Mercer of his co-operation and assisted in recording an inventory of foodstuffs and water.

Between them they worked out a ration per person comprising: 2 ozs of water, twice a day, 8 Horlicks tablets, 4 biscuits, 2 ozs of Pemmican and 4 pieces of chocolate.

At mid-day, the sun, which earlier had warmed stiffened limbs and chapped faces, now scorched exposed skin. Blisters appeared. In most minds, thoughts turned to the time for the issue of the next water ration rather than food. Lt Mercer urged everyone in his boat to exercise self-discipline; the temptation to slake thirsty throats by sipping sea water must be avoided at all costs.

* * *

With marked application, Senior Third Officer Thomas Buckingham, still floating with the corpse, scanned the sea around him, filled with the early morning tints of colour which gave a lustre to the grey-green waves as they broke over him. Buckingham was able now to discern the features of his companion:

80

'He appeared to be about middle aged, and from the cut of his clothing I took him to be one of our crew. There seemed no evidence of his having come by a violent death, and only his shoes were missing... I transferred my hold to the two cord-ends which suspended loosely from his life-jacket. My wrist watch showed 9.20 and I gathered that that was the time at which I had gone into the se on the previous evening... the timepiece being an inexpensive one had quickly become waterlogged and stopped...

'In despair, I heaved myself up as far as I could, using my companion's back with which to gain some added impetus for the occasion, and took in the horizon around me within a dozen attempts, each time scanning a different arc. At each attempt the body sank a foot or so below the surface but quickly emerged again...

'I saw to the south, and a long way off, as if they were protruding out of the sea itself, the heads and shoulders of two men... Unless I was mistaken, they were certainly supported upon something just below my range of vision... Taking a last look at the limply spreadeagled figure beside me, the saddest picture I have ever seen, and without which I would most likely never have survived the night, I released my hold and started off in the direction of the two men. By the altitude of the sun I estimated the hour to be about 9 a.m.

'Making headway through the breaking sea was a slow and tiresome business, and I had to stop frequently to rest before resuming my efforts, for I was finding my stamina limited to only a few minutes of trial... I must have been progressing this way for more than an hour before the gunwales of the boat came up over the horizon. At this stage, I rested for a longer period, confident that if the boat made any move away in the opposite direction, I would have sufficient strength to hail it. An hour later... I was within fifty yards of the boat.'

Disappointment awaited Buckingham. The boat was full, around it a mass of men. In the stern, Geoffrey Purslow, the *Laconia's* medical doctor was attending to the sick. He told Buckingham he had seen another boat not far away and that he would be advised to seek it out, as many in the water had been eaten by sharks.

'I decided to make for the boat... I made fair progress, and after several rest periods I finally had the boat in sight. Another fifteen minutes and it was within hailing distance, and I called out to those on board to hold out an oar in readiness for me to grasp...

'I was hauled into the boat with little delay, and tumbling headfirst into the bottom of the boat, I was content for the time being to lie where I fetched up, on the bottom boards, breathless, and I remember, most comfortable, and gratified to such an extent as would seldom if ever be required of me again in this uncertain world.

'My arms and legs ached painfully, and my hands and feet had taken on a most unnatural appearance through so many hours in the water.'

There were seventeen persons in the boat, sixteen Italians and one Englishman wearing full Royal Air Force uniform. The aircraftman told Buckingham that the Italians had rescued him during the night. There was spare room on this boat, so, taking charge, he decided to row it to where Dr Purslow was struggling in overcrowded conditions. The boat needed to be baled out regularly; some of the Italians were in high spirits, others were inconsolable. Buckingham remembers that he 'left them to the mercy of their thoughts, and the comforts of the water sodden religious tracts which had survived many hours in the water with them'.

When Buckingham reached Dr Purslow's boat the sea had become choppy so the boats could not be allowed to get too close to each other. His task was to save as many of the hundred persons or more in the water as quickly as possible. To accomplish this in a boat designed to carry sixty-five people, they would be required to stand upright. Purslow urged the men in the water to swim over to their new arrival, but they were reluctant. Most were exhausted, numb and dazed. One made an effort, turning back after having covered only a few yards. Eventually, with help from Buckingham, who first had to get into the sea again to convince the men there were no sharks in the immediate vicinity, seventy-three persons, mainly Italians, found refuge in his boat.

Within the hour, two more boats joined them, giving space to men still in the sea. Satisfied that a suitable seaman was in charge of each boat, Buckingham instructed them to stay close together. To assist them when darkness fell, he would burn an oil lamp at the mast-head.

In overcrowded and cramped conditions, it was impossible for anyone to lie down. Frequently, room had to be opened up to allow baling. The men nearest the sides of the boat were afforded the opportunity to sit on the gunwales, but could easily fall overboard if they fell asleep. Towards midnight the breeze strengthened and in an effort to keep warm, Buckingham took the sail out of its covering, using it as an overhead canopy.

Sharing the watch with his two British colleagues, he carefully considered what to do next. Either sail westwards toward the South American coast, or north-eastwards and the African coast. Brazil was nearly one thousand miles away and he expected the boat to cover one hundred miles assisted by the equatorial current, which sweeps westwards along that region, supported by the east trade winds. A slower daily speed was to be expected to the African coast, a journey of six hundred miles, but more hope of being spotted if an air search from British bases in Africa was underway.

Buckingham communicated with the other boats, telling them that at 9 a.m. his hoisted sail would be the signal to commence their long journey. Each boat was to follow in line, keeping the sail of the boat ahead just in sight. His simple plan gave the four boats a range of fifteen miles visibility in the north-east and south-west directions and a visibility of three miles on each side of that line.

Monday 14th September:

At dawn Buckingham extinguished the oil lamp and stowed it away in its locker. Then he wrenched the water and food tanks from their seatings, to be relocated aft where he could keep close surveillance. He was angry and distrusted the Italians whom he suspected during the night had drained almost three of the four water tanks. Arguments broke out between the Italians. To Buckingham it was apparent, even though he could not understand a word they said, that the offenders were being disciplined. In another boat, the *Laconia's* First Officer Walker took similar action, making an example of the eight Italians responsible by forcing them to fill the bare space left by the tanks and nailing planks of wood across to keep them there. If an ugly situation developed, Buckingham did not have any weapon to defend himself or his English colleagues. He still looked upon the Italians as prisoners whom he imagined must have weapons they concealed from their captors. He ordered that each prisoner turn out his pockets. His assumption was right. Twelve knives of varying descriptions were confiscated. The incident confirmed that his decision of the night to set a north-east course for Africa was the right one. In a few days they should arrive under the southern fringe of the Doldrum regions where he could expect violent thunderstorms and torrential rainfalls, unpleasant, but vital to replenish their diminished water tanks. A little later than 9 a.m. the small convoy set sail.

* * *

Dr Purslow, who, like Buckingham, had had to swim from one boat to another, was in one of the boats in Buckingham's convoy. Doris Hawkins was subsequently able to record his leadership:

'Dr Purslow and other officers checked over the equipment and food in the boat. Much of what should have been provided was missing, including the medicine chest. There were only five oars, one of which was later used as a mast; some tools and white lead; a length of rope; a bucket; a compass;

83

and a battery lamp with no spare battery. There were no rockets or flares, no sail, and only two blankets, which were later used to make a jib. The rudder was also missing.

'Dr Purslow and others made and erected a sail from the tarpaulin cover, lashed to an oar. They called him the navigating doctor, as he had had considerable experience of sailing during his student days.

'The boat... kept with the main body of boats for two or three days, but one night it... drifted off in the darkness, and in the morning only three other boats were in sight. Later the U-boat [U-156] had come upon them, and had asked if they wanted anything. Dr Purslow asked for some bandages, and a few were provided; they were also given some water and hot coffee.'

* * *

At 7.40 a.m. a signal from Dönitz read: 'All boats, including Hartenstein, take aboard only such numbers as will ensure that the boat still remains operational when submerged.'

Royal Naval Gunner John Hennessey, refreshed, noted the respect crewmen showed to the U-boat commander. He judged it took a man of tenacity and grit to contemplate the magnitude of the rescue he had initiated. Hartenstein appeared somewhat agitated. Without sleep for two days, his fighting vessel turned into a refugee centre carrying over two hundred persons, many on deck, like wraiths on the periphery of his mind, the message from Dönitz troubled him. As the situation stood, it would be impossible to dive, unless he sacrificed to the sea those left on deck. Even then, the question of remaining operational when submerged was ridiculous. The main feature of his submarine was the pressure hull, a cylindrical unit of steel, compartmentalised by bulkheads. Limits were set to the depth of a dive so as to survive the build up of external pressure. Keeping the boat in the water exactly at the depth required called for skill in the best of conditions. Action to counter the effect of underwater swells, to hold the boat in trim, demanded a combination of the ballast tanks, both fore and aft, which were alternatively flooded and blown by the electric motors with constant adjustments to the diving planes. Hartenstein thought the matter through, taking into account the possibility of attack from the air. He ordered a crewman to make a Red Cross Flag, the type painted on the side of a hospital ship, and for it to be made quickly.

Hennessey was singled out by the German commander for special confidences. He was attracted to the Royal Navy man who could survive for so long in shark infested waters. A mutual admiration sprang up between the men; he spoke openly of his regret over the condition of the women and children below decks. Very few of them could stand, their legs swollen and stiff, conscious for the first time that their hair was standing on end, thickly matted, their teeth covered with a hard white crust of salt.

The crew, accustomed to living in cramped conditions, gave up their sleeping quarters to them. From their lockers they produced jars of cold cream to ease the effects of sunburn. Bottles of eau de cologne, a regular item found on a U-boat, were passed around to wash salt spray from hands and faces. The extra numbers on board added to the normal stifling atmosphere experienced inside a submarine, built up through lingering after-smells of cooking, diesel oil and sweaty bodies. Whenever the air became thick and unpleasant, U-boat men obtained relief by placing potassium cartridges in their mouths and breathing through them; the potash helped to remove carbon dioxide from the air.

Arrayed in oddments of clothing, provided mainly from the submariners' lockers whilst their own wet clothing was dried, survivors stared inquisitively at the mass of dials, pipes, valves, switches, fans and pumps. No one heard a 'Heil Hitler' or songs such as 'Denn wir fahren gegen Engeland' (We are sailing against England). The only reminder of Nazism consisted of one small photograph of the Fuhrer tucked away in a recess.

The Germans acted as caring hosts, serving hot coffee, bread, butter and jam. At first many suffered difficulty in eating but drank everything that was offered. Water, distilled from the sea, was plentiful.

* * *

In Boat 14, under a grilling sun, sense of time blurred. Men covered their heads with knotted handkerchiefs for protection, sickened by the sight of corpses around them, some partly eaten by sharks, the upturned faces of others showing white in the sun.

Unable to move because of a broken leg, Chief Deck Steward Wallace pleaded with his friend Storekeeper Jack Moore to be more disciplined and stop drinking sea water, a short-cut to madness. Moore ignored him, becoming difficult to handle, creating further problems for Sidney Ellis, the *Laconia's* Junior Third Officer in charge of the boat. A capable officer, Ellis had instituted a system of continuous baling parties to keep the boat in good order, having like Buckingham, set course for Africa. Water rationing was strict, without favour or consideration of anyone's condition. Army Captain Wooldridge was exhibiting signs of mental trouble, and so too was Chief Purser Tom Collum who went raving mad and had to be restrained. Lt Col Baldwin, the British officer commanding the Italian prisoners of war on the *Laconia*, considered Collum dangerous, a threat to

85

them all. He was implacably decisive in placing the purser on the bottom of the boat under guard from ten Italians. Captain Atkins, Royal Artillery, thought the *Laconia's* crew, with few exceptions, a poor lot, and their officers far too old. He also considered it incomprehensible that an old ship was allowed to proceed unescorted at the mercy of U-boats, and criminal to place women and children on a ship transporting prisoners of war.

Because of the danger posed by the two merchant navy men, Atkins agreed with Baldwin a pending action for disposing of them overboard to safeguard the welfare of the majority. They sailed on into another night, sighting nothing.

The sea closed over *Laconia*'s dead.

39. Another photograph of *Laconia* survivors in an isolated lifeboat.

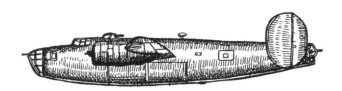

VIII

ASCENSION ISLAND

Two hundred and fifty miles away on Ascension Island, Monday 13th September merged into the personality of the previous weeks, during which the United States Air Force 1st Composite Squadron flew sixty-four sorties within a radius of two hundred and fifty miles of the island without sighting a single target. The small island had not come into the reckoning of Admiral Dönitz as a source of threat to his submarines. Intelligence reports assured him that the British owned island, only seven miles by six, was nothing more than an outcrop of volcanic debris and it did not have an airstrip or aircraft.

Unknown to him the Americans were turning it into an operational base. Urgency attended the mammoth ambitious task as, realistically, planners faced up to the many hazards ahead on a remote island entirely dependent upon shipping to bring in equipment, supplies, food and fuel. Success was conditioned by absolute secrecy, for any hint given to German Intelligence about unusual activity on Ascension presented grave consequences. Prime targets for enemy submarines would be ships and tankers heading for the island; and the added possibility of an invasion could not be discounted, as neither Britain nor America possessed sufficient ships to guard the sea lanes.

Elaborate plans for defence were implemented, to the extent of camouflaging the six tanks erected for the storage of aviation fuel and siting dummy tanks to fool a curious enemy.

Under the command of Captain Robert C. Richardson III, later to become General Richardson, member of the United States Senate, this squadron, made up of thirty officers and two hundred and nineteen men, had two flights of pursuit 'planes consisting of eighteen P-39D's designated for local island defence and five B-25 Mitchel Bombers for sea patrol.

Since its discovery by the Portuguese on Ascension Day 1501, little interest had been shown in the island of solidified lava. Britain found use for it in 1815 when she suspected the French might attempt to land a force in an effort to rescue Napoleon Bonaparte from St Helena, situated 700 miles to the south. For the next hundred years, the Royal Navy stamped its presence there until in 1922 the Eastern Telegraph Company took over the management when the navy left. The island became a dependency of St Helena and the General Manager of the Company officially appointed as representative of the Government of St Helena.

When Britain entered World War Two, a Home Guard was formed introducing a new role for the General Manager, who became its commanding officer, with the rank of Captain. Immediate attention to island defences recognised the requirement for fortification – the emplacement of twenty-five 5" guns – and the arrival of Royal Artillery personnel to man them.

Late in 1941, the Commanding Officer, Captain Cardwell, was instructed to make a survey of the island and recommend a suitable location for the construction of an air-strip. In December 1941, America entered the war and Britain granted permission for the establishment of an air-base designed to serve as a refuelling stop for military aircraft flying the ferry route from the United States to Brazil and then across the South Atlantic and Africa to the Middle East airfields. Further value was envisaged in relation to the Far East bases. Ascension had assumed a new role of importance!

On 29th March 1942, two U.S. Army Transports, escorted by two cruisers and four destroyers under the command of Col Robert Coughlin, U.S. Corps of Engineers, arrived on the island. They brought road-making equipment and 1,300 men and work began on 13th April. In co-operation with the British, on 10th May Col James Tomlinson (Royal Engineers) arrived with orders to stay on the island for the remainder of the war and care for British interests. On 12th June, the Americans informed Washington that the air-strip was sufficiently developed to be utilised for emergency situations. Work had progressed without incident, much to the relief of the British and Americans. On 15th July action stations sounded for the first time. Laid down policy declared all unannounced 'planes were to be fired upon. Such was the level of secrecy that Ascension's anti-aircraft guns opened fire upon a British Fairy Swordfish V4563 from H.M.S. *Archer*, scoring three hits before the aircraft was identified as friendly. Unaware of what was happening on the island, the pilot was instructed to drop from the air a message to the British Cable Station for transmission to the Admiralty concerning the torpedoing of S.S. *Lyle Castle*. Seeing the airstrip, the pilot chose to land. Unhurt, he was able to take off two hours later and return to his ship.

On 14th August, the American vessel *James Parker* arrived from South Carolina with the permanent garrison of men, specially trained to support and defend the island. The army task force of 1,700 officers and men was commanded by Col Ross Baldwin, an infantry officer. About one third of his force was assigned to AAF Composite Force 8012, commanded by Air Force Col James A. Ronin, the largest unit being 1st Composite Squadron commanded by Capt Robert C. Richardson III. Richardson arrived on 17th August. Planning chiefs evaluated their main threat as coming from the U-boats, which might shell the island or attempt a landing party with the objective of sabotaging gasoline storage facilities. An air attack was unlikely, taking into account the location of enemy bases. Therefore, strategy directed Richardson's squadron to patrol the sea around the island, to destroy enemy submarines and protect allied vessels in the vicinity.

By 20th August, the 1st Composite Squadron was operational. Richardson scheduled daily patrols with some aircraft on constant alert at the base, which had been named 'Wideawake Field' as a reminder of the one defeat sustained during the conversion of Ascension Island into a fortified castle. All endeavours to persuade the 'Sooty Terns' or 'Wideawakes' to move out met with stubbornness from the birds. Regularly, they returned to their nesting grounds near the airstrip before departing for another year at sea. Each effort to move them on was reciprocated with the birds' mocking cry of 'wideawake'.

Air operations were under the direction of Air Force personnel and Col Baldwin. Whenever the 1st Composite Squadron was in the air on search and patrol missions, one of the key Air Force officers, Col Ronin, Capt Richardson or Capt Willard Wilson, was available at the control tower, in communication with the pilots. The base had two radio stations: W.Y.U.C. belonged to the Americans, and was also tuned to receive reports from Allied ships in the South Atlantic. Z.B.I. was the British station in communication with Freetown, where the British Admiralty collected and correlated data on U-boat sightings to be passed on to the Americans by Lt Short, the British Royal Naval Liaison Officer attached to the task force on Ascension.

Not all the American radio equipment had been installed by 12th September and W.Y.U.C. was not in communication with either South America or Africa. At that time the Americans were entirely dependent upon Z.B.I. for communication with South America, Africa and the United States. Neither W.Y.U.C. nor Z.B.I. picked up the *Laconia's* S.O.S. or Hartenstein's message of 13th September, when the German commander asked for help in rescuing survivors.

40. *Laconia* survivors on U-506, with U-156 in background.

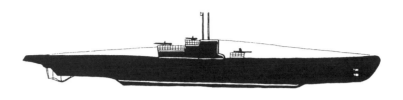

IX

THE U-BOATS ARRIVE

Tuesday 15th September:

U-506 under Lt Cdr Würdemann was the first to reach Hartenstein. The two commanders knew each other well, having been in combat together.

Würdemann was one of five commanders Dönitz sent out for operation *Paukenschlag*, Germany's first attack against American shipping. The Admiral was right in his assumption that the Americans would prove easy prey, unable to contend effectively against the wiles of a U-boat pack, as Würdemann had successfully proved. Two weeks after the entry of the United States of America into the war, Würdemann was sinking their ships. In comparison to the hard fight against the British, who from the beginning of the war exercised well prepared defensive tactics, it was almost unbelievable that American ships were sailing bright with lights. So too, towns along the coast were fully illuminated, flashing advertising signs easily distinguishable, no measures whatsoever having been taken to effect any blackening out procedure.

The life of U-boat wireless men was transformed overnight. Never before was there so much frequency to tune into. American ships did not appear to have any code of practice regarding the observance of radio silence; unknowingly they gained a new audience of intent listeners recording information on shipping positions, strength of naval escorts to convoys, down to everyday chit chat. Needless to say, the United States sustained losses at sea during those early weeks of war with Germany which she could easily have avoided.

Shortly before mid-day, Hartenstein transferred one hundred and thirty Italians to Würdemann, retaining on board U-156 fifty-five Italians and fifty-five British. An hour later U-506 sailed away to search for more boats and a rendezvous with French ships at the position where the *Laconia* sank. A further signal from Dönitz advised that the Italian submarine *Cappellini* was under orders to meet him and should arrive around the same time as the French.

THE SINKING OF THE LACONIA

On Ascension Island, Lt Short, R.N., the British Liaison Officer, handed to the Americans a message received from Freetown stating the British liner *Laconia* had been torpedoed only *a few minutes earlier* at 11.45 a.m. A position of 05° 05' south 11° 30' west was given (a considerable distance from the spot where the sinking had occurred, four days earlier). The message conveyed that the liner was carrying seven hundred passengers, but there was no mention of German submarines engaged in rescue work, of Italians, nor Hartenstein's 'en clair' radio calls for Allied ships to lend their help.

The American B-25 bombers dispatched to the area worked out from the grid reading returned with nothing to report, other than passing information to a British merchantman the *Empire Haven*. A commitment to help the ship locate lifeboats and provide air protection against enemy submarines was agreed, with reservation. The B-25s were adequate for the task but to remain over the wreck area for longer than twenty minutes would seriously impair their chances of returning to base with sufficient fuel. The Americans turned their attention to a B-24D Liberator parked on the runway, a 'plane with a longer range. The problem was it didn't belong to them. En route to the Middle East, this four engined bomber of the 343rd Bombardment Squadron developed mechanical trouble, forcing it to separate from the squadron and land at Wideawake. A decision was taken to requisition the Liberator for special service before releasing it to continue its flight to the Middle East.

At 11 a.m. in Boat 14, Captain Wooldridge died. Junior Third Officer Ellis performed a short Christian service of burial then committed his body to the deep. Ellis was beset with problems: others in his charge showed signs of deterioration, the condition of shipmate Third Engineer Jackson causing most concern. At noon he compromised his strict water rationing rule and issued a 1oz supplement to the couple of children in the boat, together with a biscuit and Horlicks tablet. During a nasty incident, Col Baldwin was forcibly attacked by Flt Lt Falkner, RAF, who manifested unbalanced behaviour and needed to be restrained.

About mid-afternoon U-506 came across Ellis' boat. It was a timely discovery, undoubtedly saving many from premature death. Würdemann replenished the lifeboat's water tanks as quickly as he could, informing Ellis of the French ships steaming towards them. Before leaving, he suggested they remain in the area as he intended to return. Boat 14's unexpected visitor certainly saved Chief Purser Tom Collum and Storekeeper Jack Moore from the fate Col Baldwin and Capt Atkins had reserved for them in the further event of untoward disturbance.

In that same afternoon, U-507, sister ship to U-506, under Lt Commander Schacht, overtook Boat 9a, taking all aboard. While English speaking officers listed each person's name, Lt Mercer noticed German crewmen stripping his lifeboat of its water and food provision tanks, before taking the boat in tow. Mercer grew suspicious of the commander's intentions. Later his attitude gave way to surprise and admiration when the German commander collected from the one hundred and fifty Italians, rescued earlier in the day, clothing he believed they could spare the British, many of whom were barely clad. He also supplied medical attention to those suffering from minor cuts and sunburn. Schacht was well organised. Generous portions of stew made up of meat-paste noodles, dried vegetables and mushrooms was served to near unbelieving survivors. Matches and cigarettes passed around. Later Mercer commented in his report:

'The submarine commander and officers were of a very fine type, all spoke English perfectly. Ridiculous though it seems – they looked kind.'

Schacht's officers were anxious to be cordial. One handed Mercer a box of cigarettes, made in Morocco, a bottle of rum and a bag of coffee. He was pleasantly unprepared to hear German officers declaring their admiration for the Royal Air Force and Royal Navy. Not wishing to directly offend Lt Mercer, the Germans held a low opinion of the British Army. One officer asked him what he thought of General Rommel, looking pleased upon hearing that a British Army officer categorised Rommel as a very capable general.

Early on Tuesday afternoon, Commander Schacht sighted a lone lifeboat and drew alongside. Mrs Davidson and her friend Mrs Walker were the only two women amongst 55 men, comprising British and Italians. Schacht suggested to the women that they would benefit from an overnight stay in the submarine as the weather forecast was not favourable. Accepting Schacht's offer they were impressed by the German crew who stretched themselves to afford the women every comfort. They took an early opportunity to lie down and get some sleep. Mrs Davidson wondered about her daughter Molly, especially as Commander Schacht's enquiries revealed that she was not on board.

Schacht took in tow a further six boats, adopting the same procedure of listing names, attending to physical needs and serving stew. In the pattern of Hartenstein, he re-distributed personnel, ensuring a seaman was in charge of each boat. Mercer was transferred to Boat 17, completely re-victualled, containing only British. Instructions were given to post a man forward on each boat keeping an axe ready to cut the tow-line if an aircraft appeared.

41. Lt Commander Harro Schacht of U-507.

42. Deck of U-506 crammed with *Laconia* survivors.

43. U-506 rescuing survivors from lifeboat.

44. British women and children on U-506 awaiting transfer to the *Annamite*.

45. Survivors on board U-506

46. U-506 with lifeboat full of survivors.

47. *Laconia* survivors on U-506.

Buckingham's small flotilla sailed on through the day, the men tightly packed together, all standing up. At mid-day they glimpsed their first sign of hope, when a submarine, which Buckingham identified as Italian, passed them by on the starboard side at full speed. The Italians on the boat failed to recognise one of their own vessels and Buckingham refrained from imparting to them her identity, considering it useful to keep such knowledge to himself. Shortly after this, an aircraft could be heard, but it was not seen and the noise of its engines died away to the northwest.

At 4 p.m. excitement grew again: approaching them astern a submarine caught them up, a man in the conning tower signalled them, using both arms. Buckingham understood the message to mean 'drop your sail'. In his mind there was no doubt it was a U-boat and he pretended he did not understand the message, refusing to obey. The submarine passed close to them, stopping fifty yards ahead across their path. Standing on her deck, looking fit and well, were members of the *Laconia's* crew. As Buckingham joined them he was tapped on the shoulder, while enjoying a cup of stew, by Executive Engineer Feldman, who in perfect English said the commander would like to see him.

Schacht questioned Buckingham closely about complaints registered by the Italians of harsh treatment while on board the *Laconia*. Buckingham responded in total disagreement. The U-boat commander did not look convinced and went away to confer with his officers. A few minutes later he ordered the British into the lifeboats to allow the Italians on deck to take their places. Buckingham, however, was to remain on the U-boat and take his turn assisting the duty officers in keeping watch for further survivors.

At 10 p.m. in a message from Freetown, the British formally requested the 1st Composite Squadron to provide air cover for the *Empire Haven* and H.M.S. *Corinthian* directed by Freetown to search for the *Laconia's* lifeboats. Warships and merchantmen were scarce, being assembled elsewhere for the invasion of North Africa; also, to avoid the greater submarine menace along the African coast, all shipping was routed further west. Again, the message did not mention the involvement of U-boats. The Americans on Ascension called in the B-24 Liberator Bomber's pilot, Lt James Harden, together with his navigator, Lt Jerome Perlman, and bomb-aimer, Lt Edgar Kellar, for briefing.

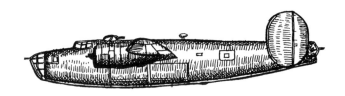

X

AMERICANS ATTACK

Wednesday 16th September:

With the advent of daylight, Commander Schacht hauled the two lifeboats alongside. Fresh water distilled during the night by the U-boat's engineers filled up the boats' storage tanks. Hot soup and bread greeted the dazed occupants, most of whom were awakening from their first night's sleep in four days. Schacht set a course for the area of the *Laconia's* sinking, which he told Buckingham he expected to reach at mid-day. At 11 a.m. a raft was sighted on which was a lone woman survivor. Two German sailors jumped overboard to go to her rescue. Buckingham commented that she was in a very distressed condition and appeared to be several months pregnant.

On Ascension Island, Captain Richardson cleared the B-24 Liberator Bomber for take off at 7 a.m. Overnight he had decided to send along Lt Raymond Ford, one of his own men, as co-pilot. Loaded with depth charges and bombs the 'plane headed north-east into a cloudless blue sky.

On Board U-156, Commander Hartenstein was pleased to learn from Dönitz that French warships were scheduled to meet him the next day. He had saved the lives of over four hundred people, a commendable accomplishment, without incident.

At 9.30 a.m. Harden saw a submarine towing two lifeboats and approaching two others. For a while the B-24 circled overhead, its crew watching the U-boats take the other boats in tow and continue on its course. The log of U-156 (mentioned in the *Memoirs* of Dönitz) describes the event:

'Shortly before the arrival of another two boats, four engined aircraft with American markings bearing 70. As proof of my peaceful intentions displayed large Red Cross Flag four yards square on bridge facing line of aircraft flight. Aircraft flew over once and then cruised in vicinity for some time. Made Morse signals 'Who are you?' and 'Are there any ships in sight?' No response. Aircraft flew off in S.W. direction.'

48. The runway on Ascension island, carved from lava rock in 91 days.

Harden reported by radio to W.Y.U.C. at Wideawake Field requesting what action they should take. According to the Americans, Harden reported having challenged the U-boat to show its national flag, without success. The submarine, however, blinked light signals they could not read clearly but were thought to be 'German, Sir'. Harden omitted to mention the Red Cross flag, which he obviously saw.

Captain Richardson conferred with Colonel Ronin, who remembers saying, 'It was a good question.' The options open were to order the B-24 back to base – or attack. They knew there were no friendly submarines in that part of the Atlantic, a matter carefully weighed, bearing in mind Freetown's dependence upon them for protection of British ships. Recalling Harden might jeopardise the safety of those ships as well as abandoning an important and legitimate military target when there was every chance of a successful attack. They realised taking action would undoubtedly place at risk the lives of men in the lifeboats. Harden pressed for an early decision as he couldn't stay in the area much longer and still have sufficient fuel to get back to Ascension. Richardson ordered: 'Sink sub!'

Harden turned back northward, finding the target as he had left it, brazenly on the surface, towing four lifeboats. Flying low, he made a winged arc above the submarine, ready for the kill. Billy Hardacre was standing near Wing Commander Blackburn, the R.A.F. officer that Hartenstein had allowed to signal the American B-24, and overheard him say, 'They won't take any notice of it,' to a seaman who believed the Red Cross flag would be recognised. Everyone in the boats and on the submarine used the half hour which elapsed since the 'plane flew off, searching sea and sky, expecting a rescue ship to be directed towards them. Now hope turned to horror as they saw bombs falling. The log of U-156 continues:

'Aircraft of similar type approached. Flew over, slightly ahead of submarine, at altitude of 80 metres (about 250 feet). Dropped two bombs about three seconds apart. While four lifeboats were being cast off, the aircraft dropped one bomb in their midst. One boat capsized. Aircraft cruised around for a short time and then dropped a fourth bomb 2-300 metres away. Realised that his bomb racks were empty. Another run. Two bombs. One exploded with a few seconds delayed action, directly under the control room. Conning tower vanished in a tower of black water. Control room and bow compartment reported taking water. All hands ordered to don life-jackets. Ordered all British off the boat. Batteries began giving off gas. Italians also ordered off – had no escape gear to give them.'

One of the bombs destroyed a lifeboat containing mainly Italians, overturning another. Able Seaman Tony Large, R.N.V.R., a survivor from the sinking of H.M.S. *Cornwall*, swam over to the upturned boat, organising efforts to right it and making the grim discovery of four British dead, trapped underneath.

Such was the creditable discipline of Commander Hartenstein that he did not turn his guns on the aircraft. Had he done so there is little doubt the expertise of his seasoned crew would have destroyed an aircraft unable to hit a sitting target. However, his restraint clearly demonstrated his peaceful intentions, a fact that was never understood at the Nuremberg Trials when Admiral Dönitz stood trial for his life, treated as if he were a Mafia godfather. When the *Laconia* incident was raised at the trial, Dönitz told the court: 'I want to mention just as an example, that all the submarines which took part in that rescue operation were lost by bombing attack at their next action or soon afterwards. The situation in which the enemy kills the rescuers while they are exposing themselves to great personal danger, is really and emphatically contrary to ordinary common sense and the elementary rules of warfare.' It must be remembered that during World War Two, due to Allied propaganda, U-boat captains and their crews were portrayed as heartless, inhumane men who murdered helpless seamen after sinking their ships. Perhaps Commander Hartenstein was influenced by the examples of Commander Schultze of the U-48 who sent radio messages to the British Admiralty requesting that a ship be sent to pick up survivors of a merchantman he had just sunk. Or how U-124 after torpedoing the British ship *Tweed* in the South Atlantic in April 1941 brought aboard survivors clinging to an upturned lifeboat which they repaired and provisioned. Then put the British sailors back to sea with a course for land, and freedom!

Sibilant noises below decks, coupled with extremely pungent smells of burning, confirmed to Hartenstein it was a risk to remain further on the surface. The force of the explosions through the water hammered the submarine until it shuddered like a wounded animal. Nursing Missionary Sister Doris Hawkins, inside the submarine at the time, said: 'It shivered and shook... It was a dreadful sensation.' Lights went out, water dripped from fractured pipes and people were thrown into each other; some of the survivors and crew on the deck were blown into the sea.

The official report from the B-24 Liberator's pilot read:

'One pass dropping three depth charges was made, one hit ten feet astern, and two were about 100 and 200 yards. Made three more runs and bombs failed to fall. This was fixed and a final run was made at 400 feet. Two bombs were dropped one on either side, not more than 15 or 20 feet away. The sub rolled over and was last seen bottom up. Crew had abandoned sub and taken to surrounding lifeboats.'

Doris Hawkins wrote 'In this crisis the German captain decided, naturally, that he must submerge at once. As he could not do so with all of us on board, he was forced to put us off into the shark-infested water. He and his commandant were genuinely distressed. He took us until we were fairly close to two of our boats, and then we found ourselves once again swimming for our lives.

'We could scarcely see the boats when we were in the water, owing to the heavy sea. One English officer helped Mary, and Squadron-Leader Wells again helped me. I am a poor swimmer, and he – a magnificent swimmer, but now a sick man – gave of his best to get me into a boat. We swam for nearly fifty minutes, and part of that time he towed me and swam for both of us. He *would* not abandon me, and finally telling me to keep going slowly, he swam off with speed and gained a boat, telling them to come back for us. The boat had only one oar, so they signalled to the second boat, whose occupants slowly made towards us. Utterly exhausted, but very thankful, Mary and I and two men were helped into the already crowded boat. I learned afterwards that Squadron-Leader Wells died ten days later – "a very gallant gentleman".

'Now we found ourselves the only two women with sixty-six men (all British, except for two Polish cadet-officers) in a thirty-foot boat. Most of the others who were in the submarine failed to reach a boat, and perished there in the Atlantic when rescue was almost at hand.'

Doris Hawkins now found herself in the same boat with Dr Purslow which had originally strayed from Buckingham's convoy.

* * *

On 10th October, twenty-eight days after the *Laconia's* sinking, one of the two lifeboats Vichy warships missed in their final search beached on the shore of the Liberian coast. They gave their account of the attack to the American Chargé d'Affaires in Monrovia:

'About four o'clock in the afternoon, an American Liberator Bomber appeared and although the submarine displayed a Red Cross Flag, the bomber launched seven depth charges one of which fell near a lifeboat, completely destroying it and drowning all passengers, who were Italian prisoners. Two others fell about three yards on either beam of the submarine, the explosion lifting it from the water and obviously causing damage. The submarine continued on the surface for about a mile and then submerged, throwing all of the survivors from the deck into the water. Many of them were drowned by suction, but the remaining lifeboats picked up a few of them.'

* * *

Common sense had prescribed Hartenstein's resolve for immediate attention to the duty of restoring his U-boat back into an effective fighting machine, which precluded any continuation of accommodating survivors. During the next hour, he transferred the British and Italians on board to nearby lifeboats, writing in his log 'Some required a little gentle persuasion.'

At 1.45 p.m. U-156 submerged and left on course 270, her role in the marathon rescue mission now ended. At 4 p.m. Hartenstein recorded:

'All damage repaired as far as possible. Damage sustained: Air search periscope jammed. Fixed eye periscope refuses to turn. Seven battery cells empty; others doubtful. Diesel cooling flange torn, D-F set not working. Sounding gear and hydrophones not working. First class repair job by technical personnel.'

U-156 was spared more serious damage, for since the beginning of 1942 the electric motors and other vital parts had been fitted with rubber mountings, greatly reducing the damage effect of depth charge explosions.

While Lt Harden was on his way back to Ascension, ready to report sinking a submarine on his first combat sortie, a signal was received from Lt Richard Atkins, pilot of a B-25 of the 1st Composite Squadron. At 10.25 a.m. he had sighted lifeboats and rafts at 05° 10' south 11° 10' west, a few miles south and east of where the B-25 bombed the U-156. That afternoon, Capt Richardson flew out to the area and found some lifeboats, passing the location to the *Empire Haven* then about twenty miles to the south. An hour later Capt Virgil Holdsworth in another B-25 found more lifeboats and this information also was radioed to the *Empire Haven*.

When Richardson returned to Wideawake, a message from Freetown to the Americans on Ascension indicated that French warships out of Dakar were headed south. The signal made no reference to the peaceful intention of the vessels. The Americans interpreted the message as meaning warships were on their way to bombard Ascension Island. Richardson linked the morning episode of Harden and the U-boat together with Freetown's news. In his thinking, it could only mean the Germans were wise to their presence on Ascension. Accordingly, the garrison prepared to defend the island. The historian of the 1st Composite Squadron wrote: 'Arrangements were made for an American Reception – the powder was dry.' As night fell, the tension was heightened when radar located a surface vessel forty miles to the north-east. For ninety minutes the radar followed the track as the vessel moved to a position fourteen miles south-east of the island. Then contact was lost. Ascension's American commanders believed it to be a submarine engaged in a reconnaissance of the island, but they were mistaken.

Late that night an urgent meeting was convened at U-Boat Headquarters, Paris. Dönitz read out Hartenstein's signal:

'FROM HARTENSTEIN: While towing four lifeboats in clear weather and displaying large Red Cross flag from bridge, was bombed by American Liberator. Aircraft dropped five bombs. Have transferred survivors to the lifeboats and am abandoning rescue work. Proceeding westwards. Repairs in hand.'

Dönitz, under pressure from his advisers to abandon the operation, was unrelenting in his determination to see it through to the end. He brought the heated discussion to an abrupt conclusion by making it very clear he would not depart from the plan so near to completion. In only a matter of hours, the Vichy warships would take over.

Around midnight he signalled his submarines:

'You are in no circumstances to risk safety of your boat. All measures to ensure safety of your boat. All measures, including abandonment of rescue

105

operations, to be ruthlessly taken. Do not rely on enemy showing slightest consideration.'

Adamant the British must have intercepted Hartenstein's appeal for help, Dönitz castigated the British attitude as 'callous'. At 1.51 a.m. he drafted a signal to Schacht and Würdemann:

'Boats will at all times be kept in instant readiness to dive and must retain at all times full powers of underwater action. You will transfer to the lifeboats any survivors you have aboard your boats. Only Italians may be retained aboard your boats. Proceed to meeting point and hand them over to the French. Beware of enemy counter measures both from the air and by submarines.'

49. A B-24 Liberator Bomber.

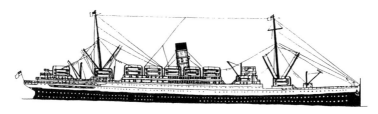

XI

THE FOG OF WAR

Thursday 17th September:

A characteristic of Admiral Dönitz was to accept reality even if the truth was unpleasant. He tended to face up to the truth rather than ignore it, perceiving the situation as it really was and making a rational, logical and intelligent decision as to how to cope with it. This was a characteristic recognised by his U-boat commanders, who respected the wise counsel of their chief, always persistent in working towards his goals, yet unafraid to re-evaluate a situation, and make necessary adjustments. He understood Hartenstein's reasons for showing a Red Cross Flag, the action of a man prepared for all eventualities, who in good faith believed he could secure similar status to a hospital ship for his submarine. Unfortunately, the action of the chivalrous commander did not produce the desired result, which prompted Dönitz to complete his morning signals to Schacht and Würdemann:

'Do not hoist Red Cross flag since: (1) it is not recognised international procedure; (2) it will not in any case and most certainly not as far as the British are concerned, afford any protection.'

* * *

Buckingham was curious about the nationality of the ship Schacht mentioned he would transfer them to. Throughout his duty watch on the submarine, the matter progressed into a mind fixation. It troubled him: a neutral ship was what he hoped Schacht meant, but his knowledge of shipping erased any expectancy of seeing a neutral flag so far south. Buckingham sensed something was wrong when Schacht, looking uneasy, angrily thrust a piece of paper into the hand of the officer of the watch to read. He wasted no time in summoning his officers for a conference, angrily turning upon Buckingham with the news that a German submarine, sixty miles away had been attacked by an aircraft whilst towing four of the *Laconia's* lifeboats. To his relief, Schacht calmed down, with decorum making it known he intended to continue towing the boats at a slow speed.

As a precaution he placed a rating in permanent residence near the towing hawser with orders to cut the tow-line if an aircraft was reported.

Supplied with a pencil and sheets of paper on which to record the names of British personnel the Germans were anxious to transmit to the Swiss Red Cross in Geneva, *Laconia's* Third Officer descended the vertical ladder to gain his first glimpse of a submarine's interior. It was not possible to move forward or aft without first selecting a foothold between the many bodies resting on the floor. He was guided to the mid-section where he found the British women and children. There was much distress about missing family members, one small girl asking if he knew of the whereabouts of her parents and two brothers. Buckingham counted twenty-five women and children and one hundred and sixty-three Italians, with fifty-two German crew. In the seven lifeboats now in tow there were three hundred and twenty British and Polish survivors; another two had been discovered while Buckingham was below. Some of the British military, like Royal Air Force Squadron Leader Vincent Mears, had removed evidence of rank, deeming their chances of escaping interrogation more favourable if they demoted themselves to 'ordinary ranks'. All Italians had been taken out of the boats. Extra look-outs were positioned, their eyes trained on the sky, wary of an enemy who would even unleash death from the skies upon the unfortunate shipwrecked. Buckingham was warned that he would be immediately shot if he made any suspicious moves in the event of an aircraft being sighted. Simultaneously, he was told the ordeal would be over in a few hours' time and he was free to share with the British below decks and in the lifeboats that they were to be handed over to a Vichy French warship. Buckingham felt increasingly relaxed: 'We left it to the U-boat to take us there. Another night of its mysteries and the powerful throbbing of the U-boat's motors shared the hours before dawn.'

* * *

At 7.20 p.m. Lt Harden and his B-24 Liberator crew took off from Wideawake Field, leaving behind them an island on full alert. They reached the search area at 9.05 a.m. flying a square pattern, scanning the sea for lifeboats. At 10.30 a.m. just two miles ahead and to his left, Harden detected the unmistakeable shape of a U-boat; increasing his speed he roared in to attack.

Würdemann gave the order to crash dive, the conning tower and deck of U-506 awash when the B-24 passed over, saved from destruction when the aircraft's two bombs failed to release. Forty-five seconds later, Harden made a second pass, dropping two five hundred pound demolition bombs and two three hundred and fifty pound depth bombs. They fell in train,

108

two landing astern the submarine and two directly on top. The U-boat quaked as the electric motors drove her downward, the one hundred and forty-two *Laconia* survivors in her compartment petrified. She plunged deep, rocked from side to side, violent concussions from the huge detonations sending her reeling in the depths, perilously perched, but undamaged. Würdemann waited.

For forty minutes Harden circled above, watching the disturbed water, at first swirling where the submarine dived, then sprayed by rising white tumults triggered by his bombs as they tumbled into the sea and exploded. Finally, the agitated sea appeared normal again, except for the patch of oil marking the spot where the submarine submerged.

Würdemann kept his nerve, using an old ploy of sending up an oil slick, designed to mislead the attacker into believing he had made a kill, or the submarine was in serious trouble. The inexperienced Harden broke off the engagement and returned to base.

This was to be the last combat mission for the B-24: the aircraft crashed in Palestine on 18th October 1942, while Harden and his crew were flying to the Middle East. They escaped injury and when Harden returned to duty he submitted his report on missions flown on 16th and 17th September. The American commander in the Middle East awarded Air Medals to Lieutenants Harden, Kellar and Perlman for the destruction of an enemy submarine on the 16th and the probable destruction of another on the 17th.

Uneasiness pervaded the garrison on Ascension Island. In nine other sorties flown by the 1st Composite Squadron on the 17th, only Lt Atkins had anything significant to report. At 3 p.m. he saw eight people on a raft.

Returning to the area next morning, Atkins found four empty lifeboats which appeared to be in good condition. Another pilot, Lt McClellan, signalled from his B-25 that he had located at 03° 45' south 13° 15' west a small vessel on a zig-zag course northward, followed by a report from Lt Phillip Main of two ships 02° 56' south, 13° 35' west, headed north-west. Main was instructed to carry out a reconnaissance, if possible identifying the ships, but remaining an observer unless fired upon. Meanwhile, a puzzled Captain Richardson queried the British at Freetown. Two hours later, at 5 p.m. the British reply was to shadow the French ships but not to interfere with them. The message went on 'It appears that they are searching for Italians from *Laconia*.'

This was the first gleaning the Americans at Wideawake had received, six days after the sinking of the *Laconia*, that any rescue for the shipwrecked was underway, by which time the whole business was completed. The cruiser *Gloire* and the sloop *Annamite* had arrived the previous evening; now they were on their way back to Dakar with 1,041 souls transferred from U-506 and U-507, the lifeboats and rafts. The sloop *Dumont d'Urville* kept her rendezvous with the Italian submarine *Cappellini*, taking aboard another forty-two survivors. The captain of the *Cappellini*, Marco Revedin, kept a war diary. His account of his rescue mission is printed here as an appendix.

On 18th September, a 'Secret Cypher' from the British in West Africa to the Admiralty and N.O.I.C. Ascension read:

'Dakar reconnaissance 15 Sep. indicate 2 cruisers and 2 destroyers had left since 15 Sep. 1 cruiser was sighted West of Freetown course 160pm 15 Sep. Reconnaissance 17th indicate 2 ships type unknown returned Dakar. Aircraft report 16 Sep. one sub with 4 lifeboats alongside full of survivors presumably from *Laconia*. Aircraft on 18th sighted group of 4 empty lifeboats. Direction finding bearings at 0301 and 0401 18th indicate 2 unknown French warships within 120 miles of position 0020° 30' south 013° 30' west. It seems possible these ships were rendezvousing sub to transfer survivors from *Laconia*. Has Admiralty any further info?'

From the beginning the British assumed Hartenstein only exerted his energies to rescuing the Italians, an assumption readily understood in the climate and circumstances of 1942. However, before the end of the year the true facts were known, facts of gravity, penetrating the false notions held about the rescue. Unlike Hitler and Goebbels, who were committed to waging psychological warfare as well, Dönitz was purely a military commander. Regrettably for him, his lapse in sparing the British Government a humiliating blow, by failing to feed into the propaganda machine the facts of the actions taken against his submarines while engaged in rescue work, in the end worked to his detriment. As early as 24th October 1942, cognizance was given to this in a 'Most Secret' message from Freetown to the British Admiralty, London:

'Germans not used bombing for propaganda.'

Accordingly, it was convenient for the British to cling to their former position, at first ignorantly accommodated in the fog of war, then occupied wilfully.

On 20th September, the Admiralty in London received the following communication from R.A. West Africa:

'Is any information concerning *Laconia* survivors recovered by Vichy ships available from U.S. sources in Dakar?'

The Americans obliged. Within days the extent of the rescue was available to the Admiralty in London who informed Prime Minister

Winston Churchill. On 27th September Churchill sent a memo to the First Sea Lord at the Admiralty:

'The report of 650 survivors being brought in from the *Laconia* and another ship shows that a very serious tragedy has taken place. Is it known what proportion are British personnel? There were nearly 3,000 people to be accounted for, so over 2,000 must have lost their lives.'

The other ship mentioned in Churchill's report referred to the British cargo ship *Trevilley* torpedoed on 14th September, whose shipwrecked were taken aboard the French sloop *Dumont d'Urville*.

On 14th November 1942, the British Admiralty received a 'Secret Message' from Freetown:

'(1) N.O.I.C. Ascension confirms that only one attack was made by Ascension based aircraft on 16 Sep. This was at 0930 in position 5' south 11° 40' west. This was claimed as a definite sinking but there is now strong evidence that this U-boat was undamaged. (2) COMMENT: Aircraft mistook British disembarked from U-boat to *Laconia* lifeboats for crew of U-boat abandoning ship.'

This is a different version to the official American report, who by their own admission knew when they attacked Hartenstein's submarine that the *Laconia* was carrying many hundreds of passengers but were oblivious of the fact she was transporting Italian prisoners of war. Furthermore, Captain Richardson ordered the attack because the German submarine represented a threat to the safety of British vessels he was committed to protect, while they searched for the *Laconia's* lifeboats.

From where then did the Americans suppose all the people on the submarine's deck and in the four lifeboats, at least three hundred persons seen by the B-24 Liberator's crew, came from? Even if Hartenstein's Red Cross flag was not recognised by international law or suspected as a bluff, the question remains. If the British communication from Freetown to the Admiralty is the true situation, it seems incredible that high ranking military commanders did not know lifeboats were not standard fixtures on a submarine, whether Allied or Axis. Flying at two hundred and fifty feet the B-24 observers saw enough people to crew six U-boats.

All too often in war, questions remain unanswered. In this case, suspicion coupled with a hasty decision from the Americans who were bent upon preserving the secrecy of their activities on Ascension Island, and the unexpected behaviour of a German U-boat commander, contributed to the drama unfolded in the South Atlantic, with the hesitant cast not fully appreciating the full scene until Act One was completed.

THE SINKING OF THE LACONIA

In a letter to this author, General Robert C. Richardson III wrote: 'In simple terms the real problem here was one of communications. Most of my crews were kids right out of flying school that could not read naval blinking lights or the Morse code. The British *never told us* that the U-156 was doing rescue although the Admiralty at Freetown knew it since they monitored naval frequencies and the Germans had gone to Geneva saying so (Red Cross). We always wondered if this was deliberate or not for notwithstanding the German free passage statement they were worried about their freighters in the area and were not the least unhappy that we went after the subs. At the same time our communications with Freetown were poor. Same with Washington.

'The basic model was quite simple. We knew there were prisoners on the *Laconia* and assumed the subs were rescuing them. Freetown asked us to protect their ships and we had picked them up in the area. No one told us of the Hartenstein free passage announcement or of the German Geneva contact. We even assumed the French were working for the Germans and prepared to attack their ships until Washington finally woke up and said lay off. The French were assured by the Germans in Dakar that there was *no possibility* of allied air in the rescue area so they went out unarmed and were more scared when they ran into us than we were when we ran into them! We of course thought they were heavily armed, when in fact they had no gun crews or working anti-aircraft systems, the ships having been laid up in Dakar for over a year.

'In view of the formal British request to protect their ships, the fact that we knew the subs were German and assumed they were rescuing their own people and would finish off the freighters next, no knowledge of Hartenstein's messages communicated to us (Ascension did not monitor the sea frequencies) and no ability to communicate with ships since our people could not read signal lamps, we assumed the Red Cross flag to be a combat bluff (not legal for combat ships to fly) and ordered the attack.'

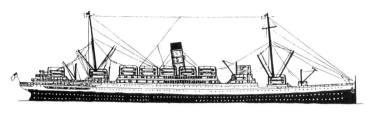

XII

IN FRENCH CUSTODY

Thursday 17th September:

Around 5 p.m. Royal Naval Gunnery Rating Robert Tinkler saw smoke on the horizon. Excitement abounded in the lifeboat, which had been abandoned by U-156 after the American attack. Eyes heavy through lack of sleep, sore through stinging spray, strained to see the warship steaming towards them. Opinions varied regarding her nationality but Tinkler was beyond caring. One thing was sure: his misery was about to end.

The French sailors on the cruiser *Gloire* hauled scrambling nets over the ship's side. Tinkler grabbed one and started to climb, others followed, negotiating the steep ascent with difficulty, eager in spirit, willing swollen, stiff limbs upward to safety. For some, totally exhausted, the exercise was beyond their physical capabilities and French sailors began the laborious task of helping them out of the lifeboat.

On board the *Gloire* Plumber Charles Gregory stared numbly at *Laconia*'s growing group of survivors, thankful for the luxury of being able to stretch his swollen, cramped legs and to move his head without touching another body. Imprisoned in the depths of the ship, below the water-line, he was hardly a candidate to offer intimidation, he thought, to the armed Frenchman standing guard as a precaution against the weary British, should they scheme to seize control of the vessel. This was a sentiment shared by William Hoyer, who with his friends David Chawe, Gerald Partridge and Third Radio Officer Cooper had arrived in style aboard *Laconia*'s powerless motor launch.

On U-507, Commander Schacht's order from his Commander-in-Chief, to return the British to the lifeboats but keep all Italians on board the submarine, troubled him. Genuinely, he wanted to complete the work he had begun, an outcome at risk if the British sensed he was under new orders. He sought for a way to conclude the business satisfactorily within the compass of his orders, in a manner unlikely to damage the morale of the British, who trusted him implicitly. Any inkling by them of possible desertion might result in them deciding to go it alone in weather about to

113

50. The French cruiser *Gloire* taken in 1938.

change for the worse. Eventually he excused his action with a reason he knew could not be contested, explaining to Buckingham he could not take bearings on the approaching rescue ship as the U-boat's radio-direction finding aerial was jammed in its housing. If further impeded by a reduced speed with lifeboats in tow, the chances of missing the planned rendezvous with the French were heightened. Rather than put this at risk he would submerge, find the rescue ship and pass on the position of the lifeboats.

Grateful Britons shook hands with the Germans before entering the lifeboats, now more comfortable due to the Italians remaining on the submarine. Schacht was emphatic that they should stay in position, stressing the importance of hanging out oil-lamps from the mast-head if rescue did not reach them before nightfall.

Buckingham talked matters over with his colleagues. Uppermost in their minds was the integrity of Schacht's word. He was their enemy, in no way obliged to organise their safety, especially as the Italians were aboard his submarine.

Finally, they agreed to give the German commander the benefit of any doubt, stay where they were for the night, but set sail at daylight if the French ship failed to appear.

Without the Italians it was easier to move about in the boats. Buckingham had not slept for the past four days and it occurred to him that none of Schacht's men had slept for two days as there was nowhere for them to sleep, all accommodation having been taken up by the women and children.

In contrast to previous days, the sky was overcast and it started to rain. Lt Mercer acquainted himself with some new passengers, two of them women, Mrs Dorothy Davidson and Mrs Walker. They were confident rescue would come within two hours' time, based upon a snippet of information passed by a German officer. Two hours later Schacht returned, Buckingham heard his name called and within minutes was standing in the conning tower face to face again with Schacht, expecting to hear definite news about the French ship's arrival time. Brief and apologetic, the German commander informed Buckingham that he should consider himself a prisoner-of-war: 'It seemed useless to ask why, but I did, and was told that the U-boat had many new devices in her equipment, and as I was a professional sailor, and an officer, it was deemed imprudent to allow me to escape... An R.A.F. officer had also been taken out of the boats, and was already in the U-boat when I was taken down there myself.'

In the meantime, Lt Mercer passed around the good news of a Vichy French warship steaming in their direction. She was picking up survivors on the way and should reach their area in approximately three to four hours time.

The weather deteriorated, squally with heavy rain, and seas ran high, making it difficult for the lifeboats to remain together. Hours went by, still no sign of the French ship, only the intensifying wind in their ears, shrieking with a note of malevolence and supremacy. Exposed to the onslaught they rode out the storm, head on to the seas, aided by the sea anchor. Overhead the sky darkened, colouring the dark forebodings in Mercer's mind of another night on the sea. However, one hour before nightfall through the gloom, Mercer saw a large ship speeding towards them. She was the *Gloire*, and close behind her was the *Annamite*.

The British and Polish officers were herded together in a small room behind the forward gun turret, confined in a space eighteen feet by twelve. They had to make the best of it on a steel floor without bedding. All other ranks were segregated into three main divisions – army, air force and navy – and incarcerated at the bottom of the ship, while the Italians, no longer prisoners, were billeted in an aero-hanger. The women and children fared better, occupying cabins surrendered by *Gloire's* officers. On board the *Gloire* Molly Davidson was re-united with her mother. Captain Ben Coutts was there, too.

During the night the seas became mountainous but at 10.15 a last boat was spotted: Boat 14 containing Junior Third Officer Ellis, Tom Collum, Jack Moore, Commander Baldwin and others. Ellis saw the *Gloire's* searchlight and sent off three flares. He was convinced they would not have survived much longer in such inclement conditions.

One of the seven boats picked up by the *Gloire* at this point was no. 12. This contained some 67 people, including Leading Stoker James William Rowson, aged 21. He kept a short diary of events which mentions 'Sighted Cruiser at 1955. Taken on board at 2010. Very hungry and weak and tired having had hardly any sleep. A total of 1000(?) picked up. Another boat picked up at 2115.' He also recorded that a church service was held on the *Gloire* at 2015 the next day for 2000 people still missing.

Soon after the *Gloire* had picked up the survivors from the seven lifeboats abandoned by U-507 after Buckingham had been taken prisoner, U-506 and U-507 had also rendezvoused. Schacht transferred his 163 Italians to the *Annamite*. Buckingham was not allowed to watch the Italians transfer to the French ship 'but when the operation of transfer was complete, there seemed signs of great relief amongst the officers and crew at having the U-boat to themselves again'. U-507 then submerged and kept a careful watch on proceedings as Würdemann transferred his nine women

51. The French sloop *Annamite.*

52. The French sloop *Dumont D'Urville* taken in 1944 at a U.S. navy yard.

and children and 142 Italians from U-506.

The *Annamite* later rendezvoused with the *Dumont-d'Urville*, the French ship which had joined the Italian submarine *Cappellini*. Forty-two Italian survivors were transferred to the *Annamite* for passage to Dakar. Commander Madelin of the *Dumont-d'Urville* continued to search for survivors, but without further success.

When they had got under way, Schacht came below and informed Buckingham and Flying Officer Smith, RAF, the second prisoner he chose to take back to Germany, that he was now continuing with his patrol but proceeding slowly towards home. They were briefed concerning their conduct during the long voyage ahead: in return for their promise of good behaviour, they would receive treatment equivalent to a U-boat officer. Schacht was as good as his word, permitting Buckingham and Smith to have access to the deck during daylight hours, to take meals with the officers and to sleep in their quarters. Buckingham wrote in his first report:

'Food was mostly dehydrated provisions. They thought well of chocolate and energising tablets amongst their meals. 50% of crew were in British Battle and Tank dress. They also were smoking Bulwark Tobacco, which they said came from the beaches of Dunkirk, left after our evacuation from there.

'In the evening crew and Captain gathered on Bridge and sang German folk songs to an accordion...

'I was given a pair of khaki trousers and discarded slippers. Landing thus attired in Lorient I was given a meal of boiled potatoes and put on a train with two guards, and for 50 hours travelled to Wilhelmshaven, N.W. Germany.'

* * *

Friday 18th September, on the *Gloire*:

At 6 a.m. the *Laconia's* survivors were aroused after a cold night lying on a bare floor. Coffee was served and the *Gloire's* officers unfolded their plan of organisation, insisting the thirty-six British and Polish officers compile a roster of Duty Officers for a twenty-four hour period, to assist French sentries in controlling men who were restive. Two hot meals were promised each day at 11.30 a.m. and 6 p.m., followed by coffee at 6.30 p.m.

The condition of *Laconia's* Third Engineer Jackson worsened during the day and he died. At sunset, British and French stood side by side as his body was committed to the deep with full naval honours.

The journey was not without incident: Lt Mercer was concerned at the aggressive attitude of French naval officers towards Lt Barnes, the only British Royal Naval officer. The lower deck men were different, friendly,

53. British women and girls on board the *Gloire*.

54. Handing out clothes to survivors on the *Gloire*.

deriving satisfaction in smuggling luxuries such as soap and cigarettes to the British. Lt Mercer, Wing Commander Blackburn and Capt McCordick spoke French fluently, learning from conversation with crewmen who secretly confessed they were Gaullists and had fought at Dunkirk, and that the Germans were using Dakar as a submarine base. But their main concern was over Lt De La Haase who was questioning women and older children about any remembrance they could glean of shipping movements after sailing from Suez. Commander Graziani, however, soon became popular with his passengers.

Several times action stations sounded and it was rumoured British naval vessels were nearby, probably H.M.S. *Corinthian* still searching for the *Laconia's* lifeboats. The *Empire Haven* had abandoned her efforts on the 18th.

Lt De La Haase was proud of his ship, repeatedly boasting how efficient were his guns, to the *Laconia's* crewmen and Royal Naval Ratings as they came up from the hold to exercise on deck, much to the satisfaction of the leering Italians whose roles were now reversed. Boatswain's Mate Le Brocq thought the French officer somewhat ridiculous, his proud guns evidently in urgent need of maintenance, their annoying squeaks bringing smiles to the faces of the British sailors.

The *Gloire* arrived at Dakar on Tuesday 22nd September, where she refuelled and provisioned. At 4.30 p.m. she sailed for the final stage of the voyage to Casablanca, arriving there two days later.

According to a Secret Cypher received on 1st October 1942 by the British Admiralty:

'Members of crew of *Gloire* stated impressed by the model behaviour of British sailors picked up, whereas the Italians were simply insufferable, insolent and arrogant. On landing at Casablanca the Italians had priority and went off first, without a word of thanks. The British, however, before setting off in the lorries lined up along the quay, gave three cheers for the captain and crew of *Gloire* and shouted, "Vive la France". Those of the ship's company who were previously pro-collaboration have now definitely changed their tune.'

Peillard records that Colonel Baldwin, who had done much to mediate with the crew concerning the needs of the women and children on board, was the last to walk down the gangplank. 'As he reached the quay to join the thousand survivors, he turned and raised his hand as a signal: "Three cheers for the *Gloire*. Hip hip hooray!..." "Hip hip...!" It was repeated by all in various accents.'

THE SINKING OF THE LACONIA

Thursday 24th September marked a new turning in the sufferings of the survivors. From the quayside they were transported to Mediouna Camp, twenty kilometres along the Marrakesh road; the women and children separated to Camp Sidi-el-Avachi, near Azemmour, Mediouna, where they stayed until liberated by American forces six weeks later.

New deprivations awaited those who had been fortunate enough to outlive the terrors of the past two weeks. Under French control, the men were subjected to inhumane conditions, far different from the care and attention received from the German sailors. Accommodated in concrete buildings with a corrugated roof, filthy, overrun with beetles, insects and mosquitos, the men slept on straw.

Royal Naval Gunnery Rating John Hennessey was stung by a red scorpion. Plumber Charles Gregory tried to feed the wild dogs roaming the camp with part of his rations. The refusal of the dogs to eat it didn't surprise him. Eight men shared a loaf of bread, the menu varying from wheat with husks to unfilleted fish, boiled as caught. Steward Wallace, under treatment from German Dr Mullard, was dependent upon his colleagues fetching water from a tap allocated to serve four hundred men.

Ben Coutts fared better. In a letter he wrote to Doris Hawkins he reported 'We were all popped into an internment camp – the women and children in one – service personnel in another... When on the third day they held a sick parade, they saw my wound [he had had a toenail removed two days before the sinking], and rushed me off to the local military hospital. Life there was much more pleasant, the only trouble being that, with my size, they couldn't get clothes for me, especially for my big feet! and I only had pyjamas and a greatcoat. However, they managed to procure a sackcloth suit, and with some boots of an ersatz material, a shirt and a tie (blue with yellow spots) and string socks I was indeed well off.

'The colonel in charge of the hospital arranged for me to go to France to be interviewed by their plastic surgeons, with a view to repatriation ... I was to go on 20th October (we arrived in Casablanca on 20th September); but God was with me, and the ship was full. I eventually left on 5th November, and the ship crawled along the North African coast, and was to put into Oran Bay, then cross to Marseilles.

'On November 8th the Allies put in their attack on North Africa, and on the night of November 7th I saw a greyhound-looking shape loom alongside, and order us to halt. A British destroyer!... I was taken off next day, and put on the senior naval officer's ship, and I saw the whole show at Oran.

'From there I was taken to Algiers, which was packed with British shipping – a magnificent sight ...

'I got a colossal welcome, and we were home in eight days ... The rest, who were interned in Casablanca, were released when the Allies landed, and were repatriated, coming back via America.'

Two other survivors remember their rescue by the *Gloire*. Andrew Zamrej and companions had floated for five days before they were found:

'On the fifth day, late afternoon, we spotted on the horizon a ship and were convinced that it was the British ship, *Robinson Crusoe*. Everybody was very excited, but later on we realized that it was the French Vichy ship, *Gloire*.

'They started picking us up and I got pulled up at about 7.30 p.m. Some of the survivors could climb up the ship's ladders, but others were hauled up by ropes because they were so weak. On the French ship I met a French sailor of Polish parentage and he help me a lot to survive, especially by advising me not to eat. He gave me a drink of rum with tea and told me to go to sleep. "Tomorrow I will give you something else". Through him I survived, but some people who ate too much were a goner.

'We were taken to Casablanca in Morocco and then to a camp, seventy km from Casablanca, where we spent 3 months, being liberated when the Americans invaded Morocco. Then we travelled to Great Britain where I joined the 1st Polish Parachute Brigade, part of the 1st Airborne Division, in time to become involved in operations at Arnhem and later on was decorated.'

The young French sailor of Polish descent gave Andrew a souvenir card of himself, inscribed on the back in French 'To my dear compatriot, saved by the cruiser 'Gloire' from the wreck of the L'aconia, 17.9.42' and signed *J. Szablewski*. The postcard is illustrated on page 125. Polish survivors presented Captain Graziani with a card of thanks designed by artist Longin Wargocki, signed by them all.

James Campbell also remembers vividly the moment of rescue. His boat had separated from the others gathered together by Hartenstein and he was lucky to be found:

'In charge of our boat was a navy P.O. and he, in his wisdom, cut us apart from the group and we started to row away. Jock Jarvie and I were given the task, in the stern, of keeping us on the given course with the aid of a compass and an oar lashed to the stern. The occupants were mainly Italians and a few Brits plus one Polish officer. It was mainly uneventful except for two occasions when Liberator aircraft flew over us and, despite a flare being set off each time, appeared to ignore us. In retrospect I think they were desperate to locate the sub.

'After five days of this on the fifth night I was desperately trying to get a bit of sleep. Difficult task in a rolling lifeboat with 86 people on board. I had my head resting on my knees when I felt a tug at my hair from one of the Italians. I was just about to swing a punch at him when he pulled my head up and, there, a short distance away, was a fully lit ship. I called up the Navy P.O. and he set off a flare and very shortly we heard the engines stopping. What a lovely sound. They came alongside and we all climbed up a rope ladder. The rest, I suppose is history.

'The ship was, of course, the Vichy French Cruiser the *Gloire* and we were looked after well, allowing for the inevitable overcrowding. In fact we had been very lucky as the *Gloire* had given up looking for the missing lifeboat (us!) and we happened to be lying in their route to Dakar.'

In later life both James Campbell and Andrew Zamrej lived in Scotland but it was not until an article on Andrew's experiences appeared in a December 1992 issue of the *Ross-shire Journal* that the two made contact, having lived for many years just a few miles from one another.

Before leaving the *Gloire*, Lt De La Haase assured the British officers that there were no Germans at the camp. However, this was a lie: upon arrival they found a small group of German Gestapo waiting for them. They selected at random members of the *Laconia's* crew for interrogation. Billy Hardacre, still scarred around his body, underwent a gruelling time, thinking it sensible to say something rather than nothing, yet careful not to divulge anything of importance.

The United States Ambassador in London informed the British Admiralty of American efforts to visit the people in the camps. The French were proving far from co-operative, as detailed in a telegram received on 28th September from the United States Consulate in Casablanca. The Consular Attaché and his wife, accompanied by Mr Leslie Heath of the 'Friends Relief Committee', visited Camp Sidi-el-Avachi to visit the women and children, only to be turned away by the Civil Controller under military orders not to admit any American consular representative, as a reprisal against the United States of America.

On 1st October, the Acting British Consul-General, Tangier, signalled the Admiralty, London:

'Casablanca authorities refused as a reprisal against the United States for their failure six months ago to inform the French Government concerning Diego Suarez prisoners.'

124

55. J. Szablewski, on the *Gloire*.

56. Andrew Zamrej today

57. Andrew Zamrej and James Campbell, *Laconia* survivors

THE SINKING OF THE LACONIA

On 7th November 1942, American soldiers liberated the camps, setting free six hundred *Laconia* survivors whom they returned to the British Isles, in most cases via the United States. John Hennessey's foot, for lack of medical attention, swelled considerably, causing him difficulty in walking on it. The Americans transferred him to the United States Ship *Anna Arundel* bound for Norfolk, Virginia, committing him to the sick bay for the whole of the voyage.

* * *

A *Laconia* survivor who was held as a prisoner of war in Mediouna Internment camp was the British War Artist, the late Edward Bawden. He had boarded the ship in Cape Town after illustrating events in the Middle East. Four pictures survive from his experience, reproduced here by kind permission of the Imperial War Museum. For the recent book *Edward Bawden, war artist, and his letters home 1940-45*, edited by Ruari McLean, he wrote a short account of his experiences which is here reproduced by kind permission of the publisher, Scolar Press:

'I must have been one of the last passengers to leave the *Laconia* when she was torpedoed. At the moment of impact the ship shuddered violently causing a hail of broken glass in the bar where I was having a drink before dinner. At once the ship began to list making the launching of half the number of life boats impossible. I saw few people on deck and no sign of panic. I didn't feel conscious of fear but as I could see no hope of escape I went below for a wrist watch bought in Cape Town for my wife: why not take it with me?

'On returning from my cabin I saw ropes hanging down on the side where life boats had been lowered and standing by one of these I was joined by a major: "After you, Sir" I said. He descended – there was a splash. Sliding down the next rope I found myself being gripped and guided into a boat. A few minutes later all the boats pulled away to a safe distance and there we sat waiting, still and silent and tense for the terrible sound of the ship's final end. I did not see it disappear because I had my arm round a little girl who had become separated from her mother and brother, but, luckily, they were later discovered on another boat.

'The last person to come aboard was a young RAF officer who was seen clinging to a raft. Night was beginning to fall so the merchant seamen unfolded a heavy tarpaulin which was fastened down to provide warmth and protection, allowing everyone to find a sleeping place wherever there was room. It was unfortunate that a young seaman had soiled himself.

'Next morning the boat was sitting still, rising and falling with the motion of the water and looking down drowned bodies were floating, often

126

at some depth, while now and again a shark appeared seemingly within touching distance nudging the side. Food and water were doled out sparingly and what remained was assessed to give a rough idea of how long it might last.

'So that day and the next four passed. Now and again the submarine was seen. An aeroplane passed overhead very high up. And waving shirts did not seem successful in attracting attention. At last a ship appeared coming directly towards us and the other boats which like our own had been shepherded by the submarine converged towards what could now be seen as a warship. As we climbed on to the deck there were pails of coffee and brandy ready for us but no friendliness. *La Gloire* was Vichy French and we were now guarded as prisoners of war.

'On reaching Casablanca, coaches were waiting but I do not remember anything about the journey inland except that in the evening a large group of us were standing spread out on a strip of treeless stony ground as the sun was sinking below the horizon. Hours later we saw it rise, on my part with relief because during the night it was eerie hearing voices now near and then more distant. A railway line was not far away and cattle trucks took us from there to near our final destination, a wired-in enclosure on a stretch of barren ground, the distance bounded by low barren hills.

'Life in the camp for the next two and a half months was uneventful: we walked about the compound aimlessly, taking exercise and talking to each other. For warmth French Foreign Legion uniforms were issued, our food was beans washed down with a coffee substitute. We slept in small wooden huts and because I woke early by habit and also possessed a watch I was given the job of rousing everyone for breakfast.

'A day came when our guards appeared to be in a restless state. An invitation was received for us to make use of the Officers' Mess so a small party walked down, opened the door and looked in. What silly monkeys we must have seemed in our ill fitting uniforms, bare legs and unshaven faces, so it was no wonder that a group of French officers round the bar turned to glance at us and then turned back. We shut the door and went back to the camp.

'Suddenly the French disappeared and the Americans arrived.'

* * *

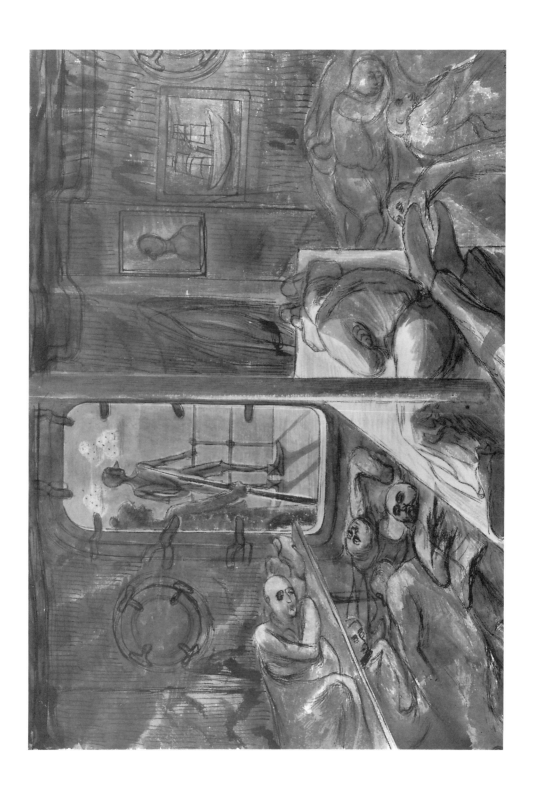

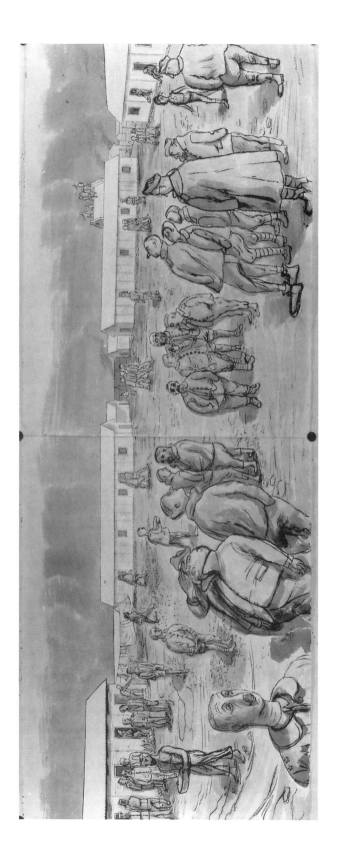

61. Edward Bawden, British War Artist, was a *Laconia* survivor. This is his second drawing of the Mediouna internment camp.

Previous pages:

58. Edward Bawden's drawing of British officers on the *Gloire*.
59. Edward Bawden's drawing of *Laconia* survivors on the *Gloire*.
60. Edward Bawden's first drawing of survivors interned in the Mediouna Camp.

On 6th December 1942, the liner *Strathaird* docked at Greenock, Scotland. Seven of the *Laconia's* crew disembarked, including Boat Deckman Robert Hicks and Butcher Edward Johnson. Most of the others, liberated from the French camps, sailed to England on the *Queen Mary* from New York. Plumber Charles Gregory was placed aboard the S.S. *Westerland* bound for Greenock. To his horror he was provided with quarters in the cargo hold. Gregory refused to descend the wooden ladder, choosing to remain on 'B' Deck for the voyage, despite protests, snowfalls and freezing winds.

* * *

Another survivor was David Chawe, already mentioned as a friend of William Hoyer. His story after rescue is preserved in a typescript at the Imperial War Museum, written by his sister Grace:

'They were interned in a camp near Casablanca with little food or comfort. They succumbed to dysentery, skin sores and lice. As soon as they realised that the Allied forces had invaded N. Africa he and several of the men broke out of camp and made their way towards Casablanca. They met up with U.S. troops who took them on to Casablanca and gave them their first decent meal in months. They were returned to camp and the U.S. Army made ready to liberate them. They were given disinfectant showers. All their hair was shaved off and they were given U.S. naval uniforms and shipped to the U.S. aboard the U.S.S. *Ancorn*.

They were fêted, wined and dined by prominent N.Y. citizens and criticized by Walter Winchel, newspaper column writer, for saying they had been helped by a humane German. David said humane he was. He had done his job, and could have left them to their fate, but he risked his life and flotilla to help them. The men were sorry to learn he did not survive the War.'

* * *

Third Officer Thomas Buckingham and Flying Officer Smith were transported to prison camps in Germany. Buckingham to a camp near Bremen and the Royal Air Force man to Stuttgart, where he died in captivity. On 25th November a German radio broadcast transmitted from Calais confirmed news of the safety of the two *Laconia* men. Buckingham closed his first report stating 'For the next 2 years and six months I was at a Marine Prison Camp 18 miles W x N from Bremen. The full strength of this camp including all colonial and British subjects was 3,100 men, all Merchant Service Officers and Ratings.

'Liberated by Guards Armoured Division on April 29th, 1945, after a pitched battle around the camp.'

62. *Laconia* survivor David Chawe, second from right, and other survivors, being toasted by Canadian prime minister after their liberation. Survivor William Hoyer identifies the man on the extreme left as Gerald Partridge. Note the shaven heads.

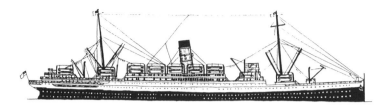

XIII

JOURNEY TO AFRICA

After leaving the U-156, Doris Hawkins' boat was also slowly sailing eastwards – towards Africa. Her account is so graphic it is worth quoting in full:

The sixty-eight of us were to be companions for many long and bitter days. Most were destined not to survive the dreadful journey in that boat. There were among our number at the beginning a lieutenant-colonel, a squadron-leader, an assistant purser, an assistant ship's engineer, a lieutenant of the Fleet Air Arm, an electrician, a pilot officer, two Polish cadet officers, and other ranks from all services, and the young ship's surgeon, Dr Geoffrey Purslow...

The boat was a thirty-foot wooden lifeboat, and by the time we were taken into it, it had a leak in one side which necessitated pumping day and night. The U-boat commandant before submerging had told us that the nearest land was 600 miles away, and had advised us to try to keep N.N.E. He added that we should "never make it". Although we had a compass, we had no skilled navigator or charts.

We were packed so tightly together that it was almost impossible even to ease our position during that first long, cold night, as we sat shoulder to shoulder. The next morning, Thursday, we started to sail to the coast, as we had no idea where the "rendezvous" was, nor whether the Vichy ships would keep their appointment. Since we had only fifteen gallons of water for sixty-eight people, and a minimum of 600 miles to go, the officers in charge of the boat decided that it was unwise to wait about, and so waste valuable time.

During the morning an American 'plane sighted us, circled low over us twice, flashed us a message, which unfortunately no one could read, and flew off. We were jubilant, and hope ran high. In a few hours a flying-boat would come and pick us all up – in a day or two a destroyer would be there seeking us, or a convoy would be diverted to rescue us. So the hopeful suggestions ran, and we believed them all in turn. Finally, however, as nothing came, we settled down and determined to make land.

At first the men rowed in shifts day and night, others taking turns at the tiller, but after some days the rowing was discontinued, as they became too weak. A jib was made from our two blankets, and we relied on the wind to carry us along.

Our daily ration of food, dispensed at first by Dr Purslow and the colonel, was as follows:

Morning. Four or five Horlicks tablets, three pieces of chocolate (size 1½" x ¾" x ½"). No water.

Evening. Two ship's biscuits (size of petit beurre, but very dry and hard): one teaspoonful of pemmican. Two ounces of water.

After a few nights a place was made where Mary and I could lie side by side, and we tried to keep each other warm by lying very close together. But the wind seemed to blow through us, and sometimes we were soaked as a wave broke over the boat. It was dark in that latitude from about 6.30 p.m. to 6 a.m.

The days passed in a dreadful monotony. Nobody had anything to do. Mary and I used to sit during those first days 'up forward' behind the sail, where there was a little shade in the mornings, for we were in equatorial waters, and the sun was almost unbearable by 10 a.m.

We all talked of our homes and families and friends – of what we would do when we were rescued and when we reached home. We discussed the things we were going to eat and drink, and spoke of most of the things we had ever eaten in the past. We were unanimous in declaring that water would always be treated with great respect in future, and that we should never again refuse a drink, or complain about our food! Mary and I were always confident, and our sense of humour persisted.

Strange as it may seem, I never failed to appreciate the beauty of the ever-changing sea and sky, and I often thought that, given better conditions, one could enjoy a similar voyage. It would, we decided, be necessary to be suitably clad, to have adequate food and drink, suitable protection from the elements when necessary, and a means of navigation and locomotion. It would, of course, be pleasant to be among one's friends. We should need books, handwork, fishing-tackle, and a few games. For those who live busy lives in noisy places, whose lives are spent under the tyranny of the telephone and door-bell, but who love the sea, nothing could be a more complete rest-cure.

Quite a number of us shared this opinion, and it gave us a good topic of conversation. As each became interested and contributed a suggestion or a criticism, we became quite enthusiastic, and thus we kept our minds from our own danger and suffering for a while. The beauties of the sea and sky are always worth noting. We saw the most lovely-coloured tropical fish through the transparent blue water, clouds of blue-green flying fish, their fins shining silver in the sunlight, as, leaving the water, they darted through the air, to strike the water again with a little splash. We saw brown gulls and other birds, flying in flocks and excitedly diving, crying and fighting as they came upon a shoal of fish. We saw porpoises tumbling through the water.

Less pleasant was the sight of the sharks' dorsal fins cleaving the surface, often following our boat with uncanny knowledge. One day we saw several whales quite close to us, their great bodies making a smooth green patch as they moved near the surface. Suddenly we would glimpse the dark forms half out of the water, and from time to time they noisily spouted jets of water into the air.

The sun always set in a blaze of glory, reflected in the sea, and left an after glow of colours which spread across the sky and lasted until the blue shadows of night stretched across and took their place. Then the moon came up, making a silver pathway across the waves, and the stars came out and twinkled encouragingly, looking larger and nearer than those in an English sky.

In the morning we watched the sun rise, for it was then that occasionally just a few drops of very fine rain fell, lasting less than five minutes usually; but we liked to feel it on our faces. So we were awake as dawn came, and streaks of light broke across the sky, and then the sun came quickly over the horizon and it was day, and hope was born anew.

One of our number was the fourth engineer of the ship, William Henderson by name, and he never spared himself in his work for the comfort and safety of all of us. He made a rudder from some pieces of wood, and two of the lads went over the side to fix it. He organized the 'pumping squad', himself taking the longest night watch, when it was coldest and most difficult to keep alert, and if anyone fell out, he was always there, ready to carry on. One day he made one of the doors covering the buoyancy tanks into floor-boards, so that 'the ladies' might be a little more comfortable at night, and two more into notice-boards, on which was printed by means of white lead: 'S.O.S. Water', this to be held aloft should any aircraft pass our way again. Another day, with great care, he removed two buoyancy tanks and discovered the position of the worst leak. Then, with the help of two other men, the place was made more or less water-tight by teasing out rope and impregnating it with white lead, and pressing it firmly into the crack.

136

Several mornings found him cold and blue, and we had to chafe his limbs to bring him back to consciousness. Those of us who finally reached safety must always remember with deep gratitude and pride Billy Henderson's selflessness and devotion to duty, on what was to prove his last voyage; for one morning we found that he was no longer breathing.

In spite of such losses, with each new day came fresh hope. Surely to-day must be the day? Was there anything on the horizon? Could that be smoke? Yes! – No – only a wisp of cloud. All day we longed for our minute water ration, which came at 5 o'clock. Our worst torture was thirst. After a time we could quite easily bear the lack of food, but the lack of water tried us sorely. When each water ration was passed along, everyone peered at it with longing, as it went from hand to hand. When we received our precious drop, we took a sip, ran it round our teeth and gums, gargled with it and finally swallowed it. We repeated this until not a drop nor a drip was left clinging to the little biscuit tin from which we drank. After five minutes we could not tell that we had had any, so quickly did our parched bodies absorb the fluid. As we grew weaker and our mouths more and more dry, we only spoke when necessary. Whenever we had a few minutes of fine rain, as occasionally happened in the very early morning, it was a pathetic sight to see all those people with their dry, brown tongues out, and heads thrown back, trying to catch 'just a few drops'. It is a sight that I shall never forget.

Our pores closed up completely after a few days, and we did not perspire at all, in spite of the intense heat. Our nails became brittle and broke easily; many of us found our cuticles peeling away, and our nails became very pale. After a few days we all became a little light-headed, and were unable to sleep, but dozed lightly, and dreamed always of water, cool drinks, fruit – and of rescue. I used to see all my friends' houses with the refrigerator doors wide open, and ice-cold food and drinks ready to be taken, but always just out of reach. I saw the cups of tea I had had in hospital, ice-creams and iced coffees as I had so often enjoyed them in Palestine; I saw myself in Cairo, with a glass of pineapple juice at Groppi's, and ripe mangoes ready to be eaten, and once more came the cup of tea!

Over and over again, teasing and tormenting, like a cinematograph show, the scenes passed and re-passed. I thought of the water I had wasted, of the dripping taps. People were washing up and cleaning floors with precious life-giving water, unconscious of our need and our longing. If only—! Returning to consciousness after these light-headed wanderings, time and time again I thought: 'Well, thank God it is all a dream. I shall wake up in a minute, and find that it is not true'; and then I would feel the boat rocking, rocking, and sit up to find only miles and miles of sea and sky – and I knew it was no dream.

We became thinner daily, and we were hollow-eyed. The men's beards grew, until they looked like pirates. All of us were insufficiently clad, only two having shoes and socks, and the sun and salt water rotted such clothing as we had. All our sore areas began to discharge pus after a few days, and continued to discharge all the time. Many of us had salt-water sores, septic fingers and toes, and boils. I had lost my glasses, and the light was very strong, so my eyes became sore and discharged pus fairly freely from the end of the first week onwards. My back never ceased aching from the time of the explosion when the ship sank, and the floor-boards made hard beds. I longed for a hospital bed with a pillow, a back-rest and an air-ring – and some massage.

We had no medical supplies at all, no dressings, no drugs, no stimulants, and, as a nurse, I had never felt so helpless. We did what we could for each other, but we could do very little, except by keeping cheerful and optimistic, and so helping to keep up morale. Doctor Purslow and I opened septic fingers and toes with a pen-knife, cleansed in sea water, and tried to explain the importance of not infecting each other.

Mary became a little weaker each day. She never suffered acutely, but just faded, and I knew that unless we were soon picked up she must die. She spoke often to me of her family, and her thoughts were constantly with her husband, fighting in the desert, or with her little sons awaiting her in the homeland. Never once did she allow the sorrow which must have been in her heart to depress those around her, and she kept her keen sense of humour all the time, and I remember how, despite our desperate position, something would amuse us, and, catching each other's eye, we would laugh, and then the men "up forward" would smile too. She was most considerate of others, and grateful for everything that was done for her. On 25th September she realised that she could not live much longer. She smiled and thanked me for taking care of her, adding: "We've had lots of fun." Quite calmly she repeated her home address, and then seemed to fall asleep, facing death as she had faced life, unflinchingly, looking forward and not back.

Throughout the night of September 25th/26th I lay with my arms around her, in a last effort to keep her warm, but this night she did not shiver and nothing disturbed her, and in the morning at 6 a.m. she just stopped breathing while asleep. Dr Purslow held a little service for her, and we tried to sing a verse of "Abide with Me", but the effort was pathetic. They lowered her into the water. I felt very much alone – the only woman with some sixty men.

As our journey continued, our numbers decreased. At first we were so crowded that Mary and I had had to spend the days behind the sail, and after she died I often spent the nights there too. Daily we saw our companions growing weaker, saw that they had not long to live, and then sometimes just found that they were no longer with us. There were some who, despite all warnings, drank salt water and succumbed, and others who became delirious, and their cries and rambling speech and their oft-repeated pleas for water were terrible to hear. One wondered how long one could remain sane.

Our tongues became hard and dry and our lips swollen and cracked. Many of us kept our teeth clean by rubbing them with a piece of cloth soaked in sea-water. When we talked, our mouths were curiously misshapen and our voices became hoarse and weak. With our exceedingly small water ration, it was impossible after a few days to eat our biscuits or malted-milk tablets. The biscuits blew out of our mouths as we chewed them, and they just would not go down. The Horlicks tablets stuck to the roof of the mouth, and stayed there. I tried to eat my pemmican ration every day, as I had read that it has high food value, but it often took an hour to swallow one teaspoonful. The chocolate dissolved easily and I was able to eat the three little squares daily, until the supply ran out.

Some of the men managed to eat at least part of a biscuit by soaking it in sea-water. One of the Polish cadet officers was able to eat his biscuit ration in this way until the end of the time, and was the only one of the survivors who had no septic sores or boils. He had endured many hardships in his life, which no doubt helped him to be strong in the face of privation, for he remained alert and helpful to the end of the voyage. When we were exhausted, he could always manage to dip up some water from the sea and pour it over our heads and limbs to refresh us, and although he could not speak any English, he was most kind and courteous to me, and his influence was always for good. His only surviving brother died beside him in the lifeboat.

One night a small flying fish came into our boat. It was divided among eight of us, and we ate it with relish. We looked with longing at the numerous but elusive fish, which were always to be seen swimming about the boat, through the blue water. The men tried to make hooks and lines, but they had nothing firm enough for a hook, and the fish were wiser and stronger than they, and none was caught. Some of our number ate small barnacles, scraped from the sides and bottom of the boat, and we chewed our skin as it peeled from sunburnt surfaces. We tried to make our mouths less dry by chewing bone buttons from clothing and rubber bands from the pemmican and biscuit tins.

Until they became too weak, most of the men used to go over the side for a dip once or twice a day, and they used to pour tins of water over my bare head and shoulders and limbs, and then we used to sit during the heat of the day with our clothing soaked in water, and with cloths which we kept perpetually wet tied over our heads. I believe that in these ways water was absorbed through the skin. By night our clothing had dried on us, and the burning heat gave way to cold.

On September 27th we saw quite clearly during the morning a three-funnelled vessel about four miles away. We were terribly excited, and made great efforts to attract the attention of the vessel's look-out. Summoning our strength, we all leapt up, and several climbed on the thwarts to see better, and waved anything at hand. We longed desperately for the rockets and flares which should have been in the boat. One man produced a petrol lighter which, miraculously, still worked, and we tore open a kapok life-jacket and set fire to it in our bucket, which was held aloft, the black smoke rising satisfactorily. Someone blew our "boatswain's whistle", lips moved in silent prayer, and faces were eager, hopeful, and one felt that all must now be well. Surely she was turning? No – not yet. "Oh! but she *is* nearer," the forward look-out cried, and we all craned our necks, and agreed. Murmurs of "Rescue," "They've seen us!" "Oh boy! navy rum," were heard excitedly on all sides, and eyes filled with tears; but our hopes were not realised. She moved on and out of sight, and we sank exhausted, terribly disappointed.

That was a silent day. Towards evening, as the colonel was about to help serve the rations, he spoke to us all. "Listen, everyone," he said; "we have had a big disappointment to-day, but there's always to-morrow. The fact that we have seen a ship means that we are near a shipping route, and perhaps our luck will turn now. Don't lose hope because of what happened this morning." But when another day passed and we had sighted nothing further, many people did give up hope. I still felt confident that somehow we should be saved; I was often conscious of the power of the prayers of my family and friends. During the time on the lifeboat there was a universal feeling after God, and a sense of dependence upon Him, and one or other of us used to lead "family prayers" at night. For the last ten days or so this was my privilege, and everyone joined in readily. Unfortunately, we had no Bible, but we had one Gospel of St John belong to a R.A.F. sergeant, and a prayer book.

It must not be imagined that there was no trouble at all. In circumstances such as these, small things seem important, and disputes arise over trifling incidents, and quite alarming things were sometimes said; no one who has not sat cramped in a small boat, with the sun beating mercilessly day after day, and tormented by thirst, can ever imagine the strain and tension through which these men went. Many of them had spent months and years in places of danger or difficulty, away from homes and families, and had already been through unforgettable experiences in the desert, Greece, Crete or in the Narvik and Mediterranean campaigns.

Doctor Purslow developed a deep infection of his left hand and arm and of his right foot and leg. I used a razor blade to open his finger, and this discharged well, but nothing came from his foot. His glands began to swell, and red lines streaked his arm and leg. He felt ill, and we were anxious. His condition did not improve at all, and as he became weaker, he relinquished his self-appointed task of handing out the water ration, and lay day and night, only moving when necessary, and scarcely speaking at all. More septic places appeared, and it became evident that he was suffering from blood-poisoning.

One morning, about nineteen weary days after the ship was torpedoed, I heard voices, and after a while realised that one was his, although I could not hear exactly what was being said. I gathered that, realising that he was a potential source of infection to the rest of us, Doctor Purslow had come to a great decision.

I stumbled to where he was sitting, and tried to speak to him; but no words came. He was quite conscious, and in a voice stronger than I had heard from him for many days, he said: "As I cannot be of any further help, and if I am now a source of danger to you all, it is better that I should go." As he heaved himself painfully up the side of the boat, I found my voice, and said: "Greater love hath no man than this, that a man lay down his life for his friends." He said: "Goodbye", and with a long look, he took that final step backward. The sea closed over him.

We were fortunate in having a following wind almost every night, and the sea in our favour, and as we grew weaker, we just sat or lay around, with one man keeping watch at the tiller, endeavouring to keep our course. When there was no wind, we felt that our limp yellow sail was an enemy; but when, small as it was, it filled out with wind, it was a friend indeed, and we hoped that we made several knots an hour. There were times when a brisk wind lashed the sea into foam and we were tossed vigorously, and it took skill to keep our little boat from capsizing. At these times we shipped water

141

and were soaked with spray. There were other days and nights when no one had strength to steer, and when we felt as though we went round in circles.

Towards the end of our third week at sea, when I could no longer eat at all, because I was devoid of saliva, and depended for life on my water ration, we ran out of water. We had not sufficient for next day's ration. We prayed for rain. Next morning we had a torrential downpour, lasting nearly six hours. We caught it in every conceivable kind of vessel, as it ran from the sail, the gunwale, the thwarts and the mast; and how we drank. Never had any of us seen or tasted anything so wonderful. We were soaked to the skin and shivering – and we revelled in it. Our dried-up bodies took on new strength as we absorbed this life-giving water, and drank as we had dreamed of doing for so long. That day I managed to eat two biscuits again, and two or three Horlicks tablets.

We collected about six gallons of water in our tanks, which we kept. That which had run from the sail was dyed bright yellow, but who cared? The water was rationed as before, but that downpour had saved our lives; our hearts were full of praise and thanksgiving to our God, who had abundantly met our need. We thought of those who were no longer with us, for by this time the colonel, as well as the doctor and indeed all our officers, had died; so had many of the men. If only this rain could have come before, so many others might have been saved.

Before sunset the rain ceased, and a pale sun came out of an overcast sky. The boat was inches deep in water, and there was nothing dry anywhere, so we set to work to get things as dry as possible before night fell; but we had a rather chilly time that night, although no more rain came. Several of us had earache; even that could not depress us now. The Polish cadet-officer and one of our own men, however, developed large painful swellings of the parotid gland, making them look as though they had mumps. The Pole soon recovered, but the Englishman's condition did not improve.

The heat continued, and we had no more rain. There was by this time room for us all to lie down, and so, by means of articles of clothing suspended from the seats, we made a little shade when the sun was hottest, and lay full length in the bottom of the boat.

We noticed an occasional *grey* gull now, and new birds; cloud-banks formed on the horizon morning and night – and we wondered whether we were nearing land. Then one day we saw a leaf in the water, and our hopes rose.

On the morning of Thursday October 8th one of the British naval ratings sat looking ahead. I was sitting near, and saw his face brighten, and he spoke to an airman. They both looked eager, and I asked what the excitement was. He beckoned to me and said: "Sister, can you see anything over there?" pointing ahead of us. "Don't disturb the others, in case it is nothing, but I think that I can see a ship."

I looked, and was sure that I could see something; but what that something was, I could not tell. After a little while we took it to be a destroyer on the horizon. It appeared to come a little nearer, and then we saw other shapes, which we took to be ships of a convoy. We watched for half an hour, and then, as the "ships" did not move onwards, we knew that our prayers were answered and our dreams realised, and that ahead of us was land! Our eyes smarted, as we roused the others, sure now that they would not again be disappointed.

Now we began speculating upon how long it would take us to reach land. Some said two days, others said four days, and one optimist thought that we should make it there in a day. We wondered where we were, and whether the coast was inhabited. We felt sure that there would be coconuts, pineapples and citrus fruit, even if there were no habitations, and several of the men promised, in their new excitement and enthusiasm, to get me the first coconut. We had an extra water ration that day. It was not tasting very good, and we were thankful that land was in sight; but we decided not to be rash, in case we could not find a stream at once.

By the end of the day we could make out trees and hills easily. We could see that there was plenty of vegetation, but we could see no signs of habit-ation. We dropped our sea-anchor for the night and longed for morning. We could detect the heavy scent of tropical vegetation, and lightning flashed all night, although only distant thunder was heard; a little rain fell.

In the morning we were greeted by an off-shore breeze which blew us slowly away from land. We were disappointed as we saw our special hill and palm trees for which we had decided to steer growing farther and farther away. However, we waited with what patience we could for the wind to change, and towards afternoon an on-shore breeze sprang up again. We then made fair progress towards the land. We could still see no houses or buildings of any kind, and no smoke or any other sign of human habitation.

Late in the afternoon, when we were about five miles from the shore, we saw a 'plane. It came towards us, and we saw that it was a flying-boat, with a Union Jack painted on its body. We waved and waved, and the 'plane circled over us. We were seen. It circled again, coming lower, and again lower still. We lifted our board with "S.O.S. Water". Someone waved from the cockpit, and then the 'plane flew off landwards. We saw them flashing, and then back came the 'plane, heading for us once more, and circled round us again. As it flew very low over us, a life-jacket came hurtling through the air, and struck the water just beside us. It was a superb shot. Attached was a linen bag containing some food, but unfortunately it broke loose and was carried away. One of our airmen, finding strength which no one else could comprehend, climbed over the boat's side, fell into the water, and swam a few strokes. He rescued the life-jacket and only an apple, a pear and a banana.

On the life-jacket was written: "O.K. Help coming! You are sixty miles south of Monrovia." None of us had any idea where Monrovia was, but we knew what "help" was, and our hearts sang.

On reaching England I saw an extract from Captain A. G. Store's voyage report, as follows:-

"9.10.42. At 16.01 we passed over a small craft about five miles off the Liberian coast. Thinking this resembled a ship's lifeboat, I turned, descending, and inspection confirmed that this evidently was a boatload of survivors from a sunken vessel. Due to a south-westerly wind, the boat had slight way on her towards the shore. The occupants, some of whom appeared to be women, were evidently delighted to see us, and held up a board on which was chalked, 'S.O.S. Water'. We circled for some time, but could find no container in which water could be dropped, so filled a double pillow-slip with fresh fruit, and a can of orange juice, also enclosing a waterproof bag containing cigarettes, matches, and a note. To this package was tied one of the Kapok life-jackets. A bombing run was made over the boat, and the bundle dropped from the starboard drift-sight hatch. It fell near the boat, and was picked up immediately by a swimmer."

On arrival in Lagos, Captain Store again reported that he had sighted a lifeboat "whose occupants were obviously in a bad way", and suggested that it might be a good idea for flying-boats to carry special water containers, on purpose for such occasions. They could be fairly small, and fitted with a small parachute to prevent their breaking on striking the water.

I understand that work is in progress in England to produce such containers; they must prove invaluable when completed. I thank Captain Store for his gift, for his cheering message to us, and for his effort on behalf of survivors in general.

When the 'plane had gone we settled down again, with the knowledge that someone would search for us ere long; but we did not expect any more help that night. We could see waves breaking on the shore and spray being flung high in the air all along the coastline, except for one spot. We knew, therefore, that there must be rocks where the spray flew high, and sand and shingle where we saw no spray. Our boat was being blown directly towards

144

this gap in the rocks. A British naval rating was at the tiller, and kept the little boat headed towards this place of safety. We prayed that all might be well, and that this last difficulty might be overcome; for by now we were powerless to help ourselves.

Night fell, and we went drifting on. We could still see the great white walls of spray. We scarcely spoke, but each sat staring fixedly ahead, unmoving, breathing fast. At last, a little before 8 p.m., we were washed up on the sand by two great rolling waves. We had beached, and our boat was held firm, on the one spot possible; anywhere else for miles on either side we should have been dashed against rocks.

We scrambled with difficulty over the boat's side, and promptly collapsed into the shallow water. We crawled on hands and knees out of reach of the tide.

The ground seemed to be rocking, rocking even as our boat had rocked, and this sensation was to bother us for several days. The men brought with them our remaining biscuits and pemmican, and a few souvenirs from the boat, and then, wet to the skin, we huddled together on the sand and gave thanks to God for the miracle He had wrought for us — sixteen survivors out of our original sixty-eight. We had travelled over 700 miles in our open boat. The senior Englishman was a sergeant of the R.A.F; of the officers there was only the Polish cadet.

The heavy scent of tropical undergrowth was in the air. Crickets were singing as I had never heard them before; only a few yards before us was the African bush. We wondered what wild animals lurked there, and just what the night held for us.

After about twenty minutes we saw a light approaching along the shore. Who could be coming? Could they be cannibals, or wild untamed savages, we wondered? Two of our men staggered forward, and found themselves face to face with a crowd of negroes, the leader of whom flung his arms around them and said in English: "Thank God, you safe!" They had watched our boat for two days, and had come to search for us, rather expecting to find a wreck and no living people.

They came up to us and began talking to us in loud, excited voices in pidgin-English, and in their own language to each other. They searched the boat, taking with them everything that they could carry. I was grieved because Mary's wedding-ring had slipped from my thin finger, and it had fallen between the floor-boards. It was too dark to find it, and I had so much wanted to keep it safely for her husband.

After a short time these men helped us to our feet, supported some of us, and carried three men who were unable to stand. They led us to a native

African village some distance away in the bush. We staggered along on our bare, swollen feet for some time, and wondered whether we should ever reach a resting-place. Suddenly we heard voices, and came through the trees into a clearing. There, by the light of flares, we saw thatched native houses; all the inhabitants of the village seemed to be standing around one house, larger than the rest, where the "priest" lived. Some were laughing, some were crying (we *were* pitiful sights), and some just stood staring stolidly and silently.

We had landed in Liberia, in West Africa...

* * *

Doris Hawkins and her companions reached the coast on the evening of 9th October. The boat to which Squadron-Leader Wells had swum after leaving U-156 with Miss Hawkins had a different experience. It was damaged by the blast from the bombing attack on U-156 and was at sea for thirty-one days until meeting a convoy on 21st October (ironically, 'Trafalgar Day') and being rescued by H.M.S. *Wistan*. Six hours after the attack, Able Seaman Large had lost the battle to keep the boat afloat but late in the afternoon of 17th September, the Italian submarine *Cappellini* salvaged the capsized boat, pulling from the water men who had watched their shipmates disappear beneath the waves, too exhausted to help them. Commander Marco Revedin was frank with the British: unlike Hartenstein, he did not propose to keep them on board. His orders were to rendezvous with a Vichy French warship and hand survivors over to their safe custody. Unfortunately, the commander didn't know the whereabouts of the warship and was anxious to get underway as soon as possible. Tony Large was grateful to the stockily built, thinly-haired Italian captain; evidently not as confident or experienced as Hartenstein, nevertheless his timely arrival had saved the lives of fifty-one men.

After a hot meal, the men returned to the lifeboat, made seaworthy and provisioned with two cases of biscuits and thirteen bottles of water. Large waited three days in the area, hoping the Italian commander, as promised, had remembered to pass on to the French their position. On the 20th, the day Revedin made contact with the French, Able Seaman Large set sail for the African coast. Petty Officer Lester, the *Laconia's* Senior D.E.M.S. Rating, converted an oar into a mast, used shirts and coat linings for a mainsail, and a broken oar was turned into a rudder. All was entrusted to their most sensitive piece of equipment – a boy scouts' compass.

Flt Lt Blackburn, RAF, took charge of the stores, working out a rationing system. By 21st October only four of the original fifty-one men were left alive, all naval personnel – Tony Large, Harry Vines, Harry Dobson

146

and Bill Riley. A number of Royal Air Force officers died in the boat, including Flt Lts Blackburn, Johnston and Hayton, Squadron Leader Wells and Flying Officer Oakes. The next day the four naval men were landed at Freetown and Commander Williams reported to the British Admiralty:

'Acting Leading Seaman Vines followed the highest traditions and his survival is proof of his cheerfulness, tenacity and resource under most difficult conditions. It is submitted that the qualities displayed by him merit recognition.'

In his determination to live, Harry Vines spent long hours fishing, slitting the fish below the head on the underside and squeezing the blood into a tin. Relief was gained by sucking the eyes and gills for moisture. The fish was skinned and hung out to dry for tomorrow's food.

In her last chapter Doris Hawkins mentioned the strong impression which a few individuals in her boat made on the few survivors:

'We who survived will remember some whose patience, tact and courage were an inspiration. Amongst others, we think of the man with the broken arm, his hand and arm swollen and painful throughout that long journey to the African coast, whose only complaint was that he was unable to row and to help with the navigating. He was a most energetic member of the 'pumping squad', and always cheerful and uncomplaining.

'We remember with gratitude the Irishman, no longer young, who was ever optimistic and comforting, and full of ingenuity over the sail and jib. He would sit considering, then, if he thought of an improvement, he would energetically undo work which had had done perhaps only an hour before, and refix the sail and ropes, so that we might take fuller advantage of the wind prevailing at the time. He was always giving us as many as possible jobs to do.

'We think, too, of the assistant purser, who inspired the forward end of the boat, and was always among the first to move if there were a job to be done. We were impressed by the quiet, unassuming way in which the R.A.F. corporal helped us in those last trying days in the boat; it was he who lent his overcoat to cover Mary at night, when the blanket was taken to make the jib. Only those who have lived through such an experience can know how big the little things seem, and how one word or one action, or one person's optimism, can change the atmosphere for everyone.'

Many stories of heroism came to light; so also did complaints from military officers on the matter of discipline and unpreparedness of the *Laconia* to transport nearly three thousand persons, compelling early enquiries to be set up.

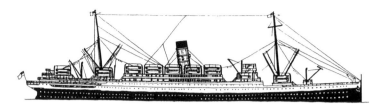

XIV

OFFICIAL ENQUIRIES

In October, the American Ambassador in Casablanca interviewed civilian and military survivors, sending the following report to the British Foreign Office:

'A sorry story with some useful suggestions:

(1) My personal experience of passage in a transport (without prisoners), an experience shared by many with whom I have yarned, is that the Merchant Navy is very reluctant to take any measures that savour of discipline.

(2) The question of who should take charge of boats crops up frequently but I think personality decides.

(3) The U-boat did not track the *Laconia* and it is extremely unlikely that they knew her route but they very likely knew of her passage from the Cape. It is evident from other sources that her smoke was seen at a great distance and one report states that she made a large arc towards the U-boat when she was rapidly going out of sight.'

According to Buckingham's report, the *Laconia* did have strong black-out rules, even extending to the lighting of cigarettes while on deck, but the funnel smoke does seem to have been ignored.

On 22nd December 1942, Lt Col Baldwin, officer in charge of the Italian prisoners, and Wing Commander Blackburn went to the War Office, London, to lodge a complaint regarding the inefficiency of the *Laconia's* crew and the poor conditions of the lifeboats. Squadron Leader Vincent Mears supported their representations by stating that the *Laconia's* rafts were tied together with rope, fastened to the bulkheads, and not one member of the crew was assigned the responsibility to release them in time of emergency. He also criticised the mode of boat drills.

Later an official statement concurred:

'O.C. Troops is very good at mustering, fairly good at inspecting but completely neglects any form of instructed seamanship in its broadest sense.'

SUMMONS

TO ATTEND A PRELIMINARY INQUIRY

BY AN OFFICER OF CUSTOMS, OR COAST GUARD, OR BY A PERSON APPOINTED FOR
THE PURPOSE UNDER SECTION 465 OF THE MERCHANT SHIPPING ACT, 1894.

ISSUED BY THE
BOARD OF TRADE.

To

Christian Name, Surname, and Occupation of Person referred to in the Summons.		Name and Port of Registry of Ship in respect of which inquiry is to be instituted.	
Name.	Occupation or rating on board Ship.	Name.	Port of Registry.
P. Wallace.	3rd Class Chief Steward	Laconia	Liverpool

57 & 58 Vict., c. 60, ss. 465 & 729.
Take Notice, That I hereby, by virtue of the provisions of the Merchant Shipping Act, 1894, require you to attend personally before me at *Receiving Wreck Office Ground Floor Cunard Building Liverpool* on *Wednes* day, the *23rd* instant, at *11.10* of the clock in the *Fore* noon, for the purpose of being examined on Oath relative to the *Casualty to the S.S. Laconia* of the said Ship : [And I also require you then and there to bring with you and produce the Official Log Book of the Ship, and all other Documents containing any information on the subject of the Casualty.]

The words within the brackets only apply in the case of a Master or other person having the charge of the Log Book, and are to be erased in all other cases.

Given under my hand at *Liverpool.*
this *19th* day of *December* 1942.

Deputy RECEIVER OF WRECK

Inspecting Officer of the Coastguard.*
Chief Officer of Customs and Excise.*
Person appointed by the Board of Trade.*

* Obliterate the words which do not apply.

** NOTE.—ANY PERSON NEGLECTING OR REFUSING TO ATTEND AS REQUIRED BY THIS SUMMONS WILL INCUR A PENALTY NOT EXCEEDING TEN POUNDS. VIDE SECTION 729 OF THE MERCHANT SHIPPING ACT, 1894.—ALL PROPER AND REASONABLE EXPENSES IN RESPECT OF A WITNESS'S ATTENDANCE WILL BE PAID.

NOTE.—*This form is to be used by Inspecting Officers of the Coast Guard, Chief Officers of Customs and Excise, and persons appointed by the Board of Trade when Witnesses refuse to attend at a preliminary Inquiry under Section 465 of the Merchant Shipping Act, 1894.*

(3299/368) Wt14122/ 38/22985 250 6/38 FHD **Gp683**

63. Summons to attend the wreck enquiry.

Next day in Liverpool, the Board of Trade held a Preliminary Inquiry into the loss of the *Laconia*. On 15th February 1943 a statement was published:

'Suggestions lifeboats leaked and not provisioned properly mainly hearsay. Depositions taken by the Receiver of Wrecks from six members of the crew including three senior officers, each of whom pays tribute to the behaviour of the crew. Taking all the circumstances into consideration and account, it is not considered any good purpose will be served by a mere formal inquiry, nor does the further evidence indicate that disciplinary action would be justified as regards the Merchant Navy crew. The experience gained will be used to the best advantage for the future.

R. Metcalfe D of St.'

That act of officialdom closed the book on the *Laconia* epic, not daring to draw attention to the grave matter of the Italian prisoners of war. Of the 1,111 persons who survived from the *Laconia*, approximately four hundred and fifty were Italians. Hartenstein's torpedoes, the sea and the American bomber accounted for the majority of their deaths, but many met death under a hail of bullets when they tried to reach the upper decks after escaping from their prison hatch; a matter not spoken about, save in hushed tones by certain crew members. No-one even seems to have raised the question as to how, thirty years after the scandalous tragedy of the *Titanic*, a ship could have sailed the Atlantic with an insufficient number of lifeboats to accommodate everyone on board.

Doris Hawkins closed her *Atlantic Torpedo* with some observations of her own:

'As I look back over these experiences, although I am no expert in matters connected with the sea I cannot but feel that a few simple readjustments in the lifeboat equipment might have made our story very different.

'Obviously the most vital need is for water. With an adequate supply, the regulation food is no doubt fairly easy to manage. The small apparatus for purifying sea water which has recently been devised should be made a compulsory part of the equipment. In my opinion concentrated fruit juice and tinned milk would, in any case, be useful additions.

'Fishing-nets and lines would take up only a small space; they would have brought us an adequate supply of fresh fish, which is full of nourishment, and very good even eaten raw, in such circumstances.

'Had the essential equipment, especially such things as the rockets and flares, medical supplies and water, been *secured* in such a way that loss would be impossible in the event of the lifeboats capsizing, I feel that many more of our number would have reached safety. There may be good explanations for all this; but I do not know them.

'It is impossible to imagine why I should have been chosen to survive when so many did not. I have been reluctant to write the story of our experiences, but in answer to many requests I have done so; and if it strengthens someone's faith, if it is an inspiration to any, if it brings home to others, hitherto untouched, all that 'those who go down to the sea in ships' face for our sakes, hour by hour, day by day, year in and year out – it will not have been written in vain.'

Some of her suggestions are now standard. The Marine Safety Agency at Southampton report that modern lifeboats are self-righting in the unlikely event of their capsizing, all equipment is secured in lockers, and fishing rods are compulsory. Fishing nets and water purifying equipment remain an option.

The final chapter of the *Laconia* affair, however, was yet to be written.

64. Cunard publicity postcard of the *Laconia*.

65. Admiral Karl Dönitz.

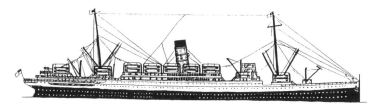

XV

THE LACONIA ORDER AND ITS AUTHOR

Imperceptibly, new technological advances dictated revision of ethical codes governing warfare at sea and Admiral Dönitz believed it was time to update his orders to U-boat commanders, removing from them the authority hitherto exercised in granting traditional assistance to the shipwrecked, once their judgement of the situation allowed it was safe to proceed. He resolved never again to risk the loss of a U-boat in circumstances similar to the *Laconia* initiative.

The ubiquitousness of Allied aircraft, which he suspected was due to Allied progress in radar detection, ushered in new signs of the times: no longer was it possible to determine the 'terminus a quo' or 'terminus ad quem' when an action might be considered over. In this discernment he was right, and was intelligently ahead of obtuse boffins at German Naval High Command who argued that Allied aircraft could only detect a submarine on the surface at close range and in calm waters. Unknown to them, British aircraft were equipped with a compact radar set effectively accurate in calm or bad weather over a greater distance than the Germans appreciated.

Despite his continual warnings to commanders, U-boat losses for the first half of September 1942, due to air-attacks, were unusually high. Evidence confirmed that far too many commanders were conditioned by a false sense of security, believing their boats were safe as there were no aircraft in sight, only to realise when an aircraft appeared that they were already at a disadvantage. The average time needed to clear the bridge, close the hatch and submerge was one minute; during this time an aircraft could cover four miles. Depth was also required to escape the lethal or damaging effect of depth charges.

In practice only boats maintaining high surface speeds were the ones which took less time to submerge. To engage in rescue work meant stopping the boat altogether, bringing extra crew on deck, negating any hope of diving if attacked.

Clearly, the bombing attacks on U-156 and U-506 angered Dönitz. Insofar as he was concerned, the enemy was prepared to sacrifice women and children in a ruthless endeavour to gain military advantage. His mind was fixed! No longer could he trust past guidelines in determining the precise moment an action could be considered over. Now a great gulf stood between them as far as the vaguely-accepted previous guidelines were concerned.

Known as 'The Laconia Order', the new order instructed:
(1) No attempt of any kind must be made to rescue members of ships sunk and this includes picking up persons in the water, putting them in lifeboats, righting capsized lifeboats and handing over food and water. Rescue runs counter to the most primitive demands of warfare for the destruction of enemy ships and crews.
(2) Orders to bring in captains and chief engineers of enemy ships remain in force.
(3) Shipwrecked people will only be rescued if their information is important for the submarine.
(4) Be hard. Remember the enemy has no regard for women and children when he bombs German cities.

Dönitz withheld sending the new 'order' to all U-boat commanders until the *Laconia* rescue mission was completed. Regrettably, for Dönitz 'The Laconia Order' constituted the most controversial charge brought against him at the Nuremberg War Crimes Trial. The wording 'destruction of enemy ships and crews' was viewed as an inhumane declaration, a licence to murder, and the prosecution counsel made use of all their expertise to prove Dönitz guilty. In the context of the *Laconia* incident, it is clear that the Admiral did not mean the annihilation of the shipwrecked, an interpretation understood by his commanders, for out of the thousands of actions involving U-boats there was only one instance when a commander murdered the shipwrecked. This was the notorious incident concerning the Greek ship *Peleus*, in March 1943. The commander of the U-boat concerned, U-852, was Heinz Eck. He was summarily tried by a British military court in Hamburg in October 1945, and executed, but he bore witness in his testimony to the court that 'The Laconia Order' did not influence his behaviour.

The Nuremberg Trial was designed to expose the evils of the Nazi regime and the men who committed its worst crimes. Dönitz was arraigned before the court as one of the men of the Nazi hierarchy whom the Allied Powers were determined to reveal had fought Hitler's war in a manner leading to criminal acts.

In Karl Dönitz, Hitler had found a man of vision. Born at Grunau, Berlin on 16th September 1891, he entered the German Navy in 1910, going to sea in the cruiser *Breslau*. At the outbreak of World War One, the *Breslau* was trapped in the Dardanelles by the Royal Navy and Dönitz returned to Germany for training at the submarine school.

In 1917 he was given command of the coastal U-boat U-68 and saw action in the Mediterranean. On 4th October 1918, while attacking a British convoy, his U-boat came under heavy shelling from a destroyer, sustaining severe damage, and had to be abandoned. Dönitz and his crew were later rescued by the Royal Navy. Five weeks later the war ended.

Returning to Germany, he continued his naval career commanding a torpedo boat flotilla. Recognition of his skills gained him command of the cruiser *Emden* and in 1935 he was promoted to commander of U-boats.

The terms of the Treaty of Versailles prevented Germany from building submarines, but the 1935 Anglo-German Navy Agreement mitigated the Versailles ruling, permitting German U-boat construction on a restricted basis. As previously discussed, the British outlook gave little credence to the value of submarines in any future war.

In the summer of 1935, Grand Admiral Raeder, Commander-in-Chief of the German Navy, handed Dönitz the commission of commanding the new U-boat arm of the transformed German Navy. It was a dream come true! Like no-one else, he retained the experience of March to May 1917, the period of the peak of German U-boat success, resulting eventually in the destruction of over eight hundred Allied ships.

Carefully, he studied the Anglo-German Naval Agreement, noting the restrictive imposition applied to tonnage, but not to the number of U-boats built. He opted for the construction of smaller boats, and by the end of 1935 ten Type VII design five hundred ton U-boats complemented his fleet of twenty-four. The performance of the new boat in tests excited him. Capable of a surface speed of sixteen knots, it behaved well when submerged. Difficult to detect on the surface, easy to manoeuvre, it was able to dive more quickly than a heavier boat in an emergency. Dönitz the visionary then turned into Dönitz the missionary, determined to convert the German Naval High Command from the darkness of World War One strategy, by combining the idea of U-boats as lone bandits with the concept of U-boat packs wreaking havoc on convoys of ships, a system of sailing more favoured by the British in the latter part of the war. In this, Dönitz was ahead of his times; his superiors viewed the rebirth of the German Navy differently. In line with British thinking, they invested energies and materials in building large battleships and cruisers. Might, to them, spelt power. U-boats, they contended, should be much larger, more heavily armed on deck, geared to inflicting damage on the enemy in a surface engagement.

Ominous signs in the late 1930s warned Dönitz that war with the old enemy, Britain, was nearer than the ageing admirals comfortably seated at Naval High Command appreciated. He stepped up his pressure to mass produce three hundred small U-boats, setting out his plan to cripple the British Isles. At all times, one hundred boats would be in action at sea against the convoys, one hundred sailing from or to combat zones with a further one hundred in German bases undergoing servicing. In his mind was the simple scheme of controlling the vital sea lanes the British depended on for imported materials, which in time of war would include fuel, ore, weapons and food. A large force of U-boats, he predicted, sinking cargo vessels bound for her island ports, could isolate the nation in a very short space of time, forcing the alternatives of submission or starvation. Fortunately for the British, his campaign failed to move men already rigid in their planning for the future shape of the German Navy and use of the submarine.

On 3rd September 1939, Britain went to war with the German nation, which had a large battle fleet, a well equipped mechanised army, a large air force – but only fifty-seven U-boats. With fewer boats, Dönitz specialised in quality training of recruits, billeting the submarine training divisions in large merchant ships. When training was completed, the crews, all volunteers, joined boats at Kiel and Hamburg, sailing across the North Sea to join the Battle of the Atlantic. Later, following the capitulation of France, crews travelled by train across Europe to sail in boats berthed in the secure pens dotted along the Bay of Biscay. Often, for the purpose of morale, Dönitz flew to the Biscay coast bases, fostering a close contact with the men.

The first eighteen months of the war was referred to as 'the happy time', a description coined by the U-boat commanders themselves. Allied shipping suffered huge losses and German U-boat 'aces' such as Günther Prien, who sank the battleship H.M.S. *Royal Oak* and claimed nearly 200,000 tons of merchant shipping, and Otto Kretschmer and Joachim Schepke became household names, featured on a par with film stars in German propaganda cinema newsreels.

As the war advanced into 1941 and 1942, Dönitz estimated that British shipping losses far exceeded their replacement rate. In this he was perfectly accurate. The entrance of the United States of America into the war in late 1941 prevented the U-boats, on the verge of a complete breakthrough, from gaining mastery in the war at sea. The Americans revolutionised the ailing Allied shipbuilding programme, turning out 'Liberty' boats in as little as twenty-one days. Dönitz strongly challenged Hitler for top priority attention to U-boat construction, but his requirements never materialised until the war at sea turned to their disadvantage.

In January 1943, Dönitz was chosen by Hitler to replace Grand Admiral Raeder as Commander-in-Chief of the German Navy. Hitler and Raeder had reached stalemate over the future of capital ships. Hitler considered them obsolescent and wanted to scrap them but Raeder insisted they were still necessary. Hitler admired Dönitz who, although not a member of the Nazi Party, had built up the U-boat arm into a fighting machine outstripping the army and air force for consistency. He saw in the U-boat Chief a pure warrior free from the political ambition tarnishing so many military subordinates. To his surprise, Dönitz concurred with Raeder in the matter of capital ships and to Raeder's surprise, Hitler accepted his new Navy Chief's opinion, never to raise the question again. On 30th January, Dönitz was named Grand Admiral and appointed Commander-in-Chief of the Navy, while Raeder became Admiral Inspector of the Navy.

Immediately, Dönitz made it clear that he wanted U-boat production doubled; from twenty to forty boats a month. He set the designers to work on a new class of submarine, able to attain a higher underwater speed and a greater underwater range by increasing the power of the electric motors. Copying the American system of building Liberty boats, the submarines were to be built in sections at inland factories, breaking the long tradition of shipyard construction. Trains would then deliver the sections to coastal ports for assembly. The first of the new type U-boats were delivered to the navy for testing in 1944. Between January and March 1945, eighty-three U-boats were assembled; however, Allied bombing destroyed forty-four of them in the dockyards. If Dönitz had been appointed Navy Chief a year earlier, there is no doubt the new U-boats would have prolonged the war.

Hitler's lack of experience in dealing with naval matters spared Dönitz the censure he poured out on the air force and particularly the army.

During World War Two, German U-boats accounted for the destruction of one hundred and forty-eight Allied naval vessels and two thousand, seven hundred and fifty-nine merchantmen. Of eleven hundred U-boats put to sea, seven hundred and fifty-three were put out of action, sending twenty-seven thousand men, including Dönitz's sons, to their deaths, and another five thousand into captivity in Allied prisoner-of-war camps. Over thirty thousand men in the British Merchant Navy lost their lives in encounters with U-boats, not counting the many thousands of merchant seamen from other nations and a large number of Royal Navy officers and men.

In the final days of the war, Dönitz was the only military chief Hitler respected. Before he committed suicide, he nominated the Grand Admiral to succeed him, as he was the only leader he believed the army, air force and navy would adhere to. The elevation of Dönitz began with a radio message dated 8.30 a.m. 30th April 1945:

'Grand Admiral Dönitz. In place of the former Reichsmarschall Goering the Fuhrer has designated you as his successor. Written authorisation on the way. Immediately take all measures required by the present situation. Bormann.'

A second radio message arrived on 1st May while Dönitz was at Plön in Schleswig-Holstein:

'Grand Admiral Dönitz (Top Secret! Only via officer). Fuhrer deceased yesterday at 3.30 p.m. Testament of April 29 appoints you Reich President, Minister Goebbels Chancellor, Reichsleiter Bormann Party Minister, Minister Seyss-Inquart Foreign Minister. On the Fuhrer's instructions the testament sent out of Berlin to you and to Field Marshal Schöorner, to assure its preservation for the people. Reichsleiter Bormann will try to get to you today to orient you on the situation. The form and time of announcement to the troops and public are left to you. Confirm receipt. Goebbels, Bormann.'

Albert Speer, Reichminister for Armaments and War Production, was present when the second radio message arrived. Dönitz was angry that Hitler had curtailed his powers by appointing his cabinet for the new President of the Reich and ordered the radio man to be sworn to silence and the message kept confidential. He refused to work with Goebbels and Bormann, agreeing with Speer that they should be arrested.

For twenty days he ruled the remnants of the Third Reich from Flensburg, staving off surrender for as long as possible, yet under no illusions as to the final outcome. The Allies later accused Dönitz of unnecessarily prolonging the war in that he ordered a continuation of the fight against the Soviet Union, insensible to his true motive. Between 23rd January and 8th May 1945, he masterminded the evacuation to the west of over two million Germans from the Eastern Provinces and the advancing Russian army. Millions of refugees, wounded German soldiers and important persons streamed into the German controlled Baltic ports. It was impossible for all of these people to escape by road and rail, outlets constantly attacked from the air and cut off by Russian land forces, so

Dönitz, inspired by the British evacuation of Dunkirk, schemed the greatest evacuation by sea the world would witness.

The armada he put together integrated naval ships with trawlers, liners with cargo boats, sailing in convoys through the tempestuous waters of the Baltic Sea. Poor visibility shielded the Dönitz plan from air attack but attracted Russian submarines to an area which, at that time, had yielded poor returns in tonnage sunk. One refugee ship, the *Wilhelm Gustloff*, a former cruise liner of 25,000 tons, sailed from Gydnia, Danzig where she had been laid up for four years, used to house U-boat men enrolled in the nearby submarine training establishment. Carrying eight thousand men, women and children, she was torpedoed and sunk on 30th January by the Russian submarine S13, with the loss of seven thousand lives, four times more than the number lost on the *Laconia*. Commander Alexander Marinesko made no attempt to rescue survivors and was later decorated for his accomplishment.

Time was running out for Dönitz and on 8th May, he was obliged to accept surrender terms. For the next two weeks he continued to conduct daily Cabinet Meetings at Flensburg, until he was arrested by the Allied Control Commission on 22nd May and taken to Mondorf in Luxembourg.

66. Dönitz

67. Captain Otto Kranzbuehler, defence counsel to Admiral Dönitz at Nuremberg.

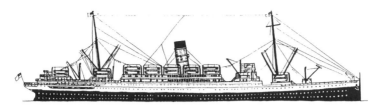

XVI

THE LACONIA ORDER
AND THE NUREMBERG TRIALS

The impetus to establish an international tribunal to try major war criminals, was not the result of a new policy. All wars ended with specific charges being brought against individuals who exceeded accepted rights, spreading misery through practices not reasonably related to the conduct of war. It was customary for the indicted to appear before the court of the country for war crimes committed against that country, sometimes standing trial before several courts, if their military forces touched more than one nation.

At the dawn of the twentieth century, attention was directed to a codification of the laws of war, for embodiment as a 'sine qua non' in international agreements. The Hague Convention of 1907 set forth requirements for starting a war, affirming the need to issue 'a reasoned declaration of war', or 'an ultimatum with conditional declaration of war'. The Geneva Prisoners of War and Red Cross Conventions of 1929 laid down rules for the treatment of prisoners and care for the sick and wounded. But none of these treaties specified means of enforcing laws governing the conduct of war or consequential retribution for their violation. Nevertheless, many nations reshaped their military law, absorbing the new requirements. Following World War One, the Allied Powers listed forty-five persons whom they considered guilty of violating international law. They permitted the German Government to conduct their trial before the Supreme Court of Leipzig; only six were convicted, a farce which dented the Allied Powers' evaluation of justice. Britain, France, Russia and the United States of America agreed that the crimes of the Nazi leaders could not be identified with one particular country. In total, twenty-three nations were at war with Germany at the price of an estimated thirty million deaths. For the accused to appear before the courts of all the belligerent nations, with their varying kinds of justice, time scale and procedure, was impracticable.

THE SINKING OF THE LACONIA

The London Agreement, signed by the four Allied Powers on 8th August 1945, established the charter for the International Military Tribunal and the unprecedented decision of a group of victors to try war criminals before the same court. The four major powers named twenty-four Nazis and six organisations for indictment.

The city of Nuremberg, the hub of Nazism, situated one hundred miles north of Munich, was selected to stage the public examination of the perpetrators of the Nazi regime. The city of Albrecht Dürer, the fifteenth century painter, had fortifications dating back to the Middle Ages. At one time the wealthiest and most important of the free imperial cities of the old Holy Roman Empire, it was singularly rich in medieval architecture. Its picturesque streets, quaint gables and carved balconies had teemed with travellers; tourist attractions included the Gothic Church of St Sebaldus, rich in sculptures and paintings, the Rathaus built in 1616 in the Italian Renaissance style, containing a great hall adorned with frescoes by Dürer, and Dürer's house itself.

When the trial opened, Nuremberg was a scarred city, the rubble and stench concealing thirty thousand dead. Beneath her ancient spires, there was barely a building undamaged; yet it was not by design the Allies chose Nuremberg, famous for the stadium created by Hitler to hold his rallies, accompanied by massive pageantry and ceremony, for it was the only city with an undamaged court and prison large enough to cater for the hundreds of people who would be involved in the trial.

The Palace of Justice, on the western edge of the city, had escaped serious damage; its court room could hold six hundred persons. There were also hundreds of offices for the lawyers and staff of the prosecuting nations.

There were no flags or splendour, only evidence of the fierce battle for the city between the German First Army and the Americans. The acrid smell of burning and destruction hung cheerlessly in the air.

Outside the Palace of Justice, the area came under the protection of the American army. Five Sherman tanks guarded the court-room, machine guns in placements, ever alert, wary of the persistent rumours of rescue bids on behalf of the prisoners, Nazi uprisings engineered by the S.S.

Now the city from which Hitler declared the Third Reich would last for one thousand years was the centre of world media attention, as Dönitz and his associates were accommodated under one roof for the trial of the century.

In harmony with Article Sixteen of the Charter of the International Military Tribunal, Dönitz was delivered a copy of the Indictment, a document of twenty-four thousand words, written in German and detailing the full charges against him. He was allowed, together with the other defendants, the right to answer the charges and choose a lawyer to conduct his defence, freedom to present evidence in his defence and cross examine witnesses summoned by the prosecution. The trial was destined to become a major topic of interest in the post-war world.

A month before the trial, scheduled to commence on 20th November 1945, Major Airey Neave, the first man to escape from the infamous Colditz Castle prisoner-of-war establishment, and later tragically murdered by the I.N.L.A., served Dönitz his copy of the 'indictment' setting out the charges he would have to answer. Signed in Berlin, it detailed the International Military Tribunal's outline of the charges under the four main counts of the 'indictment'.

(1) CONSPIRACY (including breaking treaties and involving the crimes of 2, 3 and 4).

(2) CRIMES AGAINST PEACE (starting a war).

(3) WAR CRIMES (wanton destruction, ill-treatment of prisoners of war, etc.)

(4) CRIMES AGAINST HUMANITY (extermination, persecution).

Dönitz was charged on the first three counts, much to the displeasure of the British Admiralty who opposed his inclusion among the arraigned from the outset, expressing reservations about the wisdom of a case against the German navy. The Hague Conventions of 1907 had not dealt with the use of submarines in wartime; at that time they were an unknown quantity, not seen as the menace they were to become. The London Protocol of 1936 was soon out of vogue in the early days of World War Two. The Protocol was not far seeing enough, although its authors could not be blamed; technological advances in radar and communications subjected submarines to dangers not envisaged, entitling the submarine to adopt self-preservation as its first priority.

In October 1945, the Admiralty's legal department submitted a report stating that the case against the German navy was weak, riddled with difficulties due to its vagueness, and should be withdrawn. They received an unfavourable reply from the Foreign Office: 'Typical Admiralty whitewashing of the German Navy.'

The case against Dönitz on Counts One and Two was also considered weak. The Admiralty saw him as a non-Nazi Party officer who on merit had come up through the ranks and served his country in command of the U-boat arm. Until 1943, when he was promoted to Commander-in-Chief of the German Navy, he had not been personally involved in sitting around a war table with Hitler, planning strategy. It did not appear there was a firm foundation to charge Dönitz, and the weight of the prosecution's case against him had to be placed on Count Three and prove, without doubt, that the mode of Germany's war at sea had been criminal. The Americans, however, disagreed, insisting Dönitz be incarcerated in Nuremberg Prison and be tried as a war criminal. He was too big a fish to let go, especially as Hitler named him as his successor.

Otto Kranzbuehler, a young naval officer from the German Judge Advocate's office, was chosen by Dönitz to represent him.

Among the many inconsistencies and inequities, which illustrate the judicial absurdity of sentencing Dönitz to ten years imprisonment, was the unforeseen embarrassment to the court in allowing him to use the 'tu quoque' (thou also) argument as defence. This was not a case of two wrongs making a right but was done to clarify the vague laws governing conduct of warfare at sea. Kranzbuehler, Dönitz's brilliant advocate, asked the Tribunal's permission to send a questionnaire to Fleet Admiral Chester Nimitz, Commander-in-Chief of the U.S. Pacific Fleet. They gave it. He followed up with a request to approach the British Admiralty, convincing them of his right to examine captured German documents and British naval papers. Again he was successful.

Against the charge of having waged unrestricted submarine warfare, the Tribunal had little course but to admit an order of the British Admiralty, dated 8th May 1940, authorising British warships to sink on sight all vessels in the Skagerrak. Further embarrassment followed: a deposition from Admiral Nimitz stated that on 7th December 1941, the Chief of Naval Operations in Washington directed him to: 'Execute unrestricted air and submarine warfare against Japan.' The import of the 'order' made it general practice not to attempt rescue of survivors of submarine attacks, unless such rescues could be made without risk.

Cleverly, Kranzbuehler showed to the Court that the Germans had used exactly the same tactics against enemy shipping as the Allies.

The prosecution counsel made use of all their expertise to authenticate the supposition that the Laconia Order was an inhumane declaration, a licence to murder. At first they tried to link the order with a discussion between Hitler and Japanese Ambassador Oshima, held in January 1942, in which Hitler drew attention to the energetic shipbuilding operation of the Americans, arguing that no matter how many ships were launched, they could not go to sea without trained merchant seamen. Hitler advocated thinning down their numbers with instructions to U-boats to surface after torpedoing and shoot up the lifeboats, a proposition Hitler suggested to

164

Dönitz, who rejected the idea, supported by his Commander-in-Chief, Grand Admiral Raeder. Both admirals specified the improvement of torpedoes as the only permissible way to increase enemy losses. German scientists explored how to effect the accuracy of torpedoes but not all experiments were successful. The 'Zaunkönig', designed to 'home in' on a ship's propellers, met with an initial disaster when fired from boats in a wolf pack, sinking two of their own boats.

As a junior member of the prosecution, Colonel Phillimore was either under orders to 'play down' the role of Dönitz in bringing to safety nearly seven hundred British civilians and servicemen, or he was bent on gaining a vengeance sentence. Whatever the motive, one thing is sure – he deliberately misled the Court:

'The next document I do not propose to read. It is an extract from B d U War Diary of 16th September 1942. It records an attack on a U-boat which was rescuing survivors, chiefly the Italian survivors of the Allied Liner *Laconia*.'

Phillimore's claim that Commander Hartenstein of U-156 was rescuing 'chiefly the Italian survivors' must classify his conduct as of the most questionable propriety.

Had the prosecution read the War Diary entry of 16th September, it might have distracted from the main goal of labelling Dönitz the villain of the Laconia Order. Phillimore proceeded to read to the Court the wording of the order sent to all commanding officers of U-boats.

'Now, my lord, that is, of course, a very carefully worded order. Its intentions are made very clear by the next document on the same page, which is an extract from the defendant's war diary, personally signed by the defendant Dönitz. It is the war diary entry for 17th September 1942:

"The attention of all commanding officers is again drawn – and I would draw the Tribunal's attention to the word 'again' – to the fact that all efforts to rescue members of the crews of ships which have been sunk, contradict the most primitive demands for the conduct of warfare for annihilating enemy ships and their crews."

'The last two documents on that page consist of a telegram from the commander of the U-boat, Schacht, to the defendant's headquarters, and the reply. Schacht had been taking part in the rescue of survivors from the *Laconia*. The telegram from Schacht, dated 17th September 1942, reads:

"163 Italians handed over to *Annamite*. Navigating Officer of *Laconia* and another English officer on board." And then it goes on setting out the position of English and Polish survivors in boats.

'The reply sent on 20th: "Action as in wireless telegram of 17th of September was wrong. Boat was detailed to rescue Italian allies and not for the rescue of English and Poles." It is a small point, but of course "detailed" means before the bombing incident had ever occurred.

'To sum up these documents, it would appear from the war diary entry of 17th September that orders on the lines discussed between Hitler and Oshima were, in fact, issued, but we have not captured them. It may be they were issued orally and that the defendant awaited a suitable opportunity before confirming them. The incident of the bombing of the U-boats detailed to rescue the one hundred and sixty three survivors from the *Laconia* afforded the opportunity, and the order to all commanders was issued. Its intent is very clear when you consider it in the light of the war diary entry. The wording is, of course, extremely careful, but to any officer of experience its intention was obvious and he would know that deliberate action to annihilate survivors would be approved under that order.

'You will be told that this order, although perhaps unfortunately phrased, was merely intended to stop a commander from jeopardising his ship by attempting a rescue, which had become increasingly dangerous as a result of the extended coverage of the ocean by Allied aircraft; and that the notorious action of the U-boat commander Eck in sinking the Greek steamer *Peleus*, and then machine-gunning the crew on their rafts in the water, was an exception; and that, although it may be true that a copy of the order was on board, this action was taken solely, as he himself swore, on his own initiative.

'I would make the point to the Tribunal that if the intention of the order was to stop the rescue attempts in the interests of the preservation of the U-boat, first of all it would have been done by calling attention to Standing Order 154. Second, this very fact would have been prominently stated in the order. Drastic orders of this nature are not drafted by experienced staff officers without the greatest care and an eye to their possible capture by the enemy.'

The Prosecution's case for corroborated evidence rested on two witnesses, the only two brought forward in the trial of Dönitz, neither reliable, and both U-boat officers. The first, Lt Heisig, was presented to strengthen their case that Dönitz induced a class he attended as a young midshipman, in 1942, to murder the shipwrecked. He was the only witness to maintain that Dönitz had categorically asserted this.

PHILLIMORE: Peter Josef Heisig, are you an Oberleutnant zur See in Germany?
HEISIG: I am Oberleutnant zur See in the German Navy.

PHILLIMORE: And you were captured on 27th December 1944, and now held as a prisoner of war?

HEISIG: Yes.

PHILLIMORE: In the autumn of 1942 what rank did you hold?

HEISIG: I was senior midshipman at the 2nd U-Boat Training Division.

PHILLIMORE: Were you attending a course there?

HEISIG: I took part in the training course for U-boat officers of the watch.

PHILLIMORE: Do you remember the last day of the course?

HEISIG: On the last day of the course, Grand Admiral Dönitz, who was then Commander-in-Chief of the U-boats, reviewed the 2nd U-Boat Training Division.

PHILLIMORE: And what happened at the end of this tour?

HEISIG: At the end of his visit – not at the end, but rather during his visit – Grand Admiral Dönitz made a speech before the officers of the 2nd U-Boat Training Division.

PHILLIMORE: Can you fix the date of this visit?

HEISIG: I remember the approximate date: it must have been at the end of September or the beginning of October 1942.

PHILLIMORE: Now will you give the Tribunal, speaking slowly, an account of what Admiral Dönitz said in his speech.

HEISIG: Grand Admiral Dönitz said in his speech that the success of the U-boats had declined. The strength of the enemy air control was responsible for that decline. New anti-aircraft guns had been developed which in future would make it possible for the U-boats to fight off enemy aircraft. Hitler had personally given him the assurance that U-boats would be equipped with these anti-aircraft guns before all other branches of the armed forces. It would be expected, therefore, that the successes of former times would be reached again within a few months. The Allies were having considerable difficulties in manning their ships. Some of their seamen were even trying to shirk a crossing of the Atlantic, so that the Allied authorities were compelled, if it became necessary, to retain the men aboard by force of law. Admiral Dönitz concluded that the question of personnel was a very grave matter for the Allies. The losses in men affected the Allies especially seriously because they had few reserves and also because ....

PHILLIMORE: I don't want to interrupt you, but did he say anything about rescues at all? Will you come to the crucial part of the speech, at the end, and deal with that? What did the Grand Admiral go on to say?

HEISIG: He continued, saying approximately that under the circumstances he could not understand how German U-boats could still rescue the crews of the merchant ships they had sunk, thereby endangering their own ships. By doing that they were working for the enemy, since these rescued crews would sail again on new ships.

The stage had now been reached in which total war had to be waged at sea. The crews of ships, like the ships themselves, were a target for the U-boats; thus it would be impossible for the Allies to man their newly built ships, and moreover it could then be expected that in America and the other Allied countries a strike would break out, for already some of the seamen did not want to go back to sea.

These results could be expected if our tactics would render the war at sea more vigorous. If any of us consider this war or these tactics harsh, we should also remember that our wives and our families at home are being bombed.

That, in its main points, was the speech of Grand Admiral Dönitz. The prosecution then turned the witness over for cross-examination to the counsel for the defendant Dönitz:

KRANZBUEHLER: Oberleutnant Heisig, did you yourself take part in an action against the enemy?

HEISIG: Yes.

KRANZBUEHLER: On which boat were you, and who was your commander?

HEISIG: I was on U-877 under Kapitanleutnant Finkeisen.

KRANZBUEHLER: Were you successful in action against enemy ships?

HEISIG: The boat was sunk on its way to the area of operations.

KRANZBUEHLER: How was the boat sunk?

HEISIG: By depth charges. Two Canadian frigates sighted the U-boat and destroyed it through depth charges.

KRANZBUEHLER: Since you have knowledge of the circumstances, do you maintain that the speech of Grand Admiral Dönitz mentioned in any way that fire should be opened on shipwrecked sailors?

HEISIG: No: We gathered that from his words, and from his reference to the bombing war, that total war had now to be waged against ships and crews. That is what we understood, and I talked about it to my comrades on the way back to the Hansa. We were convinced that Admiral Dönitz meant that. He did not express it clearly.

KRANZBUEHLER: Did you speak about the point with any of your superiors at the school?

HEISIG: I left the school on the same day. But I can remember that one of my superiors, whose name to my regret I do not recall, nor do I recall the occasion, once spoke to us about this subject and advised us that, if possible, only officers should be on the bridge ready to liquidate shipwrecked sailors, should the possibility arise or should it be necessary.

KRANZBUEHLER: One of your superiors told you that?

HEISIG: Yes, but I cannot remember in which connection and where. I received a lot of advice from my superiors on many things.

KRANZBUEHLER: Were you instructed at the school in the standing orders of war?

HEISIG: Yes.

KRANZBUEHLER: Did these standing orders mention anywhere that shipwrecked sailors were to be fired on or their rescue apparatus destroyed?

HEISIG: The standing order did not mention that. But I think one can assume this from an innuendo of Captain Rollmann, who was then officers' company commander – a short time before that, some teletype message had arrived containing an order prohibiting rescue measures and demanding that sea warfare should be fought with more radical, more drastic means.

KRANZBUEHLER: Do you think that the prohibition of rescue measures is identical with the shooting of shipwrecked sailors?

HEISIG: We came to this ....

KRANZBUEHLER: Please answer my question. Do you think these two things are identical?

HEISIG: No.

KRANZBUEHLER: Thank you.

The second witness produced by the Prosecution, Captain Moehle, confessed he was testifying because when he was taken prisoner the accusation against him was of issuing the Laconia Order. Moehle was a Flotilla Commander at Kiel with the responsibility of briefing U-boat commanders in the matter of their orders. He claimed that the Laconia Order was an instruction to murder the enemy shipwrecked, confirmed by his superiors, but he always warned the commanders it was a matter for conscience. Moehle's evidence was not corroborated. It was obviously the action of a frightened man trying to save his own skin, and believing Dönitz was a 'no hoper' insofar as the trial was concerned.

PHILLIMORE: Karl Heinz Moehle, you held the rank of Lieutenant-Commander in the German Navy?

MOEHLE: Yes, Sir.

PHILLIMORE: In the autumn of 1942 were you head of the 5th U-Boat Flotilla?

MOEHLE: Yes, sir, for four years.

PHILLIMORE: What were your duties as commander of that flotilla?

MOEHLE: My main duties consisted of the fitting out of U-boats which were to be sent to the front from home bases, and giving them orders of the U-Boat Command. It was my responsibility to see that out-going U-boats were provided with the new orders of the U-Boat Command ... The orders of the U-Boat Command were always very clear and unambiguous.

PHILLIMORE: Did you personally see commanders before they went out on patrol?

MOEHLE: Yes, each commander before sailing on a mission went through a briefing session at my office.

PHILLIMORE: Do you remember an order in the autumn of 1942 dealing with lifeboats?

MOEHLE: Yes. In September 1942, I received a wireless message to all commanders at sea, and it dealt with that question.

PHILLIMORE: After you got that order did you go to Admiral Dönitz's quarters?

MOEHLE: Yes. At my first visit to headquarters after receipt of the order, I personally discussed it with Lieutenant-Commander Kuppisch, who was a specialist on the staff of the U-Boat Command. At that meeting I asked him how the ambiguity contained in that order – or I might say lack of clarity – should be understood. He explained the order by two illustrations.

    The first example was that of a U-boat in the outer Bay of Biscay. It was sailing on a patrol when it sighted a rubber dinghy carrying survivors of a British 'plane. The mission, that is, being fully equipped, made it impossible to take the crew of the plane on board, although especially at that time, it appeared especially desirable to bring back specialists in navigation from shot-down crews to get useful information from them. The commander of the U-boat made a wide circle around this rubber boat and continued on his mission. When he returned from his mission he reported the case to the staff of the Commander-in-Chief of U-boats. The staff officers reproached him, saying that, if he were unable to bring these navigation specialists back with him, the right thing to do would have been to attack that crew, for it was to be expected that in less than twenty-four hours at the latest, the dinghy would be rescued by British reconnaissance forces, and they ...

PHILLIMORE: I don't quite get what you said would have been the correct action to take. You were saying the correct thing to do would have been....

MOEHLE: .... To attack the air-crew, as it was not possible to bring back the crew or these specialists, for it could be expected that the crew would be found and rescued within a short time by British reconnaissance forces, and in given circumstances might again destroy one or two German U-boats ....

PHILLIMORE: What was the second example?

MOEHLE: During the first month of the U-boat warfare against the United States, a great quantity of tonnage had been sunk in the shallow waters off the American coast. In these sinkings the greater part of the crews were rescued, because of the close proximity of land. That was exceedingly regrettable because merchant shipping not only consists of tonnage but also crews, and in the meantime these crews were again able to man newly built ships.

PHILLIMORE: From your knowledge of the way orders were worded, can you tell the Tribunal what you understood Admiral Dönitz's order to mean?

MOEHLE: The order meant, in my own opinion, that rescue measures remained prohibited, and moreover it was desirable in the case of sinkings of merchantmen that there should be no survivors.

PHILLIMORE: How did you brief commanders on this order?

MOEHLE: I read them the wording of the wireless message without making any comment. In a very few instances some commanders asked me about the meaning of the order. In such cases I gave them the two examples that headquarters had given to me. However, I added 'U-boat Command cannot give you such an order officially; everybody has to handle this according to his own conscience.'

PHILLIMORE: Do you remember an order about rescue ships?

MOEHLE: Yes. I do not remember the exact date, but I think it must have been about the same as the order of September 1942.

PHILLIMORE: Do you remember an order about entries in logs?

MOEHLE: Yes, sir. At the time, the exact date I do not remember, it had been ordered that sinkings and other acts which were in contradiction to international conventions should not be entered in the log but reported orally after return to the home port.

PHILLIMORE: Would you care to say why it is that you are giving evidence in this case?

MOEHLE: Yes, sir, because when I was taken prisoner, it was claimed that I was the author of these orders, and I do not want to have this charge connected with my name.

Moehle was then cross-examined by Naval Judge Advocate Otto Kranzbuehler.

KRANZBUEHLER: Lieutenant-Commander Moehle, since when have you been in the U-boat arm?

MOEHLE: Since the end of 1936.

KRANZBUEHLER: Do you know Grand Admiral Dönitz personally?

MOEHLE: Yes.

KRANZBUEHLER: Since when?

MOEHLE: Since October 1937.

KRANZBUEHLER: Do you know him as an admiral to whom none of his flotilla chiefs could speak?

MOEHLE: No.

KRANZBUEHLER: Or was the opposite the case?

MOEHLE: He could be approached by everybody at any time.

KRANZBUEHLER: Have you yourself been a commander of a U-boat?

MOEHLE: Yes, on nine occasions. From the beginning of the war until April 1941.

KRANZBUEHLER: How many ships did you sink?

MOEHLE: Twenty ships.

KRANZBUEHLER: After sinking ships, did you destroy the rescue equipment or fire on the survivors?

MOEHLE: No.

KRANZBUEHLER: Did you have an order to do that?

MOEHLE: No.

KRANZBUEHLER: Had the danger passed for a U-boat after the attack on a merchantman?

MOEHLE: No.

KRANZBUEHLER: Do you know that the order of September 1942 was given in consequence of an incident in which German U-boats had undertaken rescue measures?

MOEHLE: Yes, sir.

KRANZBUEHLER: You interpreted the order of September 1942 to the commanders in the sense that it should include the destruction of rescue facilities and of the shipwrecked crew?

MOEHLE: No, not quite. I gave the two examples to the commanders only if they made an inquiry, and I passed them on in the same way as I had received them from the Commander-in-Chief Submarine Fleet, and they themselves could draw that conclusion from these two examples.

KRANZBUEHLER: In which sentences of the order do you see a hidden invitation to kill survivors or to destroy the rescue facilities? Is it the sentence 'Rescue measures contradict the most primitive demands of warfare that crews and ships should be destroyed'?

MOEHLE: Yes.

KRANZBUEHLER: Does the sentence contain anything as to the destruction of shipwrecked persons?

MOEHLE: No, of crews.

KRANZBUEHLER: At the end of the order is the phrase 'Be harsh'. Did you hear that phrase there for the first time?

MOEHLE: No.

KRANZBUEHLER: Was the phrase used by the Commander-in-Chief of U-boats to get commanders to be severe to themselves and to their crews?

MOEHLE: Yes.

The long trial dragged on for ten months. In May 1946 Kranzbuehler had the opportunity of putting Dönitz on the witness stand to question him on the Laconia Order.

KRANZBUEHLER: Admiral, you have just described the enemy's supremacy in the air in September 1942. During these September days you received the report about the sinking of the British transport *Laconia*. I submit to the Tribunal the war diaries of the submarines which took part in this action. Lieutenant-Commanders Hartenstein, Schacht and Würdemann. I shall read to you the report you received on 13th September at 1.25 a.m.: 'Sunk by Hartenstein British ship *Laconia*.' Then the position is given and the message continues: 'Unfortunately with 1,500 Italian prisoners of war. Up to now picked up 90.'

Then the details and the end of 'Request orders' .... Please tell me first what impression or what knowledge you had about this ship *Laconia* which had been reported sunk and its crew?

DÖNITZ: I knew from the handbook on armed British ships which we had at our disposal that the *Laconia* was armed with fourteen guns. I concluded, therefore, that it would have a British crew of at least five hundred men. When I heard that there were Italian prisoners on board, it was clear to me that this number would be further increased by the guards of the prisoners.

KRANZBUEHLER: Please describe now the main events surrounding your order of 17th September, and elaborate first on the rescue or non-rescue of British or Italians, and secondly, your concern for the safety of the U-boats in question.

DÖNITZ: When I received this report I radioed to all the U-boats in the whole area. I issued the order: 'Schacht, Group Eisbär, Würdemann, Wilamowitz proceed to Hartenstein immediately.' Later I had to have several boats turn back because their distance from the scene was too great. Above all I asked Hartenstein, the commander who had sunk the ship, whether the *Laconia* had sent out radio messages, because I hoped that as a result British and American ships would come to the rescue. Hartenstein affirmed that and, besides, he himself sent out the following radio message in English: 'If any ship will assist the shipwrecked *Laconia* crew, I will not attack her provided I am not being attacked by ship or air force.' I gained the impression from the reports of the U-boats that they began the rescue work with great zeal.

KRANZBUEHLER: How many submarines were there?

DÖNITZ: There were three or four. I received reports that the numbers of those taken on board by each U-boat were between one and two hundred. The reports spoke of the crew being cared for and taken over from lifeboats, of the towing of lifeboats by the submarines. All these reports caused me the greatest concern, because I knew for certain this would not end well.

My concern was expressed in a message to the submarines, radioed four times: 'Detailed boats to take over only so many as to remain fully able to dive'. It is obvious that if the narrow space of the submarine – our U-boats were half as big as the enemy's – is crowded with one or two hundred additional people, the submarine is already in absolute danger, not to speak of its fitness to fight. That my concern was justified was clearly evident from the message which Hartenstein sent which said that he had been attacked by bombs from an American bomber.

KRANZBUEHLER: The message from Hartenstein reads: 'Bombed five times by American Liberator in low flight when towing four boats in spite of Red Cross flag, four square metres on the bridge and good visibility. Both periscopes at present out of order. Breaking off rescue: all off board, putting out to west. Will repair.' Admiral, would you tell us now what measures you took after Hartenstein's report?

DÖNITZ: I deliberated at length whether, after this experience, I should not break off all attempts at rescue; and beyond doubt from the military point of view, that would have been the right thing to do, because the attack showed clearly in what way the U-boats were endangered.

That decision became more grave for me because I received a call from Naval Operations Staff that the Fuhrer did not wish me to risk any submarines in rescue work or to summon them from distant areas. A very heated conference with my staff ensued, and I can remember closing it with the statement: 'I cannot throw these people into the water now, I will carry on.'

Of course, it was clear to me that I would have to assume full responsibility for further losses, and from the military point of view the continuation of the rescue work was wrong. Of that I received proof from the U-506 of Würdemann, who also reported, I believe on the following morning, that he was bombed by an aeroplane.

KRANZBUEHLER: That report, Mr President, is in the War Diary of Würdemann, an entry of 17th September at 11.43 p.m. He reported: 'Transfer of survivors to *Annamite* completed.' Then came details – 'Attacked by heavy sea-plane at noon. Fully ready for action.'

DÖNITZ: The third submarine, Schacht's, the U-507, had sent a wireless message that he had many men on board and was towing four lifeboats with Englishmen and Poles. Thereupon, of course, I ordered him to cast off these boats because the burden made it impossible for him to dive. Later he sent a long message.

KRANZBUEHLER: At 11.10 p.m. I shall read the message: 'Transferred 163 Italians to *Annamite*. Navigation Officer of *Laconia* and another English officer on board. Seven lifeboats with about 330 Englishmen and Poles, among them 15 women and 16 children, deposited at Quarter FE 9612, women and children kept aboard ship for one night. Supplied all shipwrecked with hot meal and drinks, clothed and bandaged when necessary. Four other boats anchored to a buoy in square FE 9619.'

DÖNITZ: Because I had ordered him to cast off the lifeboats and we considered this general message as a supplementary later report, he was admonished by another message; and from that the prosecutor wrongly concluded that I had prohibited the rescue of Englishmen. That I did not prohibit it can be seen from the fact that I did not raise objection to the many reports speaking of the rescue of Englishmen.

Indeed, in the end, I had the impression that the Italians did not fare very well in the rescue. That this impression was correct can be seen from the figures of those rescued. Of eight hundred and eleven Englishmen, about eight hundred were rescued and of one thousand and eight hundred Italians, four hundred and fifty.

KRANZBUEHLER: The *Laconia* was torpedoed on 12th September. The rescue took how many days altogether?

DÖNITZ: Four days.

KRANSBUEHLER: And afterwards was continued till when?

DÖNITZ: Until we turned them over to the French warships which had been notified by us.

KRANZBUEHLER: Now what is the connection between the incident of the *Laconia* which you have just described, and the order which the prosecution charges as an order for destruction?

174

DÖNITZ: Apart from my great and constant anxiety for the submarines and the strong feeling that the British and Americans had not helped despite the proximity of Freetown, I learned from this action very definitely that the time had passed when U-boats could carry out such operations on the surface without danger. The two bombing attacks showed clearly that in spite of good weather, in spite of the large numbers of people to be rescued who were more clearly visible to the aviators than in normal heavy sea conditions when few people have to be rescued, the danger to the submarines was so great that, as the one responsible for the boats and the crews, I had to prohibit rescue activities in the face of the ever-present tremendous Anglo-American Air Force. I want to mention, just as an example, that all the submarines which took part in that rescue operation were lost by bombing attack at their next action or soon afterwards. The situation in which the enemy kills the rescuers while they are exposing themselves to great personal danger is really and emphatically contrary to ordinary common sense and the elementary rules of warfare.

KRANZBUEHLER: In the opinion of the prosecution, Admiral, you used that incident to carry out in practice an idea which you had already cherished for a long time, namely, in future to kill the shipwrecked. Please state your view on this.

DÖNITZ: The whole question concerned rescue or non-rescue; the entire development leading up to that order speaks clearly against such an accusation. It was a fact that we rescued with devotion and were bombed while doing so; it was also a fact that the U-Boat Command and I were faced with a serious decision, and we acted in a humane way, which from a military point of view was wrong. I think, therefore, that no more words need be lost in rebuttal of this charge.

KRANZBUEHLER: Admiral, I must put to you now the wording of that order from which the prosecution draws its conclusions. In the second paragraph it says: 'Rescue is contrary to the most primitive laws for the destruction of enemy ships and crews.' What does that sentence mean?

DÖNITZ: That sentence is, of course, intended to be a justification. Now the prosecution says I could quite simply have ordered that safety did not permit it, that the predominance of the enemy's air force did not permit it – and as we have seen in the case of the *Laconia* I did order that four times. But that reasoning has been worn out. It was a 'much played record ...' I was now anxious to state to the commanders of the submarines a reason which could exclude all discretion and all independent decision of the commanders. For again and again I had the experience that a clear sky was judged too favourably by the U-boats and then the submarine was lost; or that a commander, in the role of rescuer, was in time no longer master of his own decisions, as the *Laconia* case showed. Therefore under no circumstances did I want to repeat the old reason which again would give the U-boat commander the opportunity to say: 'Well, at the moment there is no danger of an air attack.' That is, I did not want to give him a chance to act independently. I did not want an argument to arise in the mind of one of the two hundred U-boat commanders. Nor did I want to say, 'If somebody with great self-sacrifice rescues the enemy and in that process is killed by him, then that is a contradiction of the most elementary laws of warfare.' I could have said that too, but I did not put it that way, and, therefore, I worded the sentence as it now stands.

KRANZBUEHLER: The order of 17th September was for you the end of the *Laconia* incident?

DÖNITZ: Yes.

KRANZBUEHLER: To whom was it directed?

DÖNITZ: According to my best recollection, only to submarines on the high seas. For the various operation areas we had different radio channels. Since the other submarines were in contact with convoys and thus unable to carry out rescue measures, they could simply shelve the order. But I have now discovered that the order was sent out to all submarines, that is, on all channels; it was a technical matter of communication which, of course, could do no harm.

KRANZBUEHLER: You said that the fundamental consideration underlying the entire order was the overwhelming danger of air-attack. If that is correct, how could you in the same order maintain the directive for the rescue of captains and chief engineers?

DÖNITZ: There is, of course, a great difference between rescue measures for which the submarine has to stop, and men have to go on deck, and a brief surfacing to pick up a captain, because while merely surfacing the submarine remains in a state of alert, whereas otherwise the alertness is completely disrupted. However, there was a military purpose in the seizure of these captains, for which I had received orders from the Naval Operations Staff as a matter of principle, and in pursuit of a military aim, that is to say not rescue work but the capture of important enemies, one must and can run a certain risk. Besides, I knew that in practice that addition brought very meagre results. I might say no results at all. I remember quite clearly having asked myself: 'Why do we still pick them up?' It was not our intention, however, to drop a general order of that importance. But the essential points are, first, the lesser risk that the state of alert might not be maintained during rescue, and secondly, the pursuit of an important military aim.

KRANZBUEHLER: What do you mean by the last sentence in the order, 'Be harsh'?

DÖNITZ: I had preached to my U-boat commanders for five and a half years that they should be hard towards themselves. And when giving this order I again felt I had to emphasise to them in a very drastic way my whole concern and grave responsibility for the submarines, and thus the necessity of prohibiting rescue activities in view of the overwhelming power of the enemy air force. After all, it is very definite that on one side there is the harshness of war, the necessity of saving one's own submarine, and on the other the traditional sentiment of the sailor!

176

68. Admiral Dönitz speaking at the Nuremberg War Trials

69. The accused at the Nuremberg War Trials, front row left to right: Goering, Hess, Ribbentrop, Keitel, Rosenberg, Frank, Frick, Streicher, Funk and Schacht. Back row left to right: Dönitz, Raeder, Shirach, Saukel, Jodl, Von Papen, Seyss-Inquart, Speer, Von Neurath and Fritsche.

70. Press conference at Nuremberg, left to right: Col H.J. Phillimore, Sir David Maxwell Fyfe KC, Mr Justice Jackson, M. Kaminker (interpreter) and M. François de Menthon (French prosecutor).

71. The courthouse at Nuremberg in 1945.

KRANZBUEHLER: You heard the witness Lieutenant-Commander Moehle state in this Court that he misunderstood the order in the sense that survivors should be killed, and in several cases he instructed submarine commanders in that sense. As Commanding Officer, do you not have to assume responsibility for the misunderstanding of your orders?

DÖNITZ: Of course I am responsible for all orders, for their form and their contents. Moehle, however, is the only person who had doubts about the meaning of that order. I regret that Moehle did not find occasion to clarify these doubts immediately, either through me, to whom everyone had access at all times, or through the numerous staff officers who, as members of my staff, were either also partly responsible or participated in the drafting of these orders; or through his immediate superior at Kiel. I am convinced that the few U-boat commanders to whom he communicated his doubts remained quite unaffected by them. If there were any consequences I would, of course, assume responsibility for them.

KRANZBUEHLER: You mentioned before the discussion with the Fuhrer, during which the problem whether it was permissible to kill survivors was examined, or at least touched on by the Fuhrer. Was the question re-examined at any time by the Commander-in-Chief of U-boats or the Naval Operations Staff?

DÖNITZ: When I became Commander-in-Chief of the Navy ...?

KRANZBUEHLER: That was in 1943.

DÖNITZ: I think in the summer of 1943 I received a letter from the Foreign Office in which I was informed that about eighty-seven percent of the crews of merchant ships which had been sunk were returning home. I was told that was a disadvantage and was asked whether it was not possible to do something about it. Thereupon I had a letter sent to the Foreign Office in which I wrote that I had already been forced to prohibit rescue because it endangered the submarines, but that other measures were out of the question for me.

KRANZBUEHLER: The decisive point of the entire letter seems to be in Heading 3. 'A directive to take action against lifeboats of sunken vessels and crew members drifting in the sea would, for psychological reasons, hardly be acceptable to U-boat crews, since it would be contrary to the innermost feelings of all sailors. Such a directive could only be considered if by it a decisive military success could be achieved.' Admiral, you yourself have repeatedly spoken about the harshness of war. Are you, nevertheless, of the opinion that psychologically the U-boat crews could not be expected to carry out such an order, and why?

DÖNITZ: We U-boat men knew that we had to fight a very hard war against the great sea powers. Germany had at her disposal for this naval warfare nothing but the U-boats. Therefore, from the beginning, already in peace-time, I trained the submarine crews in the spirit of pure idealism and patriotism. That was necessary, and I continued that training throughout the war and supported it by very close personal contacts with the men at the bases. It was necessary to achieve very high morale, very high fighting spirit, otherwise the severe struggle and the enormous losses would have been morally impossible to bear. But in spite of these high losses we continued to fight, because it had to be; and we made up for our losses and again and again replenished our forces with volunteers full of enthusiasm and moral strength, just because morale was so high. And I would never, even at the time of our most serious losses, have permitted that these men be given an order which was unethical or would damage their fighting morale; much less would I myself have ever given such an order, for I placed my whole confidence in that high fighting morale and endeavoured to maintain it.

KRANZBUEHLER: You said the U-boat forces were replenished with volunteers, did you?

DÖNITZ: We had practically only volunteers.

KRANZBUEHLER: Also at the time of the highest losses?

DÖNITZ: Yes, even then. During the period when everyone knew that he took part in an average of two missions and then was lost.

KRANZBUEHLER: How high were your losses?

DÖNITZ: According to my recollections, our total losses were six hundred and forty or six hundred and seventy.

KRANZBUEHLER: And crew members?

DÖNITZ: Altogether we had forty thousand men in the submarine force. Of these, thirty thousand did not return and only five thousand were taken prisoner; the majority of the submarines were destroyed from the air in the vast areas of the Atlantic, where rescue was out of the question.

On 16th July 1946 Naval Judge Advocate Otto Kranzbuehler addressed the court in his summing up on the matter of the Laconia Order:

'I am now coming to the second basic charge of the prosecution – intentional killing of shipwrecked crews. It is directed only against Admiral Dönitz, not Admiral Raeder. The legal basis for the treatment of shipwrecked crews, for those ships which are entitled to the protection of the London Agreement of 1936, is laid down in the agreement itself. There it says that, before the sinking, crews and passengers must be brought to safety. This was done by the German side, and the difference of opinion with the prosecution concerns only the question already dealt with, namely which ships were entitled to protection under the agreement and which were not.

'In the case of all ships not entitled to protection under the agreement, sinking should be considered a military combat action. The legal basis, therefore, with regard to the treatment of shipwrecked crews in these cases is contained in the Hague Convention concerning the application of the principles of the Geneva Convention to naval warfare of 18th October 1907, although it was not ratified by Great Britain. According to this both belligerents shall after each combat action make arrangements for the search for the shipwrecked, as far as military considerations allow this. Accordingly, the German U-boats were also bound to assist the shipwrecked of steamers sunk without warning, as long as by doing so, first, the boat would not be endangered, and secondly, the accomplishment of the military mission would not be prejudiced.

'These principles are generally acknowledged. This situation was changed through Admiral Dönitz's order of 17th September 1942, in which he forbade rescue measures on principle. The decisive sentences are: "The rescue of members of the crew of a ship sunk is not to be attempted. Rescue is contradictory to the most primitive demands of warfare, which are the annihilation of enemy ships and crews."

'It has been disputed by the prosecution that this actually prohibits rescue. It looks upon this order as a hidden provocation to kill the shipwrecked, and it has gone through the Press of the world as a command for murder. If any accusation at all has been refuted in this trial, then it seems to me to be this ignominious interpretation of the order mentioned above. How was this order brought on? Beginning with June 1942, the losses of German submarines through the Allied air forces rose by leaps and bounds, and jumped from a monthly average of four or five during the first months of 1942 to ten, eleven, thirteen, finally reaching thirty-eight boats in May 1943. Orders and measures from the Command of Submarine Warfare multiplied in order to counter these losses. They were of no avail, and every day brought fresh reports of air attacks and losses of submarines.

'This was the situation when, on 12th September, it was reported that the heavily armed British troop-transport *Laconia*, with fifteen hundred Italian prisoners of war and an Allied crew of one thousand men and some women and children aboard, had been torpedoed. Admiral Dönitz withdrew several submarines from current operations for the purpose of rescuing the shipwrecked, no distinction being made between Italians and Allies. From the very start the danger of enemy air attacks filled him with anxiety. While the submarines during the following day devotedly rescued, towed boats, supplied food and so forth, they received no less than three admonitions from the Commander-in-Chief to be careful, to divide the shipwrecked, and at all times be ready to submerge. These warnings were of no avail. On 16th September one of the submarines displaying a Red Cross flag and towing lifeboats was attacked and considerably damaged by an Allied bomber; one lifeboat was hit and losses caused among the shipwrecked. Following this report the Commander-in-Chief sent three more messages with orders immediately to submerge in case of danger and under no circumstances to risk the boats' own safety. Again, without avail. In the evening of 17th September 1942, the second submarine reported that it had been taken unawares and bombed by an aeroplane.

'Notwithstanding these experiences, and in spite of the explicit order from the Fuhrer's headquarters not to endanger any boats under any consideration, Admiral Dönitz did not discontinue rescue work, but had it continued until the shipwrecked were taken aboard French warships sent to their rescue. However, this incident was a lesson. Due to enemy air reconnaissance activity over the entire sea area, it was simply no longer safe to carry out rescue measures without endangering the submarine. It was useless to give orders over and over again to commanders to undertake rescue only if their own boats were not endangered thereby. Earlier experiences had already shown that their human desire to render aid had led many commanders to underestimate the danger from the air. It takes a submarine with decks cleared at least one minute to submerge on alarm, while an aircraft can cover six thousand metres in that time. In practice this means that a submarine engaged in rescue action when sighting a plane has not time enough to submerge. These were the reasons which caused Admiral Dönitz, directly after the close of the *Laconia* incident, to forbid rescue measures on principle. This was motivated by the endeavour to preclude any calculation on the part of the commander as to the danger of air attack whenever in individual cases he should feel tempted to undertake rescue work.

'How then can the prosecution consider this order an "order to murder"? Grounds for this are said to be furnished by the discussion between Hitler and the Japanese Ambassador Oshima, in January 1942, in which Hitler mentioned a prospective order to his U-boats to kill the survivors of ships sunk. This announcement, the prosecution infers, Hitler doubtless followed up, and Admiral Dönitz carried it out by the Laconia Order. Actually, on the occasion of a report on U-boat problems, which both Admirals had to make in May 1942, the Fuhrer suggested that in future action should be taken against the shipwrecked, that is, to shoot them. Admiral Dönitz immediately rejected this action as completely impossible, and Grand Admiral Raeder unreservedly agreed with him. Both Admirals specified the improvement of torpedoes as the only permissible way to increase losses among the crews. In the face of the opposition of both Admirals Adolf Hitler dropped his proposal, and following this report no order whatever was given concerning the shipwrecked crews, let alone concerning the killing of the shipwrecked by shooting. The testimony of Lt Commander Moehle must be taken much more seriously because he had hinted to a few submarine commanders that the Laconia Order demanded, or at least approved of, the killing of the shipwrecked. Moehle did not receive this interpretation either from Admiral Dönitz himself, or from the Chief of Staff, or from his chief assistant Lt Commander Hessler, that is to say from none of the officers who alone would have been qualified to transmit such an interpretation to the chief of a flotilla.

'How Moehle actually arrived at this interpretation has in my opinion not been explained by the trial. One thing at any rate has been proven, namely, that Admiral Dönitz and his staff had not caused this briefing to be given, nor did they know anything about it.'

Dönitz was incorrect when he stated eight hundred British were saved from the *Laconia*; the total was not contested, but he was either mistaken or misinformed. What is proven that out of the thousands of actions by U-boats the Allied powers could only turn to one instance where a German submarine commander murdered the shipwrecked. Heinz Eck, commander of U-852, machine-gunned the survivors of the *Peleus* in March 1944. Two months later U-852 was sunk by the R.A.F., but Eck survived and was taken prisoner. Unfortunately for him, there were three survivors of the *Peleus* whose story was investigated. Commander Eck was tried by court martial, found guilty and executed. During his trial the U-852's engineer claimed that his captain was obeying orders as detailed in the Laconia Order. Later, he confessed his statement was not true: he was merely trying to save Eck's life.

The marathon trial ended on 31st August 1946 and the eight judges went in secret session to consider their verdicts.

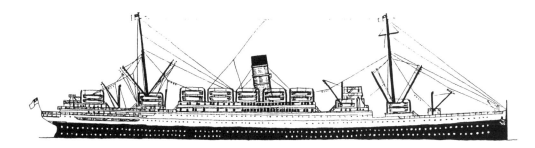

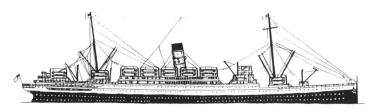

XVII

JUDGEMENT

From the outset Otto Kranzbuehler earned respect. His skilful advocacy saved Dönitz from many years imprisonment, even death. He presented his client to the Court as a military commander who performed his duty efficaciously for his country, worthy of a professional officer.

Behind closed doors, the eight judges representing the four Allied Powers, their minds conditioned to four domestic legal systems, deliberated the verdict to be pronounced on Dönitz. The American judge Biddle crusaded for his acquittal. In his opinion the deposition submitted by Admiral Nimitz, admitting that the United States of America used identical methods to Germany in pursuit of their submarine warfare, made it impossible to convict him. This was not a view shared by the British judges who argued all Admiral Nimitz had proved was that both sides broke the law. Dönitz was therefore guilty as charged. The American judge Parker was supportive, pointing out that had Dönitz not broken the rules of the 1936 London Protocol others would not have imitated. British judge Lawrence backed this view, but could not with conviction see the Laconia Order as an instrument to commit murder. Rather the ambiguity of its wording forced him to give Dönitz the advantage in this matter. And so they argued, the Russians and the French strong in pressing for a ten to twenty year prison sentence.

On 1st October 1946, judgement was passed on Grand Admiral Dönitz. On Count One of the Indictment, Conspiring to wage Aggressive War, he was declared 'not guilty' but guilty on: Count Two: Crimes against Peace – in his case waging an aggressive war.

Count Three: War Crimes – violation of the laws of war at sea. Under Article 6 of the Statutes of the Tribunal he was found guilty of committing Crimes Against Peace and War Crimes, citing his involvement in the invasion of Norway in April 1940. But the Tribunal refused to hear evidence concerning British plans for the invasion of Norway, plans which were effected a few hours before the German attack began and identical to the

German plot to seize major Norwegian ports. His condemnation was also based on the fact that in succeeding Hitler as President of the Third Reich, he ordered a continuation of the fight against the Soviet Union. Dönitz admitted this was true; regrettably, the Court did not want to understand his motive. With two Russian judges it was embarrassing to consider the evacuation of two million Germans from the Eastern Provinces before the advancing Russians.

To wage anything less than an aggressive war would have labelled him a traitor and historically it is proven that as soon as the German Navy got their people out of East Prussia into West Germany, Dönitz surrendered to the Americans.

On the question of War Crimes, the judge read to the Court: 'Dönitz is charged with waging unrestricted submarine warfare contrary to the Naval Protocol of 1936, to which Germany acceded, and which reaffirmed the rules of submarine warfare laid down in the London Naval Agreement of 1930.

'It is also asserted that the German U-boat arm not only did not carry out the rescue and warning provisions of the Protocol but that Dönitz deliberately ordered the killing of survivors of shipwrecked vessels, whether enemy or neutral. The prosecution has introduced much evidence surrounding two orders of Dönitz: war order Number 154, issued in 1939, and the so called Laconia Order of 1942. The defence argues that these orders and the evidence supporting them do not show such a policy, and has introduced much evidence to the contrary. The Tribunal is of the opinion that the evidence does not establish with the certainty required that Dönitz deliberately ordered the killing of shipwrecked survivors. The orders were undoubtedly ambiguous and deserve the strongest censure. The evidence further shows that the stipulations on rescue work were not observed and that the defendant ordered that they should not be observed. The argument of the defence is that the security of the submarine, as the first rule of the sea, takes precedence over rescue, and that the development of aircraft made rescue impossible. This may be so, but the Protocol is explicit. If the commander cannot rescue, then under its terms he cannot sink a merchant vessel, and should allow it to pass unharmed before his periscope. These orders, then, prove that Dönitz is guilty of a violation of the Protocol.

'In view of all the facts proved, and in particular of an order of the British Admiralty announced on 8th May 1940, according to which all vessels navigating at night in the Skagerrak should be sunk, and in view also of Admiral Nimitz's statement that unrestricted submarine warfare was carried on in the Pacific Ocean by the United States from the first day that nation entered the war, the sentence on Dönitz is not assessed on the ground of his breaches of the international law of submarine warfare ....'

Dönitz was sentenced to ten years of imprisonment. In determining whether a particular act was a crime, Dönitz was left at the mercy of a court decidedly of the opinion that if the represented nations had committed a similar act it was not therefore a crime. However, the charges against Dönitz were sufficiently broad to produce a finding he must be guilty of 'something'. If his sentence was 'not assessed on the ground of his breaches of the international law of submarine warfare' and the Laconia Order was not seen as a licence to commit murder on the high seas, it is very difficult to ascertain the grounds on which he was 'assessed'. The judgement on Dönitz appears to have been glossed over with a thin veneer of legal waffle which in post-Nuremberg days has puzzled leading military commanders world-wide, who wonder if the judgement was nothing more than an act of vengeance and his only crime was to be on the losing side. In jurisprudence, it is incontrovertible that Dönitz could only be sentenced and punished for a crime if he had transgressed a law in force at the time he committed the indiscretion, and if that law defined the penalty.

Submarines, like surface ships, were debarred from sinking merchant vessels without first making provision for the safety of crews. Kranzbuehler responded that Britain at the outbreak of war armed its merchant ships with orders to ram U-boats and could not therefore be entitled to the protection of the 1936 Protocol. Here he gained a victory and the Tribunal ruled Dönitz was not guilty for his conduct of submarine warfare against British merchant ships.

But the prosecution was determined not to be defeated and the Tribunal ruled that notwithstanding the practice during the 1914-18 war for Germany and Britain to declare 'operational zones' and sink neutral ships which entered those zones (a practice they were careful to point out commenced by Germany and adopted in retaliation by Britain), the Protocol made no exception for 'operational zones', even if the British Admiralty had declared the Skagerrak an 'operational zone' and neutral ships would be sunk if found there. They judged that Dönitz was guilty of a violation of the Protocol in view of his policy to sink neutral ships in designated war zones. It all amounted to a most confusing statement.

The Nuremberg Judgement confirmed at the same time approval of a code of warfare at sea which the Allied Powers did not follow themselves, and which was certain to condemn them to difficulties at some future date. The British, American, French and Russian judges established that the

186

Protocol of 1936 would govern the law of war at sea for the nuclear age. Today, submarines designed to remain submerged for weeks at a time are expected to expose themselves on the surface to comply with an antiquated law. And what happens? The first time a British nuclear submarine torpedoes an enemy vessel all the rules are broken.

During the Falklands crisis of 1982, the Argentine cruiser *General Belgrano* was sunk without warning by H.M.S. *Conqueror* outside the 'Total Exclusion Zone' declared by the British Government. It was anticipated that the hostile craft was armed with Exocet missiles, which, in a new experience of warfare at sea, had proved deadly and wickedly destructive to British Task Force ships. Not all British naval vessels were equipped with defensive projectiles against this new terror and, quite rightly, from the British assessment, the *General Belgrano* was a major threat to the large carriers H.M.S. *Hermes* and H.M.S. *Invincible*.

When the cruiser was torpedoed outside and sailing away from the 'Total Exclusion Zone' with the loss of 368 sailors out of a crew of 750, no warning was issued and no attempt to rescue her crew was made. Today, questions are still raised as to who actually gave the order for her sinking and what advice, if any, was offered about the legality of the sinking. One thing is sure, Britain's credibility was placed under the microscope when it became clear that Defence Secretary John Nott lacked information himself. On 4th May 1982 he told the House of Commons that the *General Belgrano* had been 'closing on elements of the Task Force', instead of the truth that she was heading in the opposite direction. It could be argued that the enemy ship considered itself safe outside the declared zone and was not carrying missiles, but the risk could not be taken in the light of the experience of ships lost to the missiles. Obviously, it was thought that the Argentine cruiser was sailing away to safer waters from where she would bide her time for a better moment to attack. To sink the cruiser, irrespective of the circumstances, was convenient. Whatever the truth, it was soon eclipsed 48 hours later with the sinking of H.M.S. *Sheffield*. For a time it seemed that the *General Belgrano* affair was earmarked to become nothing more than yesterday's news; but it was not to be.

If the incident had occurred in the 1940's and Britain had been overcome in the conflict, then Prime Minister Margaret Thatcher, her Naval Chief, together with the Commander of H.M.S. *Conqueror*, who as a professional officer obeyed the orders of his superiors, would have been indicted as war criminals.

Grand Admiral Dönitz served his sentence in Spandau Prison, Berlin. Six months after the rescue of the *Laconia* survivors, Commander

Hartenstein and his crew were dead, Schacht too, victims of attacks by American planes. Later, Würdemann was to share the same fate. Dönitz died on December 24th, 1980 and was buried at Aumühle, near Hamburg. There were no military honours, and no representatives of any government attended. But 5,000 naval veterans were there to pay their last respects.

Each year on the anniversary of the sinking of the *Laconia*, bereaved families of crew members received a letter from a writer who signed himself as 'A *Laconia* Survivor'. In 1967 the letters stopped and the identity of this crewman was never known. One such recipient was Mrs Doris Maddocks of Rainhill, Liverpool, daughter of John Banks. The last letter she received was, as always, accompanied by a one pound note and contained words of comfort:

'The beautiful music and rendering of Psalm 139 during this morning's 10.15 a.m. B.B.C. Daily Service was so fitting for thoughts in my mind, and too, because of yesterday's anniversary of a day now so long passed ....'

72. Early photograph of the *Laconia* from Cunard publicity material.

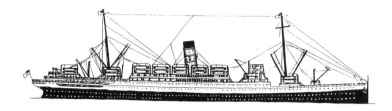

APPENDIX 1

THE *LACONIA'S* CREW MANIFEST

Officers of the Bridge

Rank	Name	Age	
Master	Capt Rudolph Sharp	56	Lost at sea
Chief Officer	Staff Capt George Steel	58	Lost at sea
Snr 1st Officer	John H. Walker	55	Rescued
Jnr 1st Officer	Edward Hall-Lucas	31	Lost at sea
Snr 2nd Officer	George Rose	45	Rescued
Jnr 2nd Officer	Charles Stokes	35	Lost at sea
Snr 3rd Officer	Thomas Buckingham	28	Taken to Germany as P.O.W.
Jnr 3rd Officer	S. Ellis	21	Rescued

Crew

Name	Age	Home Town	Position	Fate
Adams T.	31	Wallasey	Steward	Rescued
Agnew J.	38	Liverpool	Donkeyman	Rescued
Alston S.K.	54	Steyning	2nd Radio Officer	Rescued
Andrews R.W.	24	Birkenhead	3rd Electrician	Rescued
Andrews W.B.	35	Hunstanton	Steward	Lost at sea
Anwyl W.	45	Liverpool	Steward	Rescued
Archibald W.	56	Liverpool	Confectioner	Lost at sea
Armstrong W.	23	Wallasey	Steward	Rescued
Baker J.	28	Grimsby	Deckhand	Rescued
Baker W.	47	Liverpool	Steward	Rescued
Bankier T.	22	Liverpool	Fireman	Lost at sea
Banks J.G.	36	Liverpool	Steward	Lost at sea
Barnard A.	19	Liverpool	Steward	Rescued
Bearsdale F.	36	Manchester	3rd Baker	Lost at sea
Beattie F.	61	Wallasey	Chief Steward	Rescued
Beswick A.	37	Birkenhead	A.B.	Rescued
Beyer A.	19	Liverpool	Sailor	Rescued
Bird S.	20	Liverpool	Sailor	Rescued

Beisty T.	19	Liverpool	Trimmer	Lost at sea
Black W.J.	27	Liverpool	Steward	Rescued
Blackburn N.	29	Manchester	Asst Butcher	Rescued
Blair R.	34	Southend	A.B.	Rescued
Bower W.R.	28	Liverpool	Baker	Lost at sea
Broderick G.	27	Liverpool	Fireman	Lost at sea
Brown A.E.	34	Liverpool	Cabin Waiter	Rescued
Brown A.	24	Bradford	Jnr Engineer	Lost at sea
Brown V.N.	16	Liverpool	Bell Boy	Lost at sea
Bruce H.				Rescued
Buchanan S.	23	Liverpool	Steward	Lost at sea
Buckingham E.W.	27	Plymouth	Sectionman	Lost at sea
Buckley T.	49	Southampton	Steward	Lost at sea
Burke E.J.	64	Liverpool	Lift Attendant	Lost at sea
Burke T.	31	Liverpool	Asst Butcher	Rescued
Cain J.	29	Manchester	Snr 4th Engineer	Rescued
Cain S.J.	21	Wallasey	A/Pantry Steward	Rescued
Calwell J.H.	58	Belfast	Carpenter	Lost at sea
Campbell J.	46	Liverpool	Greaser	Lost at sea
Campbell J.	20	Liverpool	Steward	Rescued
Carlsen J.J.	31	Liverpool	Greaser	Lost at sea
Cartwright J.	35	Liverpool	Captain's Steward	Rescued
Chapman F.	27	Liverpool	Greaser	Rescued
Charnock J.	46	Liverpool	B.R.S.	Rescued
Chawe D.	19	Liverpool	Utility Man	Rescued
Chewles E.	42	S. Shields	Boatswain's Mate	Rescued
Chilton J.	45	Liverpool	Quartermaster	Rescued
Churchill G.	53	Liverpool	Steward	Lost at sea
Clark A.	20	Grangemouth	Jnr Engineer	Rescued
Clarke J.	36	Liverpool	Cook	Rescued
Colbourne W.H.	36	Australia	Cook	Hospitalised in Durban 29.8.42
Colligan G.L.	28	Welshpool	Steward	Rescued
Collins J.	30	Liverpool	K.P.	Rescued
Collum T.	56	Moreton	Purser	Rescued
Coogan M.	33	Dublin	A.B.	Rescued
Coogan S.	32	Liverpool	Greaser	Rescued
Cook P.R.	18	Nottingham	Cabin Waiter	Lost at sea
Cooke C.	21	Westcliffe	Steward	Lost at sea
Cooke G.R.	42	Bournemouth	2nd Steward	Rescued
Cooper D.	20	Brighton	Deckhand	Rescued
Cooper H.C.	20	London	3rd Radio Officer	Rescued
Coulton J.	21	Liverpool	Trimmer	Rescued
Courtney J.	32	Liverpool	Greaser	Lost at sea

Couttie J.	39	Birkenhead	Steward	Lost at sea
Cowan R.	56	Liverpool	Dispenser	Lost at sea
Cullimore J.A.	22	Colne	K.P.	Lost at sea
Cunningham G.	21	Liverpool	Jnr 4th Engineer	Rescued
Davies F.	18	Caistor,Lincs	Cook	Lost at sea
Davies J.R.	34	Aberdare	Cabin Waiter	Rescued
Davies S.C.	36	Wallasey	Cabin Waiter	Lost at sea
Davis H.	41	Liverpool	Asst Baker	Lost at sea
Dawe T.	29	Liverpool	Deckhand	Rescued
Deakin C.	27	Liverpool	Fireman	Rescued
Deane W.B.	41	Liverpool	Steward	Rescued
Devine S.	17	Liverpool	Sailor	Rescued
Dinlan F.P.	18	Liverpool	Pantryman	Rescued
Dixon A.	41	Wellington	1st Radio Officer	Lost at sea
Duckworth H.C.	33	Stratford	Asst Baker	Rescued
Dunkin W.	24	Liverpool	Trimmer	Rescued
Dunn F.	20	Liverpool	A.B.	Lost at sea
Duty N.	39	Bolton	Barber	Lost at sea
Edwards T.	38	Liverpool	Greaser	Rescued
Ellie S.	21	Nelson	Sailor	Rescued
Eyers F.	50	Liverpool	Steward	Rescued
Ellison F.	30	Hindley	Deckhand	Rescued
Fallon J.	20	Liverpool	Trimmer	Lost at sea
Farley T.	22	Liverpool	Asst Cook	Rescued
Faulkner S.T.	23	Alconbury	3rd Butcher	Rescued
Finn F.	20	Liverpool	Fireman	Lost at sea
Fisher A.S.	55	Liverpool	Chief Engineer	Rescued
Fisherman J.	28	London	Steward	Lost at sea
Flannery J.	49	Liverpool	Cabin Waiter	Rescued
Fleet A.W.	19	Liverpool	Cabin Waiter	Rescued
Fleet M.	58	Fleetwood	Steward	Lost at sea
Fox N.	28	Warley	Deckhand	Rescued
Foy R.	26	Manchester	A.B.	Rescued
Gellion R.	22	Liverpool	Sailor	Rescued
George W.	28	Liverpool	Cook	Rescued
Gillies J.	62	Southampton	Chief Butcher	Lost at sea
Golding J.	58	Liverpool	Steward	Rescued
Golding R.	31	London	Deckhand	Rescued
Goode A.C.	58	London	Waiter	Rescued
Greene W.	18	Liverpool	Deckhand	Rescued
Greengrass H.H.	39	Langwith	2nd Cook	Lost at sea
Gregory C.	24	Liverpool	Plumber	Rescued
Griffiths H.	29	Wallasey	Cabin Waiter	Lost at sea
Griffiths I.	55	Liverpool	Greaser	Lost at sea

191

Griffiths J.	17	Liverpool	Sailor	Rescued
Gunnelly J.N.	24	Liverpool	Quartermaster	Rescued
Hall A.	25	Liverpool	A.B.	Rescued
Halliwell J.H.	24	Liverpool	Asst Baker	Lost at sea
Hallwood L.	26	Wallasey	A.B.	Rescued
Hamilton R.	56	Liverpool	Greaser	Lost at sea
Hammond T.	57	Oldham	Baker	Lost at sea
Handley T.	18	Liverpool	Sailor	Rescued
Hanwell A.	24	Leigh	Sectionman	Rescued
Hardacre W.	20	Liverpool	Trimmer	Rescued
Harris J.F.	20	Rhyl	Deckhand	Rescued
Hassan W.	22	Liverpool	A.B.	Rescued
Hayes J.	21	Wallasey	A.B.	Rescued
Hayward J.	54	Birkenhead	Barkeeper	Lost at sea
Healey T.	20	Liverpool	Trimmer	Rescued
Heaney J.J.	22	Liverpool	Sailor	Lost at sea
Hearity E.	22	Liverpool	Trimmer	Lost at sea
Hearity J.	32	Liverpool	Greaser	Lost at sea
Henderson W.	20	Liverpool	Snr 4th Engineer	Died in lifeboat
Hennessey J.	51	Liverpool	Steward	Rescued
Heslop J.	57	Liverpool	Plumber	Lost at sea
Hicks R.J.	32	Wallasey	A.B.	Rescued
Hill C.V.	44	Sutton,Surrey	A/Barkeeper	Lost at sea
Hill G.	26	Liverpool	Cabin Waiter	Lost at sea
Hill J.	18	Birkenhead	Pantryman	Rescued
Hickey J.	22	Liverpool	Steward	Rescued
Hill R.A.	22	Liverpool	Steward	Rescued
Hill R.	22	Hove	Cook	Rescued
Holding F.	20	Liverpool	K.P.	Rescued
Hollingsworth J.	19	Liverpool	Asst Butcher	Rescued
Holman E.	30	Wallasey	A.B.	Rescued
Hoyer W.	21	Liverpool	Utility Man	Rescued
Hughes C.	20	Grimsby	Deckhand	Rescued
Hulme E.	27	Liverpool	Asst Butcher	Rescued
Hurst G.	40	Liverpool	Snr Asst Purser	Rescued
Iredale T.H.	21	Liverpool	Cabin Waiter	Lost at sea
Irish W.	36	London	Deckhand	Lost at sea
Jackson E.	29	Liverpool	Sectionman	Rescued
Jackson F.	23	Liverpool	A.B.	Lost at sea
Jackson N.L.	22	Birkenhead	Cabin Waiter	Lost at sea
Jackson W.A.	49	Glasgow	Snr 3rd Engineer	Lost at sea
James G.	26	Liverpool	Waiter	Rescued
James P.	57	Liverpool	Steward	Rescued
Jameson W.	41	Liverpool	Jnr 3rd Engineer	Rescued

Jasper G.W.	44	Liverpool	Cabin Waiter	Lost at sea
Jensen J.	42	Liverpool	Porter	Rescued
Jervis H.			Cook	Rescued
Johnson E.	19	Liverpool	Asst Butcher	Rescued
Johnston J.E.	27	Liverpool	Fireman	Lost at sea
Jones C.S.	41	Menai Bridge	Baggage Master	Rescued
Jones F.F.	31	Southport	Asst Purser	Lost at sea
Jones W.G.	36	Hereford	Sailor	Rescued
Jones N.K.	19	Birkenhead	A.B.	Lost at sea
Jones W.G.G.	24	Romford	Steward	Rescued
Jones W.O.	56	Liverpool	Steward	Lost at sea
Kelly J.	21	Liverpool	Porter	Rescued
Kennedy P.	26	Liverpool	A.B.	Rescued
Kennedy J.	32	Newcastle	Deckhand	Lost at sea
Kenny P.	15	Liverpool	Deckhand	Rescued
Kirk A.	20	Liverpool	Greaser	Rescued
Lafferty S.	24	Liverpool	Fireman	Lost at sea
Larmour W.	23	Bangor	Deckhand	Lost at sea
Law L.C.	37	Liverpool	Sectionman	Died in lifeboat
Lawford L.E.	54	Liverpool	Printer	Lost at sea
Le Brocq S.	34	Liverpool	Boatswain's Mate	Rescued
Le Coustre C.	43	Liverpool	1st Electrician	Died in lifeboat
Leal V.	30	Ryde I.O.W.	2nd Cook	Rescued
Lee J.	30	Liverpool	Quartermaster	Rescued
Lester J.	37	Dagenham	Deckhand	Lost at sea
Lewis T.H.	40	Liverpool	Chef	Rescued
Lindo S.	47	Kingston	Cook	Lost at sea
Liversage R.	46	Wallasey	Electrician	Rescued
Longden L.	50	Southport	Cook	Lost at sea
Lucas L.	23	Wokingham	Steward	Lost at sea
Lyon J.	17	Liverpool	Waiter	Rescued
Maffey F.	38	Southampton	Greaser	Lost at sea
Maloney D.	22	Liverpool	Waiter	Rescued
Marsh J.B.	36	Birkenhead	Greaser	Lost at sea
Martin J.	19	Birkenhead	Trimmer	Rescued
Mason E.	47	Neston	A/Cook	Lost at sea
Massam T.L.	37	Liverpool	Cook	Lost at sea
Masterson J.	48	Ardrossan	Steward	Rescued
Masterton A.	28	Liverpool	Cook	Lost at sea
Meeham H.	30	Liverpool	Greaser	Lost at sea
Mellis A.	44	Preston	Steward	Rescued
Merrilees F.	38	Liverpool	Hospital Attendant	Lost at sea
Moir N.F.	39	Southampton	Jnr 3rd Engineer	Lost at sea
Mooney P.	26	Liverpool	Fireman	Rescued

Moore J.	41	Wallasey	Storekeeper	Rescued
Morgan J.	30	Wolverh'ton	Steward	Lost at sea
Morley J.H.	22	Dover	Sectionman	Lost at sea
Morris P.	28	Liverpool	Steward	Rescued
Morrison H.	16	Liverpool	Bell Boy	Rescued
Morrisey E.	26	Liverpool	Cook	Rescued
Mulligan J.	35	Glasgow	Deckhand	Rescued
Murphey W.	40	Liverpool	Cook	Rescued
Murphy W.	23	Wrexham	Deckhand	Rescued
Murray O.	28	Liverpool	Sectionman	Rescued
McCallum D.W.	29	Birkenhead	Cabin Waiter	Lost at sea
McCann J.A.	60	Liverpool	2nd Engineer	Lost at sea
McCann J.	56	Liverpool	B.R.S.	Lost at sea
McCarthy J.C.	33	Liverpool	Fireman	Lost at sea
McCarthy C.	42	Liverpool	Steward	Lost at sea
McCracken J.	60	Liverpool	Greaser	Lost at sea
McCrossan S.	63	Liverpool	Steward	Rescued
McDonald C.	60	Liverpool	Steward	Died in lifeboat
McDonald D.	28	Liverpool	Greaser	Rescued
McDonald H.	55	Liverpool	Steward	Died aboard *Gloire* and buried at sea
McGee J.	24	Liverpool	Cook	Rescued
McGilvray D.	55	Liverpool	Carpenter	Lost at sea
MacKenzie M.	18	London	Writer	Rescued
McMann J.	50	Liverpool	Steward	Lost at sea
McMahon	24	Liverpool	A/Butcher	Rescued
McMurray W.E.	32	Liverpool	Cabin Waiter	Rescued
McNamara W.	40	Liverpool	Steward	Rescued
McQuillan J.	31	Liverpool	Greaser	Lost at sea
McVey F.	53	Liverpool	Cook	Died in lifeboat
Nice J.	26	Liverpool	Utility Man	Rescued
Nice L.J.	21	Liverpool	Steward	Rescued
O'Hare	42	Liverpool	Sailor	Lost at sea
O'Leary F.D.	29	Liverpool	Steward	Rescued
O'Toole M.	18	Liverpool	Sailor	Rescued
Ogle A.J.	20	Glenmorris	Electrician	Rescued
Otty J.	19	Liverpool	Sailor	Rescued
Overand H.	49	Liverpool	B.R.S.	Rescued
Owen A.	31	Liverpool	K.P.	Rescued
Parr C.	22	Exning	Steward	Rescued
Parr R.	21	Liverpool	A.B.	Rescued
Partridge A.G.	21	Dover	Sectionman	Rescued
Peck T.	52	Liverpool	Sailor	Lost at sea
Peet W.	16	Liverpool	Waiter	Rescued

Pendleton W.	38	Liverpool	A/Baker	Died in lifeboat
Perkins R.	58	Liverpool	Sectionman	Rescued
Phillips W.	49	Liverpool	Baker	Rescued
Phipps S.H.	58	Liverpool	Jnr 2nd Engineer	Lost at sea
Piggott H.	30	Liverpool	Greaser	Rescued
Pike H.	22	Liverpool	Trimmer	Rescued
Pilkington A.	25	Wallasey	K.P.	Rescued
Plant S.	42	Walsall	Deckhand	Rescued
Podmore A.	31		A/Cook	Rescued
Porter J.	20	Manchester	Deckhand	Rescued
Portet L.1	34	Liverpool	Silverman	Died in lifeboat
Poston J.W.	58	Liverpool	Steward	Lost at sea
Power E.T.	50	Liverpool	Cook	Rescued
Power J.	26	Liverpool	Cook	Rescued
Prince R.	20	Winsford	Deckhand	Lost at sea
Pugh A.	19	Fleetwood	Sailor	Rescued
Purslow G.C.	26	Leek	Surgeon	Died in lifeboat
Randall H.	25	Liverpool	Porter	Lost at sea
Rawsthorne R.	22	Liverpool	Fireman	Lost at sea
Rea R.E.	35	Southport	Cook	Lost at sea
Reeves H.N.	30	Preston	Cook	Lost at sea
Reilly O.	19	Liverpool	Sailor	Rescued
Rice H.	18	Liverpool	Sailor	Rescued
Rickard A.G.	22	Chesterfield	Utility Man	Lost at sea
Rigby J.	32	Liverpool	Chief Steward	Rescued
Riley E.	24	Liverpool	Deckhand	Rescued
Roberts H.	30	Liverpool	Steward	Lost at sea
Roberts R.	23	Liverpool	Master at Arms	Rescued
Robinson G.A.	21	Knockholt	Sectionman	Lost at sea
Ross A.	51	Liverpool	B.R.S.	Lost at sea
Roughley J.	19	Liverpool	Steward	Rescued
Rouse F.	37	King's Lynn	Deckhand	Rescued
Rouse J.	43	Gloucester	A.B.	Lost at sea
Russell J.	18	Liverpool	Sailor	Rescued
Royle J.	45	Wallasey	Boatswain	Lost at sea
Rowlins J.C.	36	Liverpool	A/Storekeeper	Lost at sea
Rowlands W.	21	Liverpool	Quartermaster	Rescued
Sarsfield C.W.	36	Liverpool	Cabin Waiter	Rescued
Scarisbrick N.	28	Liverpool	A/Linen Keeper	Rescued
Scott E.	21	Leeds	Deckhand	Rescued
Scott G.	20	Exeter	Deckhand	Rescued
Scroggie E.	38	Liverpool	2nd Baker	Lost at sea
Shannon W.	27	Liverpool	Greaser	Lost at sea
Sharkey R.	31	Liverpool	Trimmer	Rescued

Sheldon E.H.	27	Plymouth	Sectionman	Lost at sea
Slack C.	39	Liverpool	Steward	Lost at sea
Smart C.	17	Birkenhead	Waiter	Rescued
Smith A.	22	Newington	Deckhand	Rescued
Smith D.	17	Liverpool	Sailor	Rescued
Smith E.	31	Birkenhead	Cabin Waiter	Rescued
Smith J.M.	47	Liverpool	B.R.S.	Lost at sea
Smithson H.	50	Liverpool	Steward	Rescued
Sollas S.	39	London	A/Purser	Died in lifeboat
Sonne P.E.	29	Liverpool	Waiter	Rescued
Stalford T.	17	Widnes	Sailor	Rescued
Stanbury G.	40	Liverpool	A.B.	Rescued
Stephens W.G.	39	Newry 2nd	Butcher	Lost at sea
Stephenson T.	41	Liverpool	B.R.S.	Lost at sea
Strong R.	47	London	Chf Master at Arms	Rescued
Sykes H.	25	Nottingham	Steward	Rescued
Schaefer W.G.	54	Liverpool	B.R.S.	Lost at sea
Tabarn E.	18	Ormskirk	K.P.	Lost at sea
Thomas W.H.	43	Ormskirk	Steward	Rescued
Thompson D.	34	Northwich	A.B.	Lost at sea
Thompson E.	54	Liverpool	Storeman	Lost at sea
Tighe T.	40	Liverpool	Steward	Lost at sea
Tinkler R.	20	Birkenhead	Deckhand	Rescued
Took W.	57	Liverpool	B.R.S.	Lost at sea
Todhunter N.	37	Liverpool	Steward	Lost at sea
Tout R.	24	Lancing	Deckhand	Rescued
Townson J.	28	Liverpool	A.B.	Rescued
Traske L.H.	38	Southampton	Steward	Rescued
Turner A.	27	Monkseaton	Deckhand	Lost at sea
Vincent G.	41	Exeter	Cabin Waiter	Rescued
Vines H.	22	Peterborough	Deckhand	Rescued
Waghorn H.	49	Birkdale	Barkeeper	Rescued
Wainwright D.	49	Wellington	A/Barkeeper	Rescued
Walker C.	18	Liverpool	Pantryman	Rescued
Walker W.	44	Liverpool	Steward	Lost at sea
Waldeis D.	39	Liverpool	A/Barkeeper	Rescued
Wallace P.	44	Liverpool	Steward	Rescued
Walsh T.	38	Liverpool	Greaser	Rescued
Ward W.	47	Leeds	B.R.S.	Lost at sea
Wareham C.A.	35	Liverpool	Head Waiter	Rescued
Warner S.	34	Birkenhead	B.R.S.	Rescued
Washington A.	38	Bolton	Barber	Rescued
Watkinson E.	53	Liverpool	Steward	Rescued
Watters R.	44	Liverpool	B.R.S.	Rescued

Weatherall W.	48	Dewsbury	Cabin Waiter	Rescued
Webster L.	21	Gt Yarmouth	Cabin Waiter	Rescued
Weedon R.	26	Wallasey	A.B.	Rescued
Westbury G.	19	Liverpool	K.P.	Rescued
Weston J.H.	66	Liverpool	A.B.	Lost at sea
White D.	20	Honiton	Deckhand	Rescued
White J.P.	46	Liverpool	Greaser	Lost at sea
Wilwa Q.	57	Longridge	Linen Keeper	Lost at sea
Wills W.	58	Liverpool	Chief Baker	Rescued
Williams E.H.	49	Liverpool	Steward	Rescued
Williams R.	47	Liverpool	B.R.S.	Died in lifeboat
Wood R.	29	Liverpool	Steward	Rescued
Woods G.E.	19	Liverpool	Steward	Rescued
Wright H.	54	Liverpool	Snr 2nd Engineer	Rescued
Yates A.H.	41	Liverpool	2nd Electrician	Lost at sea

Civilian Passengers Lost at Sea

Name	Age	Profession	Last Address
Coombes, Peter	9	Child	Natal
De Luc, Martha	31	Housewife	Durban
De Luc, John	1	Child	Durban
De Luc, Leonie	4	Child	Durban
Greveson H.K.	31	Dredger Captain	Not known
Howe F.A.	35	Army Scripture Reader	Cairo
Lindsay, Dennis	7	Child	Natal
Moore, Jessie	26	Housewife	Malta
McMorran, Joyce	21	Housewife	Durban
Lady Grizel Wolfe-Murray	29	Independent	Scotland
Nicholas, Evelyn	48	Housewife	Malta
Qualters P.J.	26	Army Civilian	Birkdale, Lancs
Readman, Sally	1	Child	Cairo
Reynolds F.C.	62	1st Engineer (M.N.)	Not known
Stanbridge, Susan	35	Housewife	Durban
Upchurch, Bertram	24	Army Civilian	Sutton, Surrey

Crew members who 'Signed off' before Laconia's final voyage

Name	Town
Allen C.	Radcliffe
Allen J.	Liverpool
Bailey F.	Sparseton
Bakewell C.	Liverpool

197

Banker W.L.	Liverpool
Barlow S.	Liverpool
Barnes E.	Liverpool
Borrows A.	Liverpool
Bartley C.	Liverpool
Berry M.	Widnes
Bradshaw A.K.	London
Burns W.G.	Birkenhead
Canning J.	Liverpool
Carter W.	London
Caregan T.	Liverpool
Caulfield J.	Liverpool
Colbourne W.H.	Australia
Connors G.M.	St John's, Newfoundland
Crawford H.	Liverpool
Critchley J.	Rainhill
Crossley R.	London
Croucher H.M.	Massachusetts, U.S.A.
Cunningham J.	Liverpool
Daley V.	Liverpool
Davies W.	Liverpool
Donaldson W.	Fife
Dunning C.J.	Wallasey
Ebbs J.	Liverpool
Ellman M.	Liverpool
Farrell T.	Liverpool
Fitzpatrick J.	Liverpool
Fitzwilliams J.	Dublin
Flusk T.	Liverpool
France J.	Manchester
Francis E.	Richmond
Friend J.	Dover
Gellian T.	Liverpool
Greenwood A.	Goole
Gregory S.C.	Wallasey
Cresty N.D.	Wallasey
Grossmith T.H.	Liverpool
Hacking J.A.	Liverpool
Halligan J.	Liverpool
Hanlon G.	Liverpool
Hanlon J.	Liverpool
Hannon E.	Liverpool
Hardwick F.	Liverpool
Harrison W.C.	Liverpool

Healey F.	Liverpool
Hill W.J.	Liverpool
Hoffman E.	Nova Scotia
Hughes J.	Liverpool
Jenkinson T.	Liverpool
Kavanagh P.	Louth
Keating R.	Birkenhead
Keegan B.	Liverpool
Kilgour C.	Liverpool
Lafferty J.	Liverpool
Lennand K.J.	London
Lockett A.	Liverpool
Longhurst W.	Chatham
McDonald A.	Radcliffe
McGregor R.	Liverpool
McLachlan W.	Liverpool
McLurg O.	West Hartlepool
McPhillips J.	Glasgow
Masters R.	Birmingham
Morton W.	Rutherglen
Mullins A.	London
O'Connell D.	Liverpool
Osborne M.D.	Liverpool
Owens H.	Liverpool
Parkes T.C.	Liverpool
Passmore W.H.	Crediton
Piper W.	Liverpool
Prytherch R.	Liverpool
Reid A.	Liverpool
Rhodes F.	Bradford
Richards L.C.	Liverpool
Rourke P.	Birkenhead
Rushton T.	Liverpool
Ryan J.	Liverpool
Sharnock P.	London
Sims S.	Liverpool
Smallbone E.	London
Slavin T.	Liverpool
Smith A.	Newington
Smith F.	Canada
Smith G.	London
Smith F.	Hendley
Smith G.A.	Manchester
Smith R.	London

Starkey H.	Liverpool
Starkey P.	Liverpool
Steel R.	Whitley Bay
Stephenson T.	Liverpool
Stevenson S.	Wallasey
Stripe V.	London
Swinburn L.	Liverpool
Taafe A.F.	Wallasey
Thom J.	Kilmarnock
Thompson E.	Liverpool
Thorpe G.	London
Ward P.D.	Liverpool
Watson M.	Cockermouth
Watson R.	Liverpool
Welch R.	Gillingham
Wheeler C.F.	Liverpool
Whitmore W.J.	Liverpool
Wilkie T.H.	Liverpool
Williams W.	Glamorgan
Woods R.	Isle of Man
Woodworth H.	Birkenhead
Woodward L.	Nottingham

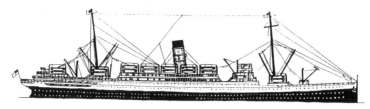

APPENDIX 2

POLISH MANIFEST

Andrychowski Józef, strz
Antyporowicz Aleksander, strz
Balicki Józef, strz
Baranowski Poniżnik, strz
Bartoszewski Bronisław, strz
Bartoszewski Piotr, strz
Brodzinski Wiesław, strz
Chlebak Emeryk, strz
Cygan Michał, plut
Czuryk Edward, strz
Debrych Jan, strz
Dobrowolski Tadeusz, strz
Dragan Jeremi, strz
Frączek Julian, strz
Godzik Władysław, strz
Groszek Zbigniew, ppor
Hampel Roman, strz
Jakowlew Bronisław, strz
Jarema Antoni, kapr
Jasiczek Leon, st. strz
Jasiukowski Józef, strz
Jaskułowski Leon, strz
Jaszczur Aleksander, strz
Jełowicki Julian, strz
Kaczmarek Teofil, plut
Kajpus Czesław, strz
Kamarnicki Czesław, strz
Kirejczuk Ludwik, kpt
Klimkowski Józef, strz
Kojpusa Bronisław, st. strz
Krauze Bronisław, strz
Kubicki Henryk, strz

Kundycki Jacek, strz
Matusiak Stanisław, kpr
Moroz Jan, strz
Moszyński Jerzy, strz
Mróz Józef, plut
Myszkowski Henryk, kpr
Olejnik Wacław, kpr
Panczyj Tadeusz, st. strz
Pietrusiewicz Stanisław, strz
Przybylik Stefan, strz
Pyrć Stanisław, strz
Rej Janusz, st. strz
Rózga Wacław, plut
Rychlicki Ludwik, kpr
Rymaszewski Stanisław, strz
Semezyński Stefan, strz
Soroko Kazimierz, strz
Spring Adam, strz
Startek Eugeniusz, st. strz
Swiderski Witold, kpr
Swolkień Kazimierz, kpr
Talarski Zdzisław, strz
Tarłowski Tadeusz, strz
Tokarski Stanisław, st. strz
Trembicki Wiesław, strz
Uher Zdzisław, strz
Walczak Tadeusz, strz
Walewski Jerzy, strz
Wargocki Longin, kpr
Węgrzyn Stanisław, strz
Wilczyński Emeryk, kpr
Wilczyński Stefan, kpr

Witek Józef, strz

Wójcik Zdzisław, strz

Wygnał Edward, kpr

Zagrajski Jerzy, strz

Zamrej Andrzej, strz

Żyłek Witold, plut

Poles Lost at Sea

Bartosz Antoni, kpr

Borkowski Tadeusz, strz

Buda Jan, strz

Bujko (or Buyko) Władysław, kpr

Darski Mieczysław, kpr

Dragan Józef, strz

Dynkowski, strz (died 27.9.1942)

Giżycki Zdzisław, strz

Górski Jozef, st. strz

Halaumbrener Zbigniew, strz

Jasiński Feliks, strz

Kosiński Kazimierz, strz

Kwieciński Józef, strz

Lacheta Zbigniew, strz

Lidmajer Zygmunt, strz

Lorenc Adam, strz

Mucha Jan, st. sierż

Niemczycki Władysław, strz

Nowak Piotr, strz

Ogiński Michał, strz

Siegel Edward, sierz

Szaluk Jan, plut pchor

Szwerdykiewicz-Kowalewski
     Edward, strz

Tymburski Bolesław, strz

Urbaniak Władysław, strz

Wardyński Zdzisław, strz

Wąsowski Józef, sierż

Weryński Stefan, strz

Wodzicki Andrzej, strz

Wójcik Ludwik, sierż

Woźniakowski Sylwester, strz

The Polish list has been supplied by survivor Andrew Zamrej. The English titles of these Polish officer cadets are:

  kpr = corporal; *st. strz* = lieut. corporal; *strz* = private; *plut* and *sierz* = sergeant;

    plut pchor = instructor sergeant cadet officer; *st. sierż* = sergeant major

Unfortunately efforts to locate a full list of the other service personnel, such as the RAF and Royal Navy passengers, and of the Italian prisoners and civilian passengers, were not productive.

APPENDIX 3
EXTRACT FROM THE WAR DIARY OF MARCO REVEDIN, 1941, THE *CAPPELLINI* SUBMARINE

On the morning of 13th September, we received the order to proceed at full speed to the area (about 800 miles away from us) where an English liner had been sunk, with 1,500 [sic] Italian prisoners on board.

On the 14th at mid-day we crossed the Equator; the sea was continually swelling because we had entered into the area of the trade winds from the SE. For the whole of the 15th September, we continued at full speed towards the shipwreck point. Finally at 8 a.m. on the 16th we sighted the first lifeboat which was sailing towards the African coast (it had red sails which were very visible from afar). In the boat there were about 50 shipwrecked people, soldiers and sailors. They were very well organised, they had a map and compass and even a radio transmitter with a pedal dynamo. They said that they were all English, shipwrecked from the liner the *Laconia* following a torpedo attack. They told me there were many other lifeboats at sea in the direction I was going in. They asked for water. I gave them a number of bottles full of water and a few bottles of wine, then I left; the shipwrecked people expressed their thanks and gave the Fascist salute. In this scene and in all those which followed I ran the ship's camera. At 11 we sighted another red sail from the *Laconia*; it was in poorer condition and certainly less well equipped than the former. On board there were 41 men (all English), 18 women, 25 children (all below 6 years old and two of them were just a few months old). When we approached the women cried and screamed and they showed us the children as well as a box with a red cross painted on top. They thought we were going to open fire on them, as they would have been led to believe by English propaganda. Given the rather precarious conditions they found themselves in, being so many on a boat which was already in a rather poor state, and considering the sea conditions which seemed to be getting worse, I offered to take on board the women and children, not being able to take the men because there were so many of them. They replied that they preferred to stay on the boat because their respective husbands were with them (the distance to the nearest coast is 780 miles). One of the women was Venetian, married to an Englishman, and she acted as an interpreter. They asked for some blankets for the children, some water, and if possible something warm. I couldn't give them blankets but I provided them with a barrel of water, 2 or 3 mess-tins of hot broth, some wine, biscuits, chocolate and cigarettes. They also asked for a map and compass but I could not give them those; instead I indicated in which direction they should be sailing to reach the coast. They said that further ahead on our present course we would find six boats full of Italians. When we left, the shipwrecked people thanked us, and they cried 'Viva il Duce,' giving the Fascist salute. They then shouted out in English 'See you when the war's over.'

At 1600 hours we arrived in the zone of the above-mentioned lifeboats. It was a real tragedy: there were 4 intact rowing boats, another one was overturned with many people hanging on to the outsides, the sea was covered in debris and corpses and there were about a hundred shipwrecked people scattered here and there in the water. Many of the corpses had had their hands cut off, others had been half-eaten by sharks; many of the shipwrecked, when they saw us, made a desperate attempt to reach us, but many died only a few metres away. I moved upwind of the area, then I stopped lengthways to the swell, so that I could drift towards the shipwrecked people and pick them up easily, sheltered from the wind.

The first 2 shipwrecked people which I took on board were Italians, and they immediately told me that on the *Laconia* there had been 1,800 Italian prisoners travelling from Suez and heading for England where they had been requested as workers. At the moment of the torpedo attack, the Italians had been divided into various holds on board. They found themselves enclosed by iron gates; when they tried to force them, the English fired at them, as there were no lifeboats or inflatables for them. It's calculated that about 1,400 Italian prisoners went to the bottom enclosed in the hull of the *Laconia*. It seems that only one hold, of about 400 Italians, managed to force open the gates and overcome their English [sic] guards. Some of these 400 managed to take life-jackets from the English, and about 90 managed to take a boat, throwing its occupants into the sea. The other boats on which there were English, New Zealanders, Poles etc. defended themselves with axes, cutting off the hands of those who grasped the sides. Only the Poles accepted a few Italians on board. In the meantime the German submarine had already broadcast by radio the presence of Italian prisoners on the *Laconia* and already other submarines like the *Cappellini* had received the order to proceed to the disaster area. Even some French warships had set sail from Dakar with the same intentions. Of the

German submarines two had already arrived. One had put on board 130 people, amongst them Italians, women and children and it had left. The other had arrived on the morning of the 16th. It had taken in tow the lifeboats and had been fishing out of the water all the Italians, English and Poles that were there. But about 3 hours before my arrival, an American 4-motor aeroplane called the 'Catalina' [sic] had arrived above them and although the submarine was sporting a large white flag with a red cross and had signalled that it was saving English shipwrecked, the aeroplane started to bomb and machine-gun the submarine and the boats, turning one of them over and completely destroying another. The German submarine, after suffering two violent bomb blasts, had sent all the shipwrecked people back on to the deck of the submarine, and then it had submerged, leaving them in the water. This is what the shipwrecked people told me. Having been given this information I had to take an unpleasant decision; given the possibility of air strikes I had to be on continual standby, ready to submerge. Therefore I could only take on board 30-40 people; what should I do with the rest? Allowing the boat to drift diagonally to the swell, towards the point where the shipwrecked people were most numerous, I began to pick out of the water as many people as I could; I immediately sent all Italians down into the submarine to be looked after and fed. The non-Italians I left on the deck to deal with later. This method of allowing the boat to drift towards the shipwrecked people brought with it an unpleasant inconvenience, namely that on the downwind side a large number of corpses began to accumulate.

Then I circled the boats; from one of them, which was full of water, I took on board 10 shipwrecked people (all English) in order to allow the others to pump the water out and to keep the boat afloat. I found another boat which was almost completely submerged and badly damaged in which there were 2 Italians, one in the prow, a Neapolitan who was shouting desperately, the other in the stern who was laughing and joking; he was playing with the water and didn't even look at us when we approached. Because of sea conditions I couldn't get too near to the boat so from about 15 metres we threw out lifelines. The Neapolitan grabbed hold and didn't let go until he had arrived on the deck of the submarine. The other one took hold of the lifeline, played around with it a bit and then threw it back into the water. I then realised he was completely mad [this was probably as much a result of drinking sea water as of his desperate situation]. When it was dark I abandoned the search but remained in the area of the boats. There were 49 Italians on board and many Englishmen on the deck, Poles, New Zealanders etc. These could only remain on deck in rather limited

73. Italian submarine *Cappellini.*

numbers, that is, only those who were down wind from the tower, otherwise the waves carried them away. In the morning there were 19; they were wet and frozen but they felt better when I gave them some hot broth, biscuits and cigarettes. Many of them were carrying life-jackets and to make them wear them I felt obliged to inform them that, because English aeroplanes were bombing whoever was trying to save the shipwrecked people, should an aeroplane be spotted I would have to submerge, leaving them outside. In the meanwhile the inside of the submarine had become to all intents a hospital. There was not one centimetre of empty space. Those coming off duty, before being able to sleep for a few hours on the floor, had to take very long turns. Amongst the shipwrecked there were 2 seriously ill with high fevers and others who were injured. One Milanese man, upon seeing the *Cappellini*, had taken off his life-jacket and swum to the ship even though one of his calves had been bitten off by a shark. The 2 most seriously ill died on the morning of the 17th and I gave them a burial at sea. [The official log of the *Cappellini* gives their names as 'Not definitely identifiable but known by the other survivors as Vincenzo or Ruggero the Nurse' and 'Infantryman Giovanni Volch di Giovanni of the class of 1912'.]

Meanwhile those vessels which had remained afloat became more and more scattered because some of them raised improvised sails while others remained rowing boats and they became blown off course by the wind as well as by the current (which was about 2 knots towards the NW); others were full of water and were just drifting with the current so I couldn't manage to keep them together. Finally, in the afternoon of the 17th, submarine command telegraphed and told me to go to a zone where there were some French ships from whom I could ask for assistance in saving the shipwrecked and I could transfer over those I had on board. I circled round the lifeboats again in order to replenish them with food and water. In those boats which were less full I distributed the shipwrecked people I had on deck. I told everybody to wait and to try to stay together while I went and called the French ships. I made the 2 English officers prisoners, then I left at full speed towards the above mentioned zone. Before dawn on the 18th, arriving in the zone of the French ships, I saw an illuminated war ship which was sailing away from me (it was certainly French). I tried to reach it at full speed but the ship was much faster than the *Cappellini*. I sent out recognition signals and then called with the heliograph but this was not seen and it continued to sail further away until it went out of sight. During this chase the sea took away various metal plates and stanchions from the deck. At dawn, having lost all hope of immediately finding the French, we submerged and implemented battle drill, to see how the submarine performed with 110 people on board. I continued the search for the French ships and in the meantime I instituted strict rationing of water and food (out of every 3 rations I made 5). I questioned the shipwrecked, who by now were 47, about their imprisonment and about their journey on board the *Laconia* and compiled a list of information. They had nearly all been made prisoners at El Alamein. There was one of them who was made prisoner at Tobruk. Amongst them there was a sergeant-major who had been an interpreter for an English command in Egypt, who therefore had some really interesting information on the fortification at Alexandria, on the distribution of some ships, on the morale of the English, etc. As to the 2 English officers, Frank Penman and Lieut. Pilot in the Royal New Zealand Airforce Arthur Edgar Boyett, officer R.T., for the moment I kept them with the other shipwrecked people and gave them the same treatment. In the meantime I was desperately looking for a ship on which to transfer at least 40 people because I realised that it was absolutely impossible to keep them all on board (at first I had thought of disembarking them on one of the Cape Verde islands but they were still very far away). Apart from difficulties with food, water and breathable air, it was impossible to teach these people in such a short period of time how one lives on a submarine, how to use the latrines, when you can move and when you can't, where to throw rubbish away etc.

I typed a letter in French with neither a signature nor the name of the *Cappellini,* in which I specified precisely the position of the 300 English and Poles that I had left in the lifeboats, which I intended to give to the first ship that I met. Finally, on the morning of the 20th and after 3 days searching I noticed smoke on the horizon. This was a critical moment because when I made the French recognition signal it didn't reply but headed straight for me. I now understood that it was a destroyer but if it was English I would have little time to submerge. It finally responded to my signal and raised a large French flag.

In order to be sure, I asked for its name. It replied immediately and it was the *Dumont d'Urville.* Then it came to a halt and lowered into the sea a motor boat and a lifeboat. The lifeboat, especially for the injured people, was rendered very uncomfortable by the rough sea, so I told the officer in the motor boat to go back on board and tell his commander to bring the ship upwind of me so we could board alongside. I gave him the letter which I'd prepared. At 11.30 the shipwrecked people disembarked. I circled around the *d'Urville* and headed east in order to hide my true course from them. I kept on board the 2 English prisoners and 6 Italians (those who had the most information, one who had 4 children and wanted to go back

209

to Italy, and a *carabiniere* who would guard the prisoners). At 12.30, whilst the French ship was still in sight, I saw the outline of a destroyer on the horizon. I submerged so as not to be seen. First I thought it was the *Annamite*, a French ship which I knew was in that area; but since on the hydrophone I could hear it had a turbine engine (whilst the *Annamite* has a steam engine), I realised it must be English. After about 2 hours I could hear nothing else and I raised the turret. I saw the destroyer stationary, very near (perhaps it was waiting for me). I submerged immediately to a depth of 90 metres. I waited until night fell, then re-emerged and found I had shaken it off. When I told the 2 English officers that they were prisoners of war, they were very happy and they told me that they'd finally finished fighting the war. They also told me that they had been afraid that I would keep them as hostages to be put on the deck in the eventuality of combat (effects of war propaganda). I had 2 beds made for them in the torpedo room. They were allowed to eat in the officers' quarters. I established a timetable when they could smoke a cigarette in the mess room and set up a guard watch amongst the shipwrecked Italians to keep an eye on them.

[The survivors from the *Cappellini* were later transferred from the *Dumont d'Urville* to the *Annamite*. The *Cappellini* returned to its main theatre of operations and attempted to engage the British cargo vessel *Bruyere*, but it had to abandon the attempt because of engine failure. It made its way slowly towards Bordeaux, arriving there on the afternoon of 17 October 1942. Its wartime adventures were not over, however. For when Italy surrendered it was seized by the Japanese at Sabang (Indonesia), handed to the Germans, seized back by the Japanese when Germany surrendered and eventually sunk at Kobe at the end of the war. All the other submarines in its class were lost in the Atlantic or the Mediterranean. Translation of the diary made by Paul Watkins from the unpublished typescript.]

74. Marco Revedin and Sub-Lt Disiervo from the Italian submarine *Cappellini*.

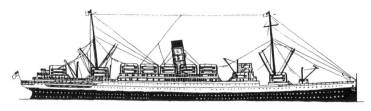

APPENDIX 4
THE ACCOUNT OF CLAUDE JONES

Claude Jones was a baggage master on the *Laconia* at the time of her sinking. He wrote this account for the 'I Was There' section in the last few issues of the *War Illustrated*. It is interesting both as a well-written contemporary account which contains a few details not recorded elsewhere and also for its moments of propaganda, notably the behaviour of the Germans, French and Italians and the absence of any mention of the Liberator attack. It appeared in issues 252 and 253 of the magazine in 1947, by which time the author had been promoted to purser on the *Wanderer*.

The alarm gongs were sounding and men, women and children were hurrying to the companion ladders. The life was dying out of the ship, for the engines were in course of being stopped. There was no indication of her sinking quickly, although no one could be sure that the unseen submarine would not slam another torpedo into her. I was in no rig suitable for a voyage in an open boat, even in the tropics, and that was the prospect conveyed by the signal to abandon ship. So instead of joining the throng swarming up the companion ladders I went back to my quarters, donned a reefer coat and life-jacket, pulled on a pair of shoes and grabbed an electric torch.

The *Laconia* was slowly settling by the head. My emergency station was Number 2 lifeboat, and it was up to me to go there by the shortest route and assist with whatever had to be done. A babel of voices and shuffling of feet suggested what is most dreaded in a crowded, sinking ship – panic. The moment I gained the open deck I was caught in a milling mob of frenzied, shouting Italians. I had to fight to avoid being knocked down and trampled on. By violent effort I broke clear, only to discover that Number 2 lifeboat, badly damaged, was hanging uselessly from a single davit. I turned back along the darkened deck, evading crazed Italians and refraining from using my torch lest it should be snatched from my hand.

The task of abandoning ship was becoming increasingly difficult. The confusion among the prisoners was serious, and another adverse factor was that the *Laconia* was not only settling deeper but taking a gradual list to starboard. Struggling Italians jammed the ladders, and I took a chance by climbing a stanchion to gain the boat-deck near Number 8 lifeboat; it was necessary to hold them at bay whilst the women and children were placed in the boats. I was ordered to help in keeping a space clear. The prisoners came at us like howling dervishes in their efforts to rush the boat. We used only our fists and feet, but elsewhere aboard the sinking ship shots were being fired by the Polish guards.[1] Throughout the whole nerve-racking ordeal the British women and children made no fuss and obeyed all commands in an orderly manner.

An officer urged us to 'get going', and I slid down the falls of Number 8 lifeboat, burning my hands red-raw and bruising body and legs against the ship's hull. I alighted between the thwarts in the boat, and was hammered flat on the floorboards by one of the Italians crashing on top of me. It was meant to hold 75. More than 100 were piled in it, and the frenzied prisoners started scrapping among themselves again, with the result that a number went over the side.

In a dazed kind of way I was aware of someone shouting 'Shove off! Shove off!' The overcrowded boat had very little free-board and was in imminent danger of being holed by bumping against the *Laconia*'s side in the heavy ocean swell. I scrambled up, helped to unhook the falls and fend off, and the boat was rowed clear with 14 Italians in the water clinging to the sides. It was then discovered that our rudder was missing. Four seamen plied a pair of oars, and elbow room had somehow to be made for them.

When the boat rose high the *Laconia* showed as a dark silhouette against the night sky – until her boilers burst and she disappeared below the waves. Lamps and torches denoted the position of other boats and the rafts, and one area of the dark waters was spread with tiny red lights like gleaming rubies. Modern life-jackets have a small red lamp attached to enable the position of the wearers to be seen in the darkness of night. The coloured lights we saw marked the men who had failed to find a place in one of the undamaged boats or on the rafts. A jacket of kapok and canvas was their one link between life and death. Our Number 8 boat was now riding so low in the water that we had only four inches of freeboard.

The night seemed unending and daybreak found only two other boats in sight; we drew within hailing distance and all set a course eastward for the African coast. A count was made of the number in our boat – 102 survivors, including many women, several children between the ages of

---

[1]   More likely to have been the English soldiers as the Poles apparently had no ammunition.

eight and fifteen, and two babies in arms. Our breakfast consisted of a biscuit, a small cube of chocolate, a Horlick's tablet and an egg-cupful of water. Two or three Italians still alongside were hitched to the boat with grab-lines under their seats, and fed with similar fare in the same quantity.

The sea rose under a freshening wind. We were all drenched to the skin, and the boat had to be baled out constantly. Even the schoolgirls with us took turn with the baling cans, and their youthful spirits transformed a grim ordeal into a semblance of gay adventure. Slow progress was made, and anxiety became acute the following night owing to a slightly heavier sea. Work at the oars took severe toll of our strength owing to the meagre rations; and those Italians hitched alongside had a grim passage, although the sea was warm. We did all we could for them short of taking them aboard, for any such attempt would have been madness, with over 100 lives at stake; nor were the other boats in any better position to help. There was no callousness toward them, quite the reverse; and happily I am able to say that they endured the intense discomfort manfully and survived the ordeal. Other Italians with us in the boat were well treated and lived to tell the tale – the true tale I hope.

Early next morning a naval rating huddled next to me bemoaned the slow progress. 'The breeze is favourable,' he said, 'what about trying to step the mast and spread a sail?' The job could be done in less than half-an-hour in harbour. But out on the ocean in our tightly-packed boat with a bare four inches of freeboard it took the entire day. The mast was under the thwarts, and slow, systematic reshuffling of many people was needed to get it out without upsetting the lifeboat. Then, with extreme care, one end had to be lifted and the mast dragged back inch by inch. Finally, at even greater peril, it had to be raised while the boat was kept head-on and rode its switchback course over the Atlantic rollers.

The mainsail was eventually clewed to the mast and gradually hoisted, while those taking no active part in rigging the boat sat tensely in expectation of being flung into the sea at any moment. Sail was set without mishap, and a seaman remained by the halliards ready to let go instantly should a squall threaten or the improvised steering with an oar fail to keep the boat on a safe course. We parted company from the other boats. Good progress was made in fair weather during the night, and hopes ran high of reaching the African coast. But our boat never made a landfall.

Once again an issue of rations was made. I sat in the stern squeezed between an R.A.F. officer and a Chief Petty Officer of the Royal Navy and received my fair whack like the rest of the tightly packed mob. That breakfast of a biscuit, small cube of chocolate, a Horlick's tablet and eggcupful of water was not my idea of a meal to start the day. My mind's eye conjured a vision of ham and eggs with buttered rolls and fragrant coffee. The remarkable thing was how the women and children who had endured the ocean ordeal for so long remained outwardly cheerful in spite of ever-present danger. No one knew how long the voyage must continue, or how soon the weather would break with disastrous result to all.

Suddenly the indigo sea was disturbed by a white flurry of foam. All except the sleeping babes-in-arms stared wide-eyed as a grey-green object thrust itself above the surface like the snout of some prehistoric monster. It was the conning tower of a submarine, and within a matter of seconds part of the hull loomed into view with the sea rolling from it in hissing cascades. The markings on it were unrecognisable; at least, no one was able to identify the nationality of the craft. We gazed, hypnotised, as it surfaced a couple of cables' lengths away on the port beam. One or two seamen of the *Laconia*'s crew were first to recover the use of their tongues; but one guess was as good as another.

The submarine cruised along slowly on a parallel course to our own. No ensign was flown, but the general appearance of the men who came out of the hatches and their guttural tones suggested that the vessel was German.

I looked at the R.A.F. officer next to me and read my own thoughts reflected in his eyes. We expected our lifeboat to be machine-gunned. There was a period of heart-searing suspense. Already in the Atlantic the sea-wolves had carried out the Nazi orders to 'sink without trace'. Cramped and helpless, we awaited tensely the grim finale to another tragedy of the sea while the Germans stood by the guns.

No further threatening move was made, however, and we began to breathe more freely. The submarine drew ahead, then slowed down and manoeuvred nearer. The commander could be seen plainly – a young man with a downy beard,[1] wearing dark-blue battle-dress and armed with a Mauser pistol. After scrutinizing us in silence for a time, he hailed our boat in fluent English: 'I am going to stop. Take down your sail and come alongside!'

The C.P.O. seated beside me gave the order 'Lower away!' and expressed the general feeling when he added, 'There's no sense in disobeying the swab.' We moved cumbrously alongside the U-boat, which had hove-to. The German commander looked down from the conning tower bridge, but did not see the Italians. These had squirmed under the

---

[1] No other accounts mention that Hartenstein had a beard. Perhaps he was simply unshaven. This might even have been Würdemann on U-506.

thwarts, where they remained hidden; the two or three still in the water were at the far side of the lifeboat and also concealed from view.

Those prisoners were scared stiff of the Huns, their allies. They knew that if taken aboard the U-boat the German captain would endeavour to repatriate them – and they wanted no more active soldiering after their experience in the Western Desert. So they kept out of sight, fearing rescue by their Hun 'friends' more than anything else that might befall them.

After a prolonged survey of us, the submarine commander brusquely asked: 'How many are in the boat?' Someone told him the number – 102. The German raised his eyebrows and, addressing our packed boatload in general, remarked: 'English seamen are all right – but ach, your Government! Why don't you British give up the war, causing all this suffering?' He spoke with disarming sincerity, apparently unaware of the irony conveyed to us victims of ruthless submarine attack. 'By hokey!' the C.P.O. muttered. 'That's rich, if you like!'

Like others, I was wondering whether this might be the same U-boat which had sunk the *Laconia* without warning. The truth about this, however, was never discovered. The U-boat commander stroked his beard and expressed his sympathy. Using his conning tower bridge as a 'soap-box', he made a speech in which he attributed our plight solely to a vicious Government who had misled the British public at the instigation of 'their overlords'. He blamed us victims only for our own blindness and folly. His speech was the familiar Nazi rigmarole such as Dr Goebbels, Lord Haw-Haw and others broadcast repeatedly. Of course, he ignored the black record of the Nazi regime and the acquiescence of the German public in the overrunning of Poland and other ill-defended countries.[1]

We were wet, cramped and weakened and in no mood for political argument – not that it is ever much good arguing with the fellow who has a machine-gun to back his opinions. We were mightily relieved when he got down to brass tacks. 'Your perfidious Government has got you into trouble,' he said, 'but I will give you what help I can. You will come on board a few at a time. And I will give you good food.'

This was a surprise indeed, and many of us were still suspicious. A U-boat commander in the role of Good Samaritan and his ship providing a hostel for British survivors! What he said, or his kindly tone, so impressed two of our Italians that they changed their mind about lying doggo. They came from under the thwarts and allowed themselves to be 'rescued'; but the others stayed out of sight. The pair that surrendered for the sake of

[1] No other accounts mention the preaching of propaganda by the German U-boat captains.

getting a meal were taken aboard the U-boat, and to do them justice they did not squeal on their comrades.

The women and children were lifted out of the lifeboat and given something to eat and drink by the Germans. Other small parties went aboard in turn, and were fed from large bowls of soup placed on the steel deck for'ard of the conning tower. The soup and bread were a godsend, but what I enjoyed even more was the chance to stretch my cramped limbs. On this occasion the sea-wolves had not run true to form! They had assumed sheep's clothing. Nevertheless, I suspected an ulterior motive by reason of what occurred while I and some of my shipmates were being fed.

One of the Germans came through the conning tower hatch and handed a small cine-camera to the young commander, who leaned over the bridge and shot a reel of film to record the scene on the foredeck. There was little doubt in my mind that this pictorial record was intended for the dual purpose of proving that a successful attack had been made against a British transport and for propaganda by demonstrating the humanity of German U-boat crews towards their victims.[1]

Refreshed by the food and comparative freedom we returned to our boat, the submarine standing by. Then the German commander addressed us again. 'It is bad,' he said, 'that women and children should suffer for the sins of a criminal Government. They have permission to come on board the Unterseeboot again. I will give them more food, and they may dry the clothes. You can trust me,' he added, when no one stirred. 'I give my word of honour they shall be well cared for.'

After some discussion the invitation was accepted. The women and children were transferred again to the U-boat and that gave blessed relief to the rest of us. It was good to be able to stretch the legs and move about without fear of capsizing. We raised sail, and the submarine cruised slowly near us. During the short tropic twilight the young commander reappeared on his bridge and made another announcement that caused us some anxiety. 'I am going to dive,' he said. 'Your women and children will stay with me to rest tonight. Tomorrow morning I will give them back. You must sail slowly and keep the course you are on now.'

The C.P.O. demanded, 'What are you going to do after that?' To this the German answered that he intended to radio a signal and try to arrange for a ship to make a rendezvous and take all of us aboard. With that we had to be content. And the Italians who were still in the water and had remained unseen were more than content when the U-boat submerged and

[1] It is not known if this film, or that taken by Revedin from the *Cappellini*, survive. The filming is mentioned by several survivors.

216

we hauled them into our boat. Those fellows had got on our nerves. We had been inclined to hand them over to the Jerries, but they had pleaded desperately to be allowed to stay where they were. Now they were curling up in the boat, catching up with much-needed sleep.

Nothing at all was seen of the U-boat during the hours of darkness. When daybreak came we scanned the sea for a sight of her periscope, wondering if the German would keep his promise and return. The sun lifted above the horizon and gilded the waves. Then, suddenly, one of our seamen, whose pre-war service had been in a whaling ship, drew attention to a burst of foam: 'There she blows!' The submarine had kept her tryst.

Whatever ruthlessness the German commander and crew were capable of in active warfare was now hidden beneath a veneer of good will. It is only fair to record that we and the survivors in two other lifeboats received generous consideration that was as gratifying as it was exceptional. Once more we were allowed to board the submarine, in batches, and fed with stew in the lee of a 4.7 gun while the seawater sluiced over our feet. Our women and children were returned dry and rested to the lifeboat, and the fact that they were soon drenched again with spray was nobody's fault. Finally, we were given some rations, water, cigarettes and matches, and the German commander ordered us to proceed on an easterly course and wished us luck before sheering off.

Our lifeboat made progress on an easterly course, switchbacking over the long Atlantic rollers. Packed like sardines, we spent a restless, uncomfortable night but enjoyed a fair breakfast, thanks to the extra rations. Haze made visibility poor, and we had no expectations of sighting a sail when, quite startlingly, at eleven o'clock in the morning, a grotesque shadow loomed into view. A ship! Rescue at last! That was the instant reaction. The vessel came nearer, and with fading hopes we saw it was another submarine.

'It's a "guinea"!' a seaman ejaculated, using the Merchant Navy slang meaning an Italian. He was correct. The approaching craft unfurled an ensign from the short staff abaft the conning tower bridge, and suspense was almost unbearable as the enemy hove-to and signalled for us to moor alongside. Here were sea-wolves of a different tribe. We could hardly expect this encounter to pass off as the previous one had, especially with Italians among us who might give a garbled account of what had occurred to many of their companions when the *Laconia* had been torpedoed. But again our prisoners went to cover under the thwarts, even less inclined for rescue by their own countrymen than by the Germans.

THE SINKING OF THE LACONIA

The Italian submarine commander spoke English, and his first question did nothing to relieve our anxiety. 'Have you seen any Italian prisoners?' he demanded. The Naval C.P.O. acted as our spokesman. 'No,' he replied. He feared, like the rest of us, that if these submariners suspected loss of life among Italian prisoners the consequences might be serious for us.

The commander looked down upon our crowded boat and asked the name of the ship that had been sunk. He repeated the question, but no one told him. He shrugged his shoulders, and put another query about the nationality of the attacker. 'We were torpedoed by a German,' the C.P.O. told him. We could not be sure of this, but it proved a good answer, because the Italian captain responded with an exclamation of disgust before interpreting to a younger officer standing by his side. One doubt kept me on tenterhooks during this second encounter. Would the Italians in our boat remain hidden and silent? They never stirred a finger or said a word – and all was well. The tide of luck again ran in our favour! Kegs of water, flasks of Chianti, boxes of biscuits and cigarettes were produced from the submarine's hatches and handed into our lifeboat. The spectre of hunger and thirst was banished once more, and the real dread now was lest the weather should worsen.

When the Italian submarine left us to continue its interrupted patrol, we exchanged farewells with a friendliness curiously inconsistent as between enemies; the years of political misunderstandings and military combat were bridged in an hour or so by compassion on one side and gratitude on the other. Discomfort and anxiety attended the further voyaging of our boat until the sixth day, which held another surprise for us. From a seemingly empty ocean our old 'friend' reappeared – the U-boat with her young bearded commander. He knew nothing of our meeting with the Italian craft, and no one enlightened him. His first concern was for the women and children, whom he took aboard again, thereby giving the rest of us a chance to move about.

'Now I will give you a tow,' he said. 'You will be made prisoners of war. Ja, it is for your own sakes, because the weather may change and you might founder. I have made a signal by radio for a French warship to meet me. Always we Germans are humane.' There was nothing we could do about it, and we made fast a rope and were towed for a couple of hours while the women and children sat on the U-boat's after deck.

Presently, to our joy, we saw four or five of the *Laconia*'s lifeboats. That German sea-wolf had been ranging like a sheep-dog to round them up, and amid emotional scenes numbers of relatives and friends were reunited for the first time since the transport was torpedoed. Then the U-boat took the

218

boats in tow and proceeded on a different course all night and part of the following day. At last the lifeboats were cast off, and the German commander made his final speech through a megaphone.

'Here you must wait,' he announced. 'Soon you will be rescued, I think, but I warn you that there will be bad trouble if you try to sail away!' When the women and children had been returned to our lifeboat, the submarine moved off and dived – and that was the last we saw of her. The boats kept together and drifted on the tide, but we were not left long in suspense. Smoke smudged the horizon and a ship hove in sight – the Vichy warship *Gloire* keeping the rendezvous in response to the U-boat's signals.

The transfer of everyone from the lifeboats took some time because many were unable to mount the rope-ladders and had to be hoisted in slings. Again there were glad reunions, for the *Gloire* had picked up many other survivors elsewhere at sea. Our life-boats were sunk by gunfire, and the warship steamed direct for Dakar; and I for one was mightily glad she arrived without 'catching a packet' from Allied air-patrols. In contrast to the open boats, our voyage was a holiday. Yet the accommodation for the men was vile, the food poor and insufficient, and we had to sleep on the steel decks without bedding, and no pillows other than our own damp life-jackets. Treatment by the French guards varied according to individual allegiance to the Vichy regime or sympathy with the Allied cause – but no open display of sympathy was made.

From Dakar some of us were taken to Casablanca, then to a grim prison camp under the ramparts of the Atlas Mountains. They gave us cubes of tough meat that the Vichy French guards called *boeuf, veau* or *mouton,* but which were easily recognized for what they were – goat. And we had a 'high' tea consisting of black bread and hard-boiled eggs. The only privileges we received at this wretched camp were accorded secretly by De Gaullists among the guards. What with dysentery and skin troubles our lot was indeed unenviable, and then prolonged gunfire from the direction of the coast one morning set us all seething with excitement.

After much suspense, we came to learn the truth of a stupendous event. The Allies had landed in North Africa! Jeeps came roaring down the rough road outside our compound. 'The Yanks! The Yanks are here!' We yelled ourselves hoarse. It was 11th November 1942, a red-letter day in our lives. We were taken to Casablanca, feasted aboard transports and cargo-carriers, and all arrangements made for our repatriation. I returned to England via Norfolk, Virginia, and New York; and another red-letter day for me came a bit later at Liverpool when I was provided with a brand-new uniform and appointed purser in the ocean-going steamship *Wanderer.*

219

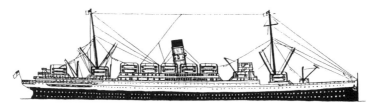

APPENDIX 5

A LACONIA SCRAPBOOK

75. Claude Jones.

76. James William Rowson.

77. Ted Johnson and Russian officers at the Battle of the Atlantic celebrations.

Liverpool.
Friday, 14th September 1962.

Dear Miss D. Banks,

The Sun will shine in the end and because of this I am seldom unhappy.

I have a drawer of memories and photographs of my own kith and kin on Rolls of Honour in church, cathedral and school with letters written by the alien pen on the alien soil where the people so very very kindly tell me of their care for the graves with the one to my especial interest. The beautiful thoughts sent by the hesitating language of a stranger tells they "tread softly here where lies an Empire's dust".

So, I understand and write you.

Please accept the enclosed tribute for yourself and with the hope from me that its potentiality will, sooner or later, achieve big things to be worthy of a sender of small ones.

I do submit to being influenced by the axioms of Psalm 19, and would like to again write:— "Let the words of my mouth, and the meditation of my heart, be alway acceptable in God's sight".

I am ending these communications, but will earnestly retain my heart-felt wishes for you because of the circumstances which have brought us together.

Very sincerely,
A Laconia survivor.

Miss D. Banks,
111, Hazel Road, Huyton,
near Liverpool.

78-79. Letters from anonymous survivor sent to Mrs Maddocks, daughter of John Banks, steward on the *Laconia*.

13th September 1967.

Dear Mrs Maddox,

My kind regards for you and trust you are well.

The beautiful music and rendering of Psalm 139 during this morning's 10.15 (BBC) Daily Service was so fitting for thoughts in my mind, and too, because of yesterday's anniversary of a day now so long passed that I could, in simple faith, pass something on to you.

The enclosed is very mundane but I hope you will accept it.

Yours very sincerely,
A Laconia survivor.

(368, Warrington Road,
Rainhill,)
Lancs.

CUNARD WHITE STAR LIMITED

S.S. "LACONIA"

Date..............................

Name ...Wm. Hoyer...

Rating ...Waiter... Art. No. ...567...

BOAT No. ...1... Position..............................

EMERGENCY STATION—
....

FIRE STATION—
...Mgt. 9 B. Loy. El. First door Fut'k Gally...

EMERGENCY SIGNAL—
A succession of more than **six** short blasts on the steam whistle, followed by **one** long blast, and supplemented by the sounding of the electric gongs

FIRE SIGNAL—A rapid ringing of the ship's bell

ALERT
3 Short rings of electric gongs

C909

S.S. "LACONIA"

No. ...567...   Name ...W. Hoyer...

Tc Date ...12 MAY 1942...

Rating ...Waiter...

TOTAL PAY FOR	£	s.	d.
...4... months ...14... days at £ 14/11/4	73	13	9

DEDUCTIONS			
Insurance H		19	-
,, U		15	10
Superannuation			
1d. in £		6	7
Tobacco	2	-	10
Cash	12	1	-
Fines			
Slop Chest			
Working Rig			
Advances			
Allotments	38	-	-
TOTAL £	54	1	10

Deductions 54 1 10

Balance Due £ 19 11 11

Ship's Stamp and Date.
Skeepstempel en Datum.

LACONIA

IDENTIFICATION
IDENTIFIKASIE

This is to certify that
Hiermee word verklaar dat

Mr./mnr. ...Wm. Hoyer...
Mrs./mev.
Miss/mej.

is a registered member of the crew of the vessel
'n geregistreerde lid is van die bemanning van die skip

LACONIA .... (name of ship)
.... (naam van skip)

.... Master of Ship
Skeepsmeester.

...W. Hoyer...
Signature of Holder.
Handtekening van toonder.

This document must be surrendered to the Master of Ship before departure thereof.
Hierdie dokument moet aan die Meester van die skip oorhandig word voordat dit vertrek.

FORM A 185A   L.P. 11 356

CUNARD WHITE STAR LIMITED.

CREW LANDING CARD · U.S.A.

Date ...10 AUG 1942...   LACONIA

Ship ....

Name ...Wm. Hoyer...

Rating ...Waiter...   Line No. ....

Sheet No. ....

85-86. Guns on the *Laconia* taken in 1941.

84. Another painting of the *Laconia*, this time used by the Sperry Corporation.

87. The author after interviewing Albert Speer.

CUNARD WHITE STAR LIMITED

SHIPPING DEPARTMENT

TELEGRAMS : "CUNARDSTAR, LIVERPOOL"
TELEPHONE : ADVANCE 7000

KINDLY QUOTE
SHIPPING
IN YOUR REPLY.

CUNARD BUILDING,

LIVERPOOL. 3.

BERKELEY SQUARE HOUSE,
W.1.

27th July, 1943.

14th October, 1942.

Mrs. Myfanwy Hamilton,
    59, Pilch Lane East,
        Huyton,
            LIVERPOOL.

Dear Madam,

        We much regret to have to advise you that we
have been informed the ship in which your husband was serving
has been lost by enemy action.

        We are extremely sorry that up to the moment his
name does not appear in the list of those who have been saved
but we are not without hope that there may be lists of additional
survivors to come forward.

        We will communicate with you again immediately
should any further news come to hand.

                Yours faithfully,
                CUNARD WHITE STAR LIMITED.

Dear Madam,

        It is with the deepest regret that I have
learned that your husband, Mr. Robert Hamilton,
who was serving in the Merchant Navy as
Refrigerator Greaser has been recorded as
missing – presumed drowned – whilst on service
with his ship.

        By command of His Majesty The King the
names of those members of the Merchant Navy who
have given their lives in the service of their
country are recorded in the Merchant Navy Roll
of Honour. I am now adding Mr. Hamilton's
name to the Roll of Honour, and, as I do so, wish
to express my admiration for the services he
rendered and to convey to you and your family
my profound sympathy in your sad bereavement.

        Your husband worthily upheld the noble
traditions of the Merchant Navy and I may perhaps
hope that the realisation of this fact may help
to soften the heavy blow which has fallen upon
you.

                Yours sincerely,

                MINISTER OF WAR TRANSPORT.

Mrs. Myfanwy Hamilton.

BUCKINGHAM PALACE

        The Queen and I offer you our
heartfelt sympathy in your great
sorrow.

        We pray that your country's
gratitude for a life so nobly given
in its service may bring you some
measure of consolation.

                George R.I.

**88-91. Collection of official letters
relating to Robert Hamilton.**

This scroll commemorates

R. Hamilton, Greaser
Merchant Navy

held in honour as one who
served King and Country in
the world war of 1939-1945
and gave his life to save
mankind from tyranny. May
his sacrifice help to bring
the peace and freedom for
which he died.

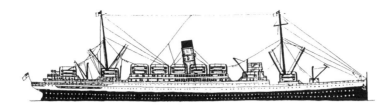

PICTURE CREDITS AND BIBLIOGRAPHY

1.   (T. H. Grossmith), *author's collection.*
2.   (Doris M. Hawkins), *from Mrs Norah K. King, Worthing.*
3.   (Cunard postcard), *courtesy of Philip Rentell.*
4.   (Cunard postcard, Panama Canal), *courtesy of Philip Rentell.*
5.   (Rear view of the *Laconia*), *courtesy of the Liverpool University Cunard Archive.*
6-8.   (Ships' plans), *from* The Shipbuilder *(October, 1921).*
9.   (Rear view of the *Laconia*), *courtesy of the* Liverpool Daily Post & Echo.
10.   (*Laconia* on trials), *courtesy of Joseph Griffiths, Liverpool.*
11   (*Laconia* general view), *courtesy of John Clarkson's 'Ships in Focus' archive.*
12-16. (*Laconia* interior views), *courtesy of the National Maritime Museum, London.*
17.   (Ivor Novello cruise), *courtesy of Douglas Ashworth, Llandudno.*
18.   (*Laconia* with *HMS Hood*), *courtesy of Douglas Ashworth, Llandudno.*
19.   (Fancy dress ball on *Laconia*), *courtesy of Douglas Ashworth, Llandudno.*
20.   (Inglenook fireplace), *courtesy of the National Maritime Museum, London.*
21-22. (Paintings from Cunard publicity brochures), *courtesy of the National Maritime Museum, London.*
23.   (*Laconia* general view), *courtesy of the National Maritime Museum, London.*
24.   (*Laconia* after 1928 refit), *courtesy of the University of Liverpool, Cunard Archive.*
25.   (View of Aden from *Laconia*), *courtesy of K. Bates, Liverpool.*
26.   (Hartenstein), *courtesy of Horst Bredow, U-Boot Archiv, Cuxhaven, Germany*
27.   (*Laconia*, general view), *courtesy of Keith Lewis, Bromborough, Wirral.*
28.   (Captain Sharp), *from Léonce Peillard's* U-Boats to the Rescue *(London, Jonathan Cape, 1963, origin unknown).*
29.   (U-156 in harbour), *courtesy of Bibliothek für Zeitgeschichte.*
30.   (Hartenstein), *courtesy of Horst Bredow, U-Boot Archiv.*
31.   (Lifeboat with *Laconia* survivors), *from* U-Boats to the Rescue.
32.   (U-156), *courtesy of Bibliothek für Zeitgeschichte.*
33.   (Plan of U-156), *from* U-Boats to the Rescue.
34.   (*Laconia* survivors on deck of U-156), *courtesy of Horst Bredow, U-Boot Archiv.*
35.   (Map), *by Martin Smith for Paul Watkins Publishing.*
36.   (Würdemann), *courtesy of Horst Bredow, U-Boot Archiv.*
37.   (Robert Tinkler), *supplied by himself.*
38.   (William Hoyer), *supplied by himself.*
39.   (*Laconia* survivors), *from* U-Boats to the Rescue.
40.   (*Laconia* survivors on U-506), *courtesy of Horst Bredow, U-Boot Archiv.*

41. (Harro Schacht), *courtesy of Horst Bredow, U-Boot Archiv.*
42. (U-506 crammed with *Laconia* survivors), *from* U-Boats to the Rescue.
43. (U-506 rescuing survivors), *courtesy of Horst Bredow, U-Boot Archiv.*
44. (Women and children survivors), *courtesy of Horst Bredow, U-Boot Archiv.*
45. (Survivors on U-506), *courtesy of Horst Bredow, U-Boot Archiv.*
46. (U-506 with lifeboat), *courtesy of Horst Bredow, U-Boot Archiv.*
47. (*Laconia* survivors on U-506), *courtesy of Horst Bredow, U-Boot Archiv.*
48. (Runway on Ascension Island), *from Ivan Dmitri's* Flight to Everywhere *(New York, 1943).*
49. (B-24 Liberator Bomber), *from Ivan Dmitri's* Flight to Everywhere.
50. (*Gloire*), *courtesy of Bibliothek für Zeitgeschichte.*
51. (*Annamite*), *courtesy of Bibliothek für Zeitgeschichte.*
52. (*Dumont D'Urville*), *courtesy of Bibliothek für Zeitgeschichte.*
53. (Women and girls on *Gloire*), *from* U-Boats to the Rescue.
54. (Handing out clothes on *Gloire*), *from* U-Boats to the Rescue.
55. (French sailor's postcard), *from Andrew Zamrej, Kildary, Ross-shire.*
56-57. (Andrew Zamrej and James Campbell), *photos by Andrew Allan originally taken for the* Ross-shire Journal, *supplied by Andrew Zamrej.*
58-61. (Drawings by Edward Bawden), *courtesy of the Imperial War Museum, London.*
62. (David Chawe), *courtesy of the Imperial War Museum.*
63. (Summons to attend wreck enquiry), *from the author's collection.*
64. (Postcard of *Laconia*), *from the author's collection.*
65. (Dönitz), *courtesy of La Documentation Française*
66. (Dönitz), *from the author's collection.*
67. (Kranzbuehler), *courtesy of Hulton Deutsch Picture Library.*
68-69. (Nuremberg War Trials), *courtesy of Hulton Deutsch Picture Library.*
70. (Press conference at Nuremberg), *courtesy of Hulton Deutsch Picture Library.*
71. (Courthouse at Nuremberg), *from the author's collection.*
72. (*Laconia* from Cunard publicity material), *courtesy of the National Maritime Museum, London.*
73. (Italian submarine *Cappellini*), *courtesy of Bibliothek für Zeitgeschichte.*
74. (Marco Revedin and Sub-Lieutenant Disiervo), *from* U-Boats to the Rescue.
75. (Claude Jones), *from* The War Illustrated, *issues 252 and 253 (1947).*
76. (James Rowson), *courtesy A. C. Rowson, Essex.*
77. (Ted Johnson with Russian officers), *supplied by Ted Johnson.*
78-79. (Letters from anonymous *Laconia* survivor), *courtesy of Mrs Maddocks, Liverpool*
80-83. (William Hoyer's collection of *Laconia* ephemera), *courtesy of William Hoyer.*
84. (*Laconia* from Sperry Corporation), *originally printed in* The Sperry Gyro-Compass and Gyro-Pilot. Pamphlet no. 237 (London, Sperry, n.d. probably 1930s), *from the publisher's collection.*
85-86. (Guns on the *Laconia*), *courtesy of Fred B. Grahame, Ontario.*
87. (Author with Albert Speer), *author's collection.*
88-91. (Collection of official letters), *courtesy of Mrs D. Edwards, West Kirby, Wirral.*

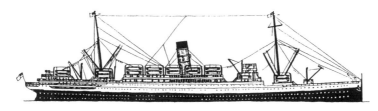

BIBLIOGRAPHY

Discussions of the *Laconia* incident in print are few and far between, but the following publications provided some information to supplement the original sources. Some of these titles provide traditional descriptions of the *Laconia* sinking as a war crime. Airey Neave, for example, calls the sinking 'a crime against humanity', but labels the attack by the B-24 as 'due to a misunderstanding'.

Bekker, C. D., *Swastika at Sea. The Struggle and Destruction of the German Navy 1939-1945* (London, Kimber, n.d., c.1953), pp.26-34.
Cary, Alan L., *Famous Liners and their Stories* (London, Sampson, c.1935).
Dmitri, Ivan, *Flight to Everywhere* (New York, Whittlesey House, 1944).
Dönitz, Karl, *Memoirs. Ten Years and Twenty Days* (London, Weidenfeld, 1958)
Grahame, Fred B., *My Radar Service Record in WWII* (Dundas, Ontario, Magra, 1993)
Hawkins, Doris M., *Atlantic Torpedo* (London, Gollancz, 1943).
McLean, Ruari, *Edward Bawden, War Artist, and his Letters Home 1940-45* (Aldershot, Scolar, 1989).
Neave, Airey, *Nuremberg. A Personal Record of the Trial of the Major Nazi War Criminals in 1945-46* (London, Hodder, 1978).
Peillard, Léonce, *U-Boats to the Rescue* (London, Jonathan Cape, 1963).
Rentell, Philip, *Historic Cunard Liners* (Truro, Atlantic Transport, 1986).
Roskill, S. W., *The War at Sea 1939-45*, 4 vols (London, HMSO, 1954-61).
Russell, Lord (of Liverpool), *Scourge of the Swastika. A Short History of the Nazi War Crimes* (London, Cassell, 1954).
Terraine, John, *Business in Great Waters. The U-Boat Wars 1916-1945* (London, Leo Cooper, 1989).

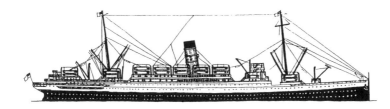

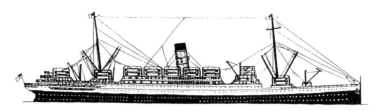

INDEX

INDEX

229

INDEX

INDEX

INDEX